Assembly Virginia. General

Acts of the General Assembly of the State of Virginia

Assembly Virginia. General

Acts of the General Assembly of the State of Virginia

ISBN/EAN: 9783744759144

Printed in Europe, USA, Canada, Australia, Japan

Cover: Foto ©ninafisch / pixelio.de

More available books at **www.hansebooks.com**

ACTS

OF THE

GENERAL ASSEMBLY

OF THE

STATE OF VIRGINIA,

PASSED AT CALLED SESSION, 1862,

IN THE

EIGHTY-SEVENTH YEAR OF THE COMMONWEALTH.

RICHMOND:
WILLIAM F. RITCHIE, PUBLIC PRINTER.
1862.

ACTS

PASSED AT THE

CALLED SESSION, 1862.

CHAP. 1.—An ACT to provide for the production, distribution and sale of Salt in this Commonwealth.

Passed October 1, 1862.

1. Be it enacted by the general assembly, that the governor of this commonwealth may adopt every such measure and do every such act as in his judgment may be necessary and proper to be done, in order to secure the possession, production or distribution to convenient places, of such quantity of salt as will in his judgment be sufficient to supply the people of this commonwealth: and to that end, may bind the faith of the commonwealth for the performance of such contracts and engagements as he may determine to be necessary and proper; and may exercise full authority and control over the property and franchises of any person, firm or company in this commonwealth, whenever he shall judge it to be necessary and proper to exercise the same, in order to secure the possession, production or distribution of the quantity of salt aforesaid: provided, that nothing herein contained shall be construed to authorize the purchase of the Smyth and Washington or Kanawha salt works, or any freehold interest therein. *Powers of governor*

Faith of commonwealth, how pledged

Washington and Smyth salt works not to be purchased

2. If, in the opinion of the governor, in order to obtain a speedy and sufficient supply of salt, it shall be expedient to do so, he may seize, take possession of and hold and exercise full authority and control over the property, real and personal, of any person, firm or company, and any engines, machinery or fixtures and other property or thing necessary for the production of salt in this commonwealth, whenever he shall judge it to be necessary to exercise the power hereby conferred, in order to secure the production and distribution of the quantity of salt aforesaid. *Property, how seized, &c.*

3. If, by the exercise of the power conferred by the second section of this act, any property should be taken in relation to which there may be existing contracts with the Confederate States, or any of the states of the Confederate States, or with any county, city or town in this commonwealth, entered into by virtue of an act of the *What contracts to be respected*

Contracts with counties, &c. to be respected

4   SALT.

<small>What contracts with individuals to be respected</small>
general assembly, entitled an act to authorize the county courts to purchase and distribute salt among the people, and provide payment for the same, passed May ninth, eighteen hundred and sixty-two, or any contract with individuals for the benefit of any county, city or town, which contract may have subsequently been adopted by such county, city or town, under the act aforesaid: provided, that such contracts with and for said counties, shall not be respected for a larger amount of salt than the twenty pounds for each inhabitant proposed by the lessees to be furnished in the proposition on which said act was founded, the same shall be respected, and the supply of salt

<small>When contracts with other states to be disregarded</small>
or salt water so contracted for shall be furnished. If a sufficient supply of salt water cannot be obtained at the wells now producing salt water, for the production of a sufficient supply of salt for the people of the state, or cannot promptly be obtained from new wells, then the governor is empowered to disregard, in whole or in part,

<small>When other states to be furnished</small>
such contracts with the states of the Confederate States; but if a surplus of water may exist, then the governor is directed to furnish to the other states of the Confederate States, out of any surplus of salt water that may remain after the supply of a sufficient quantity

<small>Proviso</small>
to the state of Virginia: provided, that nothing in this act shall be so construed as to authorize the governor to prevent the owners of salt property, or their assignees, from manufacturing and selling salt from salt water, or fossil salt remaining after all the uses of the state, under the provisions of this act, are supplied.

<small>When rail roads may be taken</small>
4. The governor may take control of any rail road or canal in this state, if necessary for the transportation of salt for distribution, or for the transportation of fuel or other thing necessary for the production of salt; but the power conferred by this section shall not be so exercised as to interfere with the transportation of troops, munitions of war and army supplies, by the confederate government.

<small>Places of distribution</small>
5. The governor shall designate places in the commonwealth from which the sale and distribution of such salt may be made to citizens

<small>Rules and regulations Publication</small>
of this commonwealth, and prescribe rules and regulations for the sale of the same, and the prices at which it shall be sold. When such prices shall be so prescribed and published for two weeks in some newspaper published in the city of Richmond, the sale of such salt at any higher price than the price so prescribed, shall be a misdemeanor, and the sale of each bushel, or any part of a bushel thereof, at a rate higher than the price so prescribed, shall be a sepa-

<small>Violation of rules a misdemeanor</small>
rate offence. Any violation of the rules and regulations so prescribed, shall be a misdemeanor. Upon conviction of any person under this act, he shall pay a fine of not less than one hundred nor more than two thousand dollars.

<small>Agents, how employed Bond</small>
6. If the governor shall find it necessary to employ agents to receive money for the sales of salt, he shall require them to give bond,

with such penalty as the governor may require, with good security, to be approved by the governor, payable to the commonwealth, with condition to pay all money received from the sale of salt, into the treasury, to the credit of the commonwealth, at the end of each month. *How payable*

7. The sum of five hundred thousand dollars is hereby appropriated, to be paid out of the treasury, upon warrant to be issued by the auditor of public accounts, upon the orders of the governor in writing, to be given only in payment of liabilities incurred for the purposes of this act. *Amount appropriated* *Orders of governor*

8. For the use of any of the property, real or personal, which may be used, occupied, possessed or controlled by the governor, a board of assessors, to be composed of five persons not members of the general assembly, who shall be appointed by a joint vote of the two houses, a majority of whom may act and shall concur, shall assess reasonable compensation or damages; which shall be paid on the written order of the governor, upon a written assessment, to be signed by a majority of the members of the board, with their affidavits that such assessment is, in the opinion of the board, reasonable and just. Such assessment shall be delivered to the governor, to be filed by him in the office of the secretary of state; and a copy thereof shall be forwarded by the secretary to the person, firm or company who may be entitled to the compensation or damages; and unless such person, firm or company shall, within thirty days after such copy shall be delivered to them, refuse, by written objections, to accept the same, such assessment shall be deemed to be final. If the governor, on behalf of the state, or if any such person, firm or company shall, within thirty days after such assessment shall have been so filed with the secretary of the commonwealth, file such written objections with the secretary of the commonwealth, and in the office of the circuit court of the city of Richmond, an appeal shall lie from such assessment to the said circuit court; and the proceedings thereon in said court shall be according to the provisions of chapter fifty-six of the Code of Virginia, as far as the same are applicable thereto, except that the commonwealth shall not be required to pay the compensation or damages to the party entitled thereto, nor into court, before the decision of the appeal. No order shall be made, nor any injunction awarded by any court or judge, to stay any proceedings of the governor, or his authorized agents, under this act. The board shall be convened at such times and places as the governor may order, and shall be paid each the sum of four dollars per day, and actual expenses incurred in traveling; to be paid by warrants to be issued upon the orders of the governor. *Damages, how assessed* *Board of assessors* *Damages, how paid* *Assessment delivered to governor* *When assessment final* *When appeal allowed* *Injunction not to be granted* *Board, how convened*

9. This act shall be in force from its passage, and shall continue in force until the expiration of the present war. *Commencement*

PUBLIC DEFENCE.

CHAP. 2.—An ACT to further provide for the Public Defence.

Passed October 3, 1862.

Duty of governor.
Slaves, how called out
Number limited
Per centage in counties
Compensation
Value of slaves, when to be paid
Further provisions
Burden of proof
Slaves hired, how regarded

1. Be it enacted by the general assembly, that the governor of this commonwealth shall, when requested by the president of the Confederate States, be and he is hereby authorized and required from time to time to call into the service of the Confederate States, for labor on fortifications, and other works necessary for the public defence, for a period not exceeding sixty days, a number of male slaves between the ages of eighteen and forty-five years, not exceeding ten thousand at any one time, and not exceeding in any county, city or town five per centum of the entire slave population thereof. Such requisition shall be apportioned ratably among all the slaveholders in the several counties, cities and towns on which the requisition shall be made. The sum of sixteen dollars per month for each slave shall be paid by the Confederate States to the holders of the slaves, and soldier's rations, medicines and medical attendance furnished; and the value of all such slaves as may escape from the confederate authorities and not return to their owners, or be seized or killed by the public enemy, or may, by want of due diligence on the part of the authorities of the Confederate States, in any manner be lost to the owners, shall be paid by the Confederate States to the owners of such slaves, and in like manner compensation shall be made for any injury to slaves arising from a want of due diligence on the part of the authorities of the Confederate States; and in those cases the burden of proof shall be on the authorities of the Confederate States to discharge the latter from liability to the former. Slaves hired by individuals having other slaves, shall be regarded as in the possession of their owners, and classed accordingly in regard to confederate service.

Notice to counties, how given
Requisitions, how filed
Summons
How directed

2. Be it further enacted, that so soon as the governor shall call out a force of slaves from any or all of the counties, cities and towns of the commonwealth, under this act, he shall give notice thereof to the several counties, cities and towns on which the call may be made, by causing to be filed with the clerks of the several county and corporation courts, copies of the requisitions made on their respective counties, cities and towns. It shall be the duty of the said clerks forthwith to issue a summons to all the acting justices of their respective counties or corporations, requiring them to meet at the courthouse of the county or corporation on a day to be named in the summons, not later than three days from the filing of the requisition, to carry the same into effect; which summons shall be directed to and executed by the sheriff of the county or sergeant of the corporation, as the case may be.

Duty of county courts

3. It shall be the duty of the several county and corporation courts, after being duly summoned as aforesaid, and not less than five justices

being present, to call to their assistance the commissioners of the revenue of their respective counties and corporations, and after ascertaining the entire slave population thereof, to apportion, without delay, the requisitions aforesaid, ratably among all the slaveholders of the county or corporation, throwing into classes, when necessary, the holders of but one or few slaves, and ascertaining, by lot, or by agreement between the parties, the slave or slaves to be sent to the fortifications from such classes: provided, that in no case of a soldier in the confederate army, owning or hiring but one male slave, shall the said male slave be subject to requisition under this act. *Commissioners of revenue* *Requisitions, how apportioned* *Classes, when to be made* *Proviso as to soldiers*

4. So soon as the apportionment aforesaid shall be made, it shall be the duty of the courts of the several counties and corporations to require each slaveholder to deliver, on a day and at a place to be appointed by the court, not more than three days from the date of the order, his quota of slaves to the sheriff or sergeant, as the case may be, to be delivered by such sheriff or sergeant to an agent or officer of the Confederate States. All slaves delivered by the holders on the day and at the place designated as aforesaid, to be returned at the expiration of sixty days. Slaves not delivered in accordance with the order of the court, shall be seized by the sheriff or sergeant, as the case may be, and delivered to the agent or officer of the Confederate States authorized to receive them, who shall thereupon execute a separate receipt to each owner for the slave or slaves, naming them, so delivered by him, and may be held on the terms and conditions aforesaid, for a period not exceeding ninety days. *Slaves, when to be delivered to sheriff* *Sheriff to deliver to officer or agent* *Slaves, when to be returned* *When slaves may be seized*

5. The clerk and sheriff or sergeant shall attend the sessions of the court as in other cases; and the court shall continue in session from day to day until the business shall be completed. *Duration of courts*

6. Should any county or corporation court fail or refuse to discharge the duties hereby imposed upon them, it shall be the duty of the clerk of such court immediately to notify the governor thereof; and thereupon it shall be the duty of the governor, by officers and agents of his own selection, with the aid of the commissioners of the revenue of the respective counties, cities and towns, who are hereby directed to render such aid when required, to impress into the service of the Confederate States, from any such county, city or town, the proportion of slaves demanded by him from such county or corporation, not exceeding five per centum of the entire slave population thereof, apportioning the same among the slaveholders, as herein above set forth, as near as may be, and holding the same not longer than ninety days for the uses and upon the terms and conditions set forth in the first section of this act. *When court fails to discharge duty imposed* *Powers of governor* *When slaves may be impressed* *How long they may be retained*

7. In making the requisitions authorized by this act, the governor is requested to equalize the burden, as nearly as may be, among the *Burden to be equalized*

PUBLIC DEFENCE.—MILITARY AFFAIRS.

Regard to be had to number of slaves previously furnished

several counties, cities and towns of the commonwealth, and amongst the citizens thereof, having, when practicable, due regard to the number of slaves heretofore furnished by any counties or corporations, or the citizens thereof, under any call heretofore made by the president or secretary of war, or any officer of the confederate army.

When certain number of slaves furnished, privilege of owner

8. So soon as a requisition may be made upon any county, city or town, it shall be lawful for any number of persons who may be required to furnish not less than thirty nor more than forty slaves, to place such slaves in charge of an agent or overseer selected by such owners, who shall deliver them to the confederate authorities, at the place where the labor is to be performed, at the expense of the Con-

Overseer, how appointed

federate States; and such agent or overseer, if a fit and proper person, shall be employed by the confederate government as the agent or overseer in charge of the slaves during their service of sixty days.

Subsistence, how commuted

9. The owner of any slaves may furnish subsistence and provisions to his slaves, and in such event shall be allowed commutation in money in lieu of rations, at the rate of sixty cents a day.

10. All slaves sent voluntarily by their owners and accepted by the agents of the confederate government, shall stand on the same footing as if sent in pursuance of the proceedings required by this act.

Acceptance by Confederate States

11. Any request for slaves made by the president on the governor under this act, shall be regarded an assent to and acceptance of all its provisions by the Confederate States.

Commencement

12. This act shall be in force from its passage.

CHAP. 3.—An ACT for the dismissal of Militia Officers for treason or disloyalty.

Passed October 6, 1862.

When militia officers may be removed by governor

1. Be it enacted by the general assembly, that whenever any officer of the militia shall be guilty, in the opinion of the governor, of treason or disloyalty, it shall be lawful for the governor to remove such officer; and the vacancy thereby occasioned shall be filled in the mode now prescribed by law. The senate shall at all times have power to reverse the action of the governor; and thereupon the commissions issued in consequence of such dismissal, shall be

Proviso

void: provided, that no officer shall be dismissed, except in cases where he cannot be arrested and served with the charges and specifications against him, as is at present provided by law.

Reasons to be assigned by governor

2. It shall be the duty of the governor, in all cases of removal, to assign his reasons therefor, in writing, and communicate the same to the next general assembly.

Commencement

3. This act shall be in force from its passage.

CHAP. 4.—An ACT amending and re-enacting an act amending and re-enacting the 2d section of chapter 22 of the Code of Virginia, respecting persons exempt from all military duties, and providing the mode of exemption, passed February 18th, 1862.

Passed October 1, 1862.

1. Be it enacted by the general assembly, That the act amending and re-enacting the second section of chapter twenty-two of the Code of Virginia, respecting persons exempt from all military duties, and providing the mode of exemption, passed February eighteenth, eighteen hundred and sixty-two, be amended and re-enacted so as to read as follows: *Act 1862 amended*

"§ 2. The following persons only shall be exempt from the performance of all military duties, to wit: the vice-president of the Confederate States; the officers, judicial and executive, of the government of the Confederate States; the members of both houses of congress, and the clerk of each house; all custom house officers; the lieutenant governor, and all the members of the general assembly, during the term for which they were elected or appointed; the secretary of the commonwealth, and his clerks; the clerks of the house of delegates and senate; the judges of the court of appeals and circuit courts, attorneys for the commonwealth, and the justices of the peace; the clerk of each of said courts, and of each county and corporation court; judge of hustings court; the sheriff of each county, and the sergeant and collector of taxes of each corporation having a hustings court, and the commissioners of the revenue; the attorney general, the treasurer, two auditors, register of the land office, superintendent of the penitentiary, and their clerks and assistants; every minister of the gospel licensed to preach according to the rules of his sect; superintendents of the public hospitals, lunatic asylums, and the regular nurses and attendants therein, and the teachers employed in the institution for the deaf and dumb and blind; one physician to each two thousand population, to be selected by the board herein after constituted; the president, the general superintendent and two local superintendents of the southern telegraph companies, in no case to exceed four persons; the president and superintendent of transportation of each rail road company; the president, secretary and chief collector of each canal company. No one shall be exempt from draft by reason of his being an agent of a commissary or assistant commissary, or quartermaster or assistant quartermaster, whether said commissary or assistant commissary, or quartermaster or assistant quartermaster be in the service of the Confederate States or of this state, or by reason of his holding any office or commission in the militia: and whenever any militia officer is drafted for actual service, his commission shall be vacated." *Who exempted*

2. If the constituted authorities of any city shall, within twenty days after any draft has been made therefrom, apply to the governor *Officers of city, how exempted*

for the purpose, he shall exempt from actual military service any drafted person who may be, at the time of the draft, an officer of such city, or in its service; in connection with its gas or water works or fire and police departments; and if within twenty days after any draft, the president and superintendent of any rail road, canal and telegraph company shall certify, upon their honor, to the governor that the services of any drafted person, who is an officer or employee of such company, are necessary to the efficient operation of the said road, the governor may, in his discretion, exempt such person from actual military service. Any person exempted under this section shall be deemed to be detailed for duty in the post or place he filled at the time he was drafted, without pay as a soldier; and in case he shall leave the service of such city or company, he shall at once be remanded to the military service for which he was drafted; and if any such person shall fail, for ten days after leaving such service, to report himself to the governor or to some military officer for duty as a soldier, he shall be proceeded against as a deserter. The governor shall promptly cause the places of all persons exempted under this section to be filled by further draft from the respective counties, cities and towns from which such persons were drafted. It shall be the duty of the president or mayor of the city, or company, as the case may be, promptly to report to the governor the name of any person so exempted, who may have left the service for which he was detailed.

Powers of governor

When exempt remanded to service

How places of exempts to be filled

Duty of mayor, &c.

Boards of exemption, how constituted

3. Immediately after the passage of this act, the governor shall issue his proclamation, requiring the organization of a board of exemptions in each county and corporation, to consist of the presiding justice or recorder, and any two justices whom such presiding justice or recorder may associate with him. In case the presiding justice or recorder cannot for any cause act, the chief clerk of the hustings or county court shall summon any three justices, who shall constitute such board. Such clerk shall act as clerk of the board. In case there be no such clerk present and capable of acting, the clerk of the circuit court shall act; or if no such board should be organized, the governor may designate any three justices of the county or corporation, who shall constitute the board, and appoint their own clerk.

Powers of boards of exemption

4. The board shall have cognizance of all questions of exemption, and shall adjudge the sufficiency of the excuse given by any person, who, by reason of his failure to report his name for enrollment, as required by the act entitled an act for ascertaining and enrolling the military force of the commonwealth, passed February eighth, eighteen hundred and sixty-two, may have been enrolled among the drafted levies, as prescribed in said act. For punishing contempts and compelling the attendance of witnesses, the board shall have the powers of a county court.

MILITARY AFFAIRS.—REDRESS OF LOYAL CITIZENS. 11

5. In no case shall the board grant a discharge upon a claim of exemption for bodily infirmity, unless at least two physicians of respectable standing, being duly sworn, shall prove before said board that the bodily infirmity is of a permanent character, and is such as will disqualify the claimant for discharging the duties of a soldier. Discharges for physical infirmity, how granted

6. Every claim for exemption or excuse shall be filed with the clerk of the board, who shall issue process for such witnesses as the claimant or enrolling officer may require; and within five days after a draft is made, and on a day to be designated by the board, the trial of cases of exemption and excuse shall commence; and the same shall be disposed of in a summary manner as speedily as may be. The clerk of the board shall promptly report to the adjutant general the name of each person exempted or excused by the board. *Exemptions, how tried*

7. For every failure to discharge any duty prescribed in this act, the members of the board and the clerk may each be fined not less than ten nor more than one hundred dollars. *Penalties on board for failure*

8. All acts and ordinances and parts of acts and ordinances inconsistent with this act, are hereby repealed. *Repealing clause*

9. This act shall be in force from its passage. *Commencement*

CHAP. 5.—An ACT to redress Loyal Citizens injured by the exercise of usurped power.

Passed October 2, 1862.

Whereas disloyal persons have conspired to overthrow the legitimate authority of this commonwealth, and for that purpose have established within the limits thereof an usurped government, whose power is exercised to the injury and oppression of the loyal people of this state within its influence: and whereas the general assembly is desirous of providing redress to such injured persons against such conspirators: Therefore, *Preamble*

1. Be it enacted by the general assembly, that every person who, since the seventeenth day of April, Anno Domini eighteen hundred and sixty-one, has been or shall be guilty of establishing or of attempting to establish, without the authority of the legislature, any government within the limits of this state, separate and apart from the existing government, or who has held or exercised, or who may hereafter hold or exercise, in such usurped government, any office, civil or military, legislative, executive or judicial, or any authority, howsoever conferred, dependent on a recognition or establishment of such usurped government, or who has been or may hereafter be a *Penalties imposed upon persons guilty of establishing usurped government, &c. Holding office under such government*

surety in bond or otherwise, under any requirement or practice of such usurped government, for any one who has held or may hereafter hold any such office or authority, shall be incapable, by deed or otherwise, of selling, conveying, devising or encumbering any real estate situate in this state. Every deed or other instrument intended to operate on such estate, and every acknowledgment, proof or certificate of the execution thereof, and the record thereof, wheresoever made, shall be null and void.

<small>Incapable of conveying real estate</small>

2. The estates of all persons mentioned in the preceding section, which they are thereby incapacitated from conveying, shall be and are hereby declared to be subjected and devoted to the redress and indemnification of all persons, loyal to this commonwealth, who have been or may be injured by the exercise of any office or authority, civil or military, legislative, executive or judicial, howsoever conferred under the said usurped government: provided, however, that all just liens on such estates, existing on the said seventeenth day of April eighteen hundred and sixty-one, shall not be impaired.

<small>Estates of persons, how subjected to redress of loyal citizens</small>

<small>Proviso as to liens, &c</small>

3. This act shall be in force from its passage.

<small>Commencement</small>

CHAP. 6.—An ACT to protect and indemnify Citizens of Virginia.

Passed October 3, 1862.

Whereas an act or acts have recently been passed by the congress of the United States, authorizing the confiscation of the property and the emancipation of the slaves of loyal and true citizens of the state of Virginia and of the Confederate States; and it being the duty of the legislature of Virginia to protect her citizens, and as far as practicable, indemnify them from the evil consequences of the iniquitous legislation of the United States:

<small>Preamble</small>

1. Be it therefore enacted by the general assembly, that any judge or commissioner, acting under the authority of the United States government, or any of its laws, who shall, by any judgment, decision or decree, subject to confiscation or sale the property of any citizen of this commonwealth, or any clerk who shall issue process for the sale of any such property, or any marshal, sheriff or commissioner who shall sell the same, they the said judge, commissioner, clerk, marshal and sheriff, or either of them, and their securities, or any or either of them, and the purchaser or purchasers of any such property, and their personal representatives, shall be jointly and severally liable to any citizen of Virginia, or to his personal representative, whose property has been so confiscated or sold, for double the value of such property, with interest thereon, at the rate of six per centum per annum, from the time of the seizure or sale of such

<small>Judge or other officer of United States</small>

<small>Clerk, &c.</small>

<small>Purchasers of property How liable to loyal citizen</small>

property; and judgment therefor may be obtained in any court of record in this commonwealth, against such judge, commissioner, clerk, marshal and sheriff, or either of them, or against their securities, or any or either of them, or against the purchaser or purchasers of such property, or their personal representatives, upon motion in such court, upon ten days' previous personal notice, or upon thirty days' notice published in any newspaper in the city of Richmond, or in any paper published in this state. *Judgment, how obtained* *Notice, how given*

2. The remedy hereby given shall not prejudice the right of such citizen from taking possession or otherwise recovering possession of such property, or any part thereof; or if such possession should be obtained, the right of such citizen to the benefit of such liability imposed by this act, shall not be prejudiced thereby; and the right to obtain, or when obtained, to enforce such judgment, shall not be impaired by reason of the recovery of the possession of the property so sold or confiscated. *Rights of citizen not to be prejudiced* *Judgment to be enforced*

3. Be it further enacted, that any officer or agent of the United States government, who shall let or lease, or cause to be let or leased the property of any citizen of Virginia, the said officer or agent, and his securities, and the person or persons to whom the property was so let or leased, and his or their personal representatives, shall be liable to any such citizen of Virginia, or to his personal representative, for double the value of the property for the time which it was so let or leased, and for all waste or damage to which the property may have been subjected during that time; to be recovered in the manner mentioned in the first section of this act: and the court in which any case arising under this act may be pending, is authorized to have summoned and impannelled a jury to ascertain any question of fact material to the correct adjudication of the case. *As to leases* *How liable* *Waste or damage* *How recovered* *Jury, how impannelled*

4. Be it further enacted, that any judge, commissioner, or other officer or agent of the government of the United States, who shall, by any judgment, decree or decision, emancipate or cause to be emancipated the slaves of any citizen of Virginia, the judge, commissioner, or other officer or agent of the United States government, or either of them, and their securities, or either of them, shall be liable to any citizen of Virginia, or his personal representative, whose slaves have been so emancipated, for double the value of the slave or slaves; to be recovered in the manner mentioned in the first section of this act. *Penalty for emancipation* *Judge, &c. how liable* *Amount of liability*

5. Be it further enacted, that any person in this commonwealth, or the security of any such person, who shall hereafter hold or accept any office, trust or appointment, civil or military, legislative, executive or judicial, under or by authority of the government of the United States, or under or by the pretended authority of the usurped *Persons holding office, &c.*

14   REDRESS OF CITIZENS.

government, pretended to have been established since the seventeenth day of April eighteen hundred and sixty-one, within the limits of this state, separate from the existing and true government, and without the authority of the legislature; and all persons in this commonwealth who shall voluntarily aid in supporting or continuing such usurped government, or who shall aid or in any way give aid and comfort to the enemy, or who shall in any way aid, encourage or assist in carrying into effect any of the confiscation or emancipation laws of the government of the United States within this state, or who shall in any way aid, encourage or assist in carrying into effect any proclamations of the president of the United States providing for such confiscation or emancipation, shall, in addition to all penalties now imposed by any law of this commonwealth, be liable for double the value of any property that may be seized or sold under such confiscation and emancipation laws or proclamations, to any good and loyal citizen of this commonwealth, who may be injured thereby, or to his or her personal representative, with interest thereon, at the rate of six per centum per annum, from the time of such seizure or carrying away of any slave; and may be proceeded against, severally against each, or jointly against any number so liable, in said courts, in the manner herein before mentioned. Any person instituting a suit, or prosecuting a suit already commenced, or suing out execution on any judgment or decree heretofore rendered in any court or before a justice of the peace assuming to act and proceed under authority of such usurped government, or in violation of an ordinance passed by the convention of Virginia on the thirtieth day of April eighteen hundred and sixty-one, to suspend proceedings in certain cases, or in violation of an act of the general assembly passed on the twenty-ninth day of March eighteen hundred and sixty-two, entitled an act to suspend sales and legal proceedings in certain cases, and to repeal an ordinance to provide against the sacrifice of property, and to suspend proceedings in certain cases, or shall seize or sell any property, real or personal, under pretence of any authority whatever, in violation of said ordinance or last named act, shall pay to the party against whom such suit shall be commenced or prosecuted, or execution issued, or whose property shall be seized or sold as aforesaid, double the value of the thing claimed by such suit, judgment, decree, execution or other process by which property may be seized or sold. There shall not be more than one satisfaction of any judgment for the same thing.

How liable

How as to suits

Liability

Satisfaction of judgment

Record evidence not required

6. No record proof shall be required of the election or appointment of any of the officers mentioned in this act; but acting in such offices shall be deemed sufficient.

When property sold or confiscated

7. Be it further enacted, that any officer or agent, civil or military, in the service of the United States government, who shall subject or expose to sale or confiscation the property of any citizen of Virginia,

they the said officer or agent, and the purchaser or purchasers of said property, and their personal representatives, shall be jointly and severally liable to any citizen of Virginia, or to his personal representative, whose property has been so sold or confiscated, for double the value of such property, with interest thereon, at the rate of six per centum per annum, from the time of the seizure or sale of such property; and judgment may be obtained therefor in the manner mentioned in the first section of this act; and the citizen whose property has been so sold or confiscated, or his personal representative, in addition to the remedy herein given, shall be entitled to take possession or otherwise recover possession of the property so sold or confiscated. *By whom Liability Judgment, how obtained Possession*

8. A lien is hereby created and declared to exist on the real and personal estate of the persons against whom such liability may exist, from the passage of this act. *Lien created*

9. This act shall be in force from its passage. *Commencement*

CHAP. 7.—An ACT amending an act prescribing the Oath to be taken by any person who applies for a License.

Passed October 6, 1862.

1. Be it enacted by the general assembly, that the first section of an act entitled an act to prevent the circulation of small notes, passed March third, eighteen hundred and fifty-four, as amended by chapter seventy-two, passed March thirty-first, eighteen hundred and sixty-two, be amended and re-enacted, so that as amended it shall read as follows: *Act of 1854 amended*

"§ 1. That it shall be the duty of commissioners of the revenue and courts, to whom application may be made for a license, to require from each and every person who may apply for a license, an oath that he will not pay out within the limits of this commonwealth, notes of any denomination, issued by banks, corporations or individuals, without authority of law; and it shall be the duty of every commissioner of the revenue and court, to whom such application shall be made, to withhold the license until the oath aforesaid shall be taken. But this section shall not apply to any person who has commenced or who has continued business without making application for and obtaining a license, and who is or may be subject to a tax in the former case to four times, and in the latter to twice the amount of tax otherwise imposed: in which case, the assessment may be made and license granted without the oath required." *Duty of commissioners of revenue and courts License, when withheld To whom section does not apply*

2. This act shall be in force from its passage. *Commencement*

SHERIFFS.—TRIAL.

CHAP. 8.—An ACT extending the time for the qualification of the Sheriffs of Orange and Culpeper Counties.

Passed September 19, 1862.

Preamble

Whereas, by reason of the occupation of the counties of Orange and Culpeper by the public enemy, the sheriffs elected for said counties, at the late elections, have been unable to qualify: Therefore,

Sheriffs of Orange and Culpeper, when to qualify

1. Be it enacted by the general assembly, that the sheriffs elected for the counties of Orange and Culpeper, at the late spring elections, be allowed until the first day of January eighteen hundred and sixty-three, within which to qualify and give the bonds of office.

Commencement

2. This act shall be in force from its passage.

CHAP. 9.—An ACT to provide for the qualification of Sheriffs and other public officers prevented from qualifying within the period now prescribed by law, by reason of the public enemy.

Passed October 2, 1862.

When sheriff, &c. may qualify in certain cases

1. Be it enacted by the general assembly, that whenever, by reason of the occupation or the threatened invasion by the public enemy, of any county, city or town of this commonwealth, the sheriff, commissioner of the revenue or other public officer elected for such county, city or town, may be unable to qualify and give the bonds of office within the period now prescribed by law, it shall be lawful for such sheriff or other public officer to qualify and to give the bonds of office at any time within the period of ninety days after such occupation or threatened invasion by the public enemy shall have ceased.

Commencement

2. This act shall be in force from its passage.

CHAP. 10.—An ACT to amend and re-enact section 1st of chapter 80 of the Acts of 1861-2, passed March 27th, 1862.

Passed October 4, 1862.

Acts of 1861-2 amended

1. Be it enacted by the general assembly, that the first section of chapter eighty of the Acts of eighteen hundred and sixty-one and two, entitled an act to provide for the trial of persons charged with offences committed in counties in possession of the enemy, or threatened with immediate invasion, passed March twenty-seventh, eighteen hundred and sixty-two, be amended and re-enacted so as to read as follows:

When county in

"§ 1. Be it enacted by the general assembly; that whenever any

TRIAL.—DISTILLATION. 17

county or corporation in this state shall be in the possession of the <small>Possession of enemy</small>
enemy, or shall be threatened with invasion, so as to make it probable
that the jurisdiction of the courts thereof cannot be safely exercised
therein, it shall be the duty of the judge of the circuit to which such <small>Powers of judges and justices</small>
county belongs, and any judge of the state or any justice of the
peace shall be empowered to cause all persons charged with felony
in such county or corporation, to be brought before him, by warrant
directed to any officer in the commonwealth, to be by him executed,
and to commit him for examination before an examining court of <small>Commitment, how made</small>
some county or corporation not in the possession of the enemy or
threatened with invasion, the most convenient to that where the
offence shall have been committed."

2. This act shall be in force from its passage. <small>Commencement</small>

CHAP. 11.—An ACT legalizing the manufacture of Alcohol.

Passed October 1, 1862.

1. Be it enacted by the general assembly, that it shall be lawful <small>Alcohol, how distilled</small>
for any person to engage in the distillation of any grain for the pur-
pose of converting the product of such distillation into alcohol, subject, however, to the provisions of this act.

2. That before any such person shall engage in such distillation, <small>Permission, how obtained</small>
he shall obtain permission therefor from the governor of the com-
monwealth; and such permission shall only authorize the manufacture of alcohol for medical, hospital, chemical and manufacturing
purposes.

3. That the legal standard of alcohol shall be not less than ninety <small>Legal standard</small>
per centum of pure alcohol.

4. No alcohol so manufactured shall be sold by the manufacturer <small>To be gauged and inspected Inspector, how appointed</small>
until the same shall have been gauged and inspected by a gauger to
be appointed by the governor for each county, city or town in which
such permission shall be granted.

5. For every cask or other vessel of alcohol inspected under this <small>Fee of gauger</small>
act, the gauger shall receive of the manufacturer the sum of ten
cents; and it shall not be lawful for the manufacturer to dispose of <small>Cask, &c. to be marked by gauger</small>
any cask or other vessel, unless it shall have the mark of the gauger,
specifying the quantity and quality of the alcohol therein contained:
and if any alcohol shall be presented by the manufacturer of a less <small>When gauger to condemn</small>
standard than herein prescribed, it shall be the duty of the gauger to
condemn the same, and cause it to be thrown away in his presence.

2

Sales, how reported

Penalties

6. Every sale of alcohol made by the manufacturer shall be reported to the governor, or such other authorities as may be prescribed by him; and any manufacturer of alcohol who shall attempt to sell to any one, except for the purpose herein before mentioned, or who shall violate any of the provisions of this act, shall be subject to all the penalties prescribed by an act to prevent the unnecessary consumption of grain by distillers and other manufacturers of spirituous or malt liquors: and any person who shall alter or remove from any cask or other vessel of alcohol, the mark placed upon it by the gauger, shall be liable to pay a fine of not less than one hundred dollars; to be recovered by motion, after ten days' notice, before any court of the commonwealth; one-half to the informer, and the other half to the commonwealth.

Fine for removal of gauger's mark

Sale of alcohol as a beverage prohibited

7. All persons who shall directly or indirectly be concerned in vending, or using or promoting the use of any alcohol as and for a drink, shall be subject to the same penalty as is prescribed in the foregoing section (to be recovered and disposed of in the same manner as is therein prescribed); and each offence of the provisions of this section shall be deemed a separate offence, and subject to the same penalties.

Statement to be made to commissioner of revenue

Tax

8. Every person who shall, by virtue of the provisions of this act, engage in the manufacture of alcohol, shall, at the period in which he shall list his property for taxation, furnish to the commissioner of the revenue of the said county, city or town in which said manufacture shall be carried on, a statement, to be verified under oath, of the number of gallons he shall have sold; and said commissioner shall thereupon assess him with a tax of thirty cents for each gallon so sold, and return the same to the sheriff or collector of the revenue of the county, city or town, who shall proceed to collect the same, and account therefor in the mode prescribed for the collection and payment of the revenue of the state.

License, how revocable

9. Any license granted under this act shall be revocable at the discretion of the governor; and it shall be his duty to revoke such license when he shall have reason to believe it is abused by being perverted from the uses intended by this act.

Rights suspended on indictment

What, on conviction

Oath, how taken

Whisky not to be distilled

Bond, how given

10. That upon a presentment or indictment by any grand jury of the city or county, in which such alcohol may be distilled, for a violation of this act, the rights granted thereby shall be suspended; and if the party be convicted on such presentment or indictment, shall be from that time ipso facto revoked: provided, that before any person is licensed under this act, he shall take an oath, the form of which shall be prescribed by the governor, to the effect that no whisky distilled shall be sold or given away, or otherwise used than to be converted into alcohol: provided further, that no license shall be

DISTILLATION.

granted under this act until the applicant shall have given bond, with good security, to be filed with the auditor of public accounts, in a penalty of two thousand dollars, payable to the commonwealth of Virginia, conditioned that all the whisky made by him under his license shall be converted into alcohol, and that the applicant shall pay all the taxes that may be chargeable on such distillery, whether assessed or not: provided, that no person shall obtain such license, unless he shall have been previously recommended by the court of the county or corporation in which such distillery is proposed to be erected, as a suitable and proper person for exercising such privilege in such county or corporation. *Conditions*

Recommendation by county court

11. This act shall be in force from its passage. *Commencement*

CHAP. 12.—An ACT to amend and re-enact an act entitled an act to prevent the unnecessary consumption of Grain by Distillers and other manufacturers of Spirituous and Malt Liquors.

Passed October 2, 1862.

1. Be it enacted by the general assembly, that the first section of an act passed on the twelfth day of March eighteen hundred and sixty-two, entitled an act to prevent the unnecessary consumption of grain by distillers and other manufacturers of spirituous and malt liquors, be amended and re-enacted so as to read as follows: *Act of 1861-2 amended*

"§ 1. It shall not be lawful for any person hereafter to make or cause to be made any whisky, or other spirituous or malt liquors, out of any corn, wheat, rye or other grain, except for medicinal or hospital purposes, in execution of a bona fide contract heretofore made, or hereafter to be made with the chief purveyor of the medical department of the Confederate States government, or with the medical director of the Virginia state line: and any person so offending shall be deemed guilty of a misdemeanor, and upon conviction thereof, shall be fined for every offence not less than one hundred dollars nor more than five thousand dollars, and be subject to imprisonment in the county jail not exceeding twelve months, at the discretion of the court." *Distillation prohibited*

Exceptions

2. This act shall be in force from its passage. *Commencement*

CHAP. 13.—An ACT to amend and re-enact section thirty-third of chapter first of the Acts 1861-2, concerning a License to distill Ardent Spirits from Fruit, &c.

Passed October 2, 1862.

Acts of 1861-2 amended

1. Be it enacted by the general assembly, that section thirty-third of chapter one of Acts of eighteen hundred and sixty-one and two be amended and re-enacted so as to read as follows:

License to distill fruit, &c.

"§ 33. On every license to distill ardent spirits from fruit, vegetables, syrups, molasses, sugar cane or sugars, the tax shall be thirty dollars. If such distillery has been in operation for the preceding year or any part thereof, there shall be an additional tax of ten cents per gallon on the quantity of liquor manufactured at such distillery

Tax

for the year next preceding, or for any part thereof: provided, that if the amount distilled in any one year shall exceed five hundred gallons, the tax shall be sixty dollars for every such license; and if the amount distilled shall exceed one thousand gallons, the tax shall be seventy-five dollars for every such license. A license for the business authorized by this section shall be obtained as other licenses are obtained, and with like penalties for a failure to obtain the same, notwithstanding the exemption provided for in the act passed March thirtieth, eighteen hundred and sixty, entitled an act making regula-

Proviso

tions concerning licenses: provided no license or tax shall be required of any person for manufacturing thirty-three gallons in one year out of the fruit, vegetables, syrups, molasses, sugar cane or sugars of his own production, for his own use."

Commencement

2. This act shall be in force from its passage.

CHAP. 14.—An ACT to repeal the Fence Law of Virginia as to certain Counties, and to authorize the County Courts to dispense with Enclosures in other Counties.

Passed October 3, 1862,

Preamble

Whereas a considerable portion of the territory of the commonwealth having been ravaged by the public enemy, and a great loss of labor, fencing and timber thereby sustained, it is rendered difficult if not impossible for the people of many counties and parts of counties, to keep up enclosures around their farms, according to existing laws:

Code repealed as to counties designated

1. Be it therefore enacted by the general assembly of Virginia, that the first section of the ninety-ninth chapter of the Code of Virginia, so far as it applies to the counties of Hanover, Henrico, New Kent, Charles City, James City, York, Warwick, Elizabeth City, Alexandria, Fairfax, Fauquier, Stafford and King George, be and the same is hereby repealed.

FENCE LAW.—JAILORS' FEES.

2. Be it further enacted, that the county courts of the counties of Augusta, Frederick, Clarke, Warren, Rappahannock, Norfolk, Princess Anne, Mercer, Shenandoah, Page, Prince William, Spotsylvania, Hampshire, Berkeley, Caroline and Nansemond, shall have power, all the justices having been summoned, and a majority thereof being present, to dispense with the existing law in regard to enclosures, so far as their respective counties may be concerned, or such parts thereof, to be described by metes and bounds, as in their discretion they may deem it expedient to exempt from the operation of such law. *Powers of county courts in other counties*

3. If any horses, mules, cattle, hogs, sheep or goats, or any animal of either of the preceding classes, shall enter into any grounds in the counties enumerated in the first section of this act, in which the existing law of enclosures has been repealed, or into the grounds of any other county or counties or parts of counties in which the courts thereof shall repeal the existing law of enclosures, after such repeal, the owner or manager of any such animal shall be liable to the owner or occupier of such grounds for any damages arising from such entry; for every succeeding trespass by such animal, the owner thereof shall be liable for double damages; and after having given at least five days' notice to the owner or manager of such animal, of two previous trespasses, the owner or occupier of such grounds shall be entitled to such animal, if it be found again trespassing on said grounds. *Damages for entry of animals, &c. When owner liable for double damages*

4. Provided, however, that this act shall apply to and be in force in the counties of Elizabeth City, York and Warwick only for the period of three years, dating from the declaration of peace between the Confederate States and the United States. *Proviso*

5. This act shall be in force from its passage. *Commencement*

CHAP. 15.—An ACT to increase Jailors' Fees for keeping and supporting Prisoners.

Passed September 24, 1862.

1. Be it enacted by the general assembly, that jailors shall hereafter be allowed sixty cents per day for keeping and supporting persons confined in the jails of this commonwealth: provided, that the county or corporation courts of the commonwealth may establish, in their discretion, a different rate, not less than thirty-five cents nor more than eighty cents per diem. *Jailors' fees. Power of county courts*

2. This act shall be in force from its passage, and shall continue in force until six months after the ratification of a treaty of peace between the Confederate States and the United States, unless sooner repealed or amended. When this act expires, the law on this subject, in force immediately before the passage of this act, shall be deemed to be revived and continued in force. *Commencement. When law revived*

CHAP. 16.—An ACT amending the seventeenth section of chapter thirty-six of the Code of Virginia, concerning the manner of making Returns of Delinquents.

Passed September 26, 1862.

Code amended

1. Be it enacted by the general assembly of Virginia, that the seventeenth section of chapter thirty-six of the Code of Virginia be amended and re-enacted, so as when amended it shall read as follows:

List, how arranged

"§ 17. In the lists mentioned in the preceding section, the names of the persons charged with the taxes shall be placed alphabetically and in the order in which they respectively appear on the commissioners' books. The lists mentioned secondly shall be in the following form:

List of real estate in the county of   , delinquent for the non-payment of taxes thereon for the year   .

Name of person.	Residence.	Estate held.	Quantity of land.	Description and situation of land.	Distance and bearing from courthouse.	Amount of taxes.	Why returned delinquent.

Oath of officer

And the sheriff or collector returning such list shall, at the foot thereof, subscribe the following oath: 'I, A B, sheriff (or deputy sheriff) of the county of   , do swear that the foregoing list is, I verily believe, correct and just; and that I have received no part of the taxes for which the real estate therein mentioned is returned delinquent; and that I have used due diligence to find property within my county liable to distress for the said taxes, but have found none.'"

Commencement

2. This act shall be in force from its passage.

CHAP. 17.—An ACT to legalize the Records and Proceedings of the County Court of Essex County, at the June, July and August Terms of said Court held at Miller's Tavern in said County.

Passed October 2, 1862.

Preamble

Whereas it has been represented to the general assembly of Virginia, that in consequence of the suspension of the mail between the seat of government of said state and the county of Essex, by reason of the federal army being around the city of Richmond, till after the fourth day of July eighteen hundred and sixty-two: And whereas the federal gun boats were constantly plying between the mouth of the Rappahannock river and Fredericksburg, from the early part of the month of April eighteen hundred and sixty-two to the fifth day of September eighteen hundred and sixty-two, and the said gun boats still have the command of the said river: And whereas the courthouse of the said county is situated on the margin of said river: And whereas the interruption of the mail between the seat of government and the county seat of said county, during the period first aforesaid, prevented any application to the governor of Virginia to designate, by proclamation, some other place in the said county to hold the sessions of the county court of said ounty during the continuance of the causes aforesaid, as by law the governor is authorized to do; and it was further considered impo tic to publish any notice of the place where the sessions of the said court might be held, lest the enemy might get information of the same, and interrupt the proceedings of the said court:

1. Be it therefore enacted by the general assembly, that all acts and things done by the said county court of Essex county, at the place in said county known by the name of Miller's tavern, at the June, July and August terms of said court, which appear from the order book of said court to have been done at the courthouse of said county, though done at Miller's tavern aforesaid, which might have been legally done at the courthouse of said county, are hereby declared and made legal and valid, as if the same had been done at the courthouse of said county. *Acts of county court legalized*

2. This act shall be in force from its passage. *Commencement*

CHAP. 18.—An ACT for the relief of Judge George W. Thompson.

Passed October 4, 1862.

1. Be it enacted by the general assembly, that the ordinance of the late convention suspending the payment of the salary of George W. Thompson, one of the circuit judges of this commonwealth, is hereby repealed; and the auditor of public accounts is directed to issue his warrant or warrants for the salary due to said judge, in the same manner as if said ordinance had not been passed. *Ordinance repealed, Salary, how paid*

2. This act shall be in force from its passage. *Commencement*

CHAP. 19.—An ACT repealing an act for the relief of Ephraim Bee.

Passed September 26, 1862.

Act of 1858 repealed

1. Be it enacted by the general assembly, that the act entitled an act authorizing Jonathan M. Bennett to convey by deed to Ephraim Bee of the county of Doldridge, certain forfeited and delinquent lands sold in the county of Jackson, but now in the county of Roane, upon the payment of a balance of purchase money, passed February eighteenth, eighteen hundred and fifty-eight, be and the same is hereby repealed.

Commencement

2. This act shall be in force from its passage.

CHAP. 20.—An ACT to authorize the Governor to settle the Account of Sampson Jones, Agent of Mrs. Jane A. Griffin.

Passed September 29, 1862.

Governor authorized to settle account

1. Be it enacted by the general assembly, that the governor of this commonwealth be and he is hereby authorized to settle the account of Sampson Jones, agent for Mrs. Jane A. Griffin, for supplying the public guard with rations from the first day of April eighteen hundred and sixty-one to the first day of October eighteen hundred and sixty-two, under a contract for that purpose with Captain Dimmock, commandant of the public guard; and that he ascertain the actual loss sustained under said contract, by reason of the great advance in the price of provisions during the same period; and that he authorize the said Jones, agent as aforesaid, to be paid his actual loss under said contract.

Terms

Commencement

2. This act shall be in force from its passage.

CHAP. 21.—An ACT to amend the Charter of the Town of Danville.

Passed October 6, 1862.

Act of 1854 amended

1. Be it enacted by the general assembly, that the third section of the act passed March seventh, eighteen hundred and sixty-two, entitled an act to amend an act entitled an act amending the charter of the town of Danville, passed March fourth, eighteen hundred and fifty-four, and incorporating into one the subsequent acts amendatory thereof, be amended and re-enacted so as to read as follows:

Jurisdiction of hustings court

"§ 3. The jurisdiction of said court, except as to matters of police, which shall belong to the council, shall correspond with that of the county courts as established by law; and the said court shall continue to have jurisdiction, and the said mayor and aldermen shall continue each to have the powers of a justice of the peace, not only within the said corporate limits, but also for the space of one mile without and around the limits of said town, in all matters arising within the said town or in the said space of one mile, according to the laws of the commonwealth and the ordinances of the town, and shall execute the same in like manner and under like responsibilities, and receive the like compensation for services rendered by them as the justices of the county courts within this commonwealth receive: provided, however, that not more than three aldermen shall receive compensation for any one day of such service in court, unless such court be one in which a greater number than three aldermen are required by law. The said aldermen shall classify themselves for service in court, in like manner as justices of the peace in counties are classified by law; and any presentment in said court by a grand jury for an offence against the said laws, committed within the jurisdiction of said court, may be presented in said court in like manner, and like proceedings be had thereon as in the county court of Pittsylvania; and the said court of hustings shall bear the same relation to the circuit court for the town of Danville, as the county court of said county bears to the circuit court thereof; and appeals may be taken, and writs of error, supersedeas, certiorari and any other judicial writs may be sued out and prosecuted in like manner as is done in the county courts of the commonwealth." *Aldermen, how classified*

Powers of hustings court

2. This act shall be in force from its passage. *Commencement*

RESOLUTIONS.

No. 1.—Joint Resolutions guaranteeing to the people of the Northwestern section of the State the construction of a Rail Road connecting that portion of the State with the Seaboard, at the earliest day practicable.

Adopted October 4, 1862.

Whereas, by the secession of Virginia from the late Union, and her accession to the Confederacy, the northwestern section of the state has become a border on a foreign and hostile nation, and has no direct intercourse in trade and travel with other and more favored portions of the state, and the prosperity of that as well as other sections of the state will be greatly promoted by a closer union and more frequent intercommunication: And whereas, on the seventeenth day of January eighteen hundred and sixty-two the general assembly of Virginia did resolve to "maintain the jurisdiction and sovereignty of the state of Virginia, to the uttermost limits of her ancient boundaries, at any and every cost;" and the congress of the Confederate States, on the twenty-second day of January eighteen hundred and sixty-two, by resolution, did "pledge all the resources of the Confederacy to uphold her determination" aforesaid: Therefore, *Preamble*

1. Resolved by the general assembly of Virginia, that increased facilities of trade and travel between the northwestern section of the state and the capital and seaboard, are demanded alike by the welfare of that section and the permanent interests of the whole state, in peace and in war, and that justice and sound policy require that such facilities be established without unnecessary delay. *Rail road connection required*

2. Resolved, that the general assembly declare, as an assurance to the citizens of the said northwestern section, that the available resources of the commonwealth shall be liberally devoted to the construction of a rail road which shall connect that section with the interior and seaboard of the state, whereby the enterprise, energy and resources of that section may be encouraged and developed, at the earliest practicable date. *Assurance of general assembly*

3. Resolved, that in the opinion of this general assembly, immediately on the conclusion of the existing war, the state should cause experimental surveys to be made, to ascertain the best, cheapest, shortest and most practicable route for a rail road connection between that part of the state and the capital. *Surveys ought to be made*

No. 2.—Joint Resolution authorizing the Branch of the Exchange Bank of Virginia at Richmond to declare a dividend for the six months ending 30th June 1862.

Adopted October 4, 1862.

Preamble

Whereas it is represented that the Exchange Bank of Virginia at Norfolk is within the lines of the public enemy, and that no dividend of profits for the six months ending on the thirtieth day of June eighteen hundred and sixty-two can be declared in the mode prescribed by law: Therefore,

Dividend, how to be declared

Resolved by the general assembly, that for the six months ending on the thirtieth day of June eighteen hundred and sixty-two, the branch of the Exchange Bank of Virginia at Richmond may declare a dividend of profits, not exceeding three per centum on the capital stock of said bank, and when so declared, shall pay the state's dividend, the tax thereon, and the bonus on the capital of said bank into the treasury.

No. 3.—Resolution instructing the Board of Public Works to adopt measures to meet the demand for Wood in the cities of Richmond and Petersburg.

Adopted October 6, 1862.

Duty of board of public works

Resolved by the general assembly, that the board of public works be instructed to adopt such measures as they may deem most expedient, to require the different rail road companies whose roads terminate in the cities of Richmond and Petersburg, to furnish a sufficient number of wood cars for the transportation of wood into the said cities, to supply the demand for the same, and that they cause the same to be transported to the said cities at a reasonable rate of tolls. To accomplish which, the said board are required to use all the power conferred on them by law for the supervision and control of said companies:

Proviso

provided, that if the said companies be opposed to the transportation of wood, the burden thereof be apportioned equitably among them, and in such a manner as not to interfere with their transportation for the confederate government.

No. 4.—Joint Resolution authorizing Justices of the Peace to issue Marriage Licenses in certain cases.

Adopted October 6, 1862.

When license issued by justice

Resolved by the general assembly of Virginia, that it shall be lawful for any justice of the peace in either of the several counties of this commonwealth, where the office of clerk of the county court shall be vacant, or where, by reason of the presence of the public enemy, or by their expected presence, the said clerks shall be absent from their respective counties, to issue licenses for the solemnization of marriages, upon the parties applying therefor complying with the provisions of the statute authorizing the issue of said licenses. The Duty of justice said justices shall return to the said clerks, whenever they shall resume the duties of their office, copies of said licenses so issued, together with the bonds taken, to be recorded, and have the same force and validity as if issued by the clerks of the respective counties.

No. 5.—Resolution authorizing the Governor to fill Vacancies in the office of Assessor, under the act to provide for the production, sale and distribution of Salt, &c.

Adopted October 4, 1862.

Resolved by the general assembly, that any vacancy that may Power of governor occur in the office of assessor, under the act passed October third, eighteen hundred and sixty-two, entitled an act to provide for the production, distribution and sale of salt in this commonwealth, either by death, resignation, removal or otherwise, may be filled by appointment of the governor of this commonwealth.

No. 6.—Resolution in relation to the Adjournment of the General Assembly.

Adopted September 30, 1862.

Resolved, that the general assembly, when it adjourns on Monday next, will adjourn to meet on the first Wednesday in January eighteen hundred and sixty-three, unless sooner convened by the governor, in pursuance of the power vested in him by the constitution.

INDEX.

ADJOURNMENT.
Resolution as to adjournment of general assembly, 29

AGENTS.
For sale of salt, may be appointed, 4
Their bonds, 4-5
Of quartermaster or commissary, not exempt from military service, 9

ALCOHOL.
Its manufacture legalized, 17
Permission, how obtained, 17
To what purposes limited, 17
Legal standard, 17
To be gauged and inspected, 17
Gauger, how appointed; his fee, 17
Cask not to be sold without gauger's mark, 17
Alcohol below standard to be condemned, 17
Manufacturer to report sales to governor, 18
Penalties on manufacturer for violating provisions of act, 18
Fine for removal of gauger's mark, 18
For selling alcohol as a beverage, 18
Manufacturer to furnish list of sales to commissioner of revenue, 18
What tax then to be assessed, 18
License to manufacture, how revocable, 18
Rights under license suspended upon presentment for violation of act, 18
Upon conviction, license revoked, 18
Oath to be taken against selling the whiskey before conversion into alcohol, 18
Applicant for license to give bond, 18
Condition of bond, 19
Applicant must be recommended by court, 19

ANIMALS.
Entering grounds where fence law is repealed, owner liable, 21

APPROPRIATION.
To carry into effect salt act, 5
How payments from it to be made, 5

ARDENT SPIRITS.
See Alcohol.
See Spirituous and malt liquors.

ASSESSMENT.
See Board of assessors.

BANK DIVIDEND.
Richmond branch of Exchange Bank may declare dividend, 28

BANK NOTES.
What oath required of applicant for license, as to circulation of, 15
Exception, 15

BEE, EPHRAIM.
Act authorizing conveyance of forfeited lands to him repealed, 24

BOARD OF ASSESSORS.
For property taken under salt act, how composed, 5
To assess compensation or damages, 5
How assessment certified and paid, 5
When it is final, 5
Appeal from assessment, and proceedings thereon, 5
How board convened and paid, 5
Vacancy in office of assessor, how filled, 29

BOARD OF PUBLIC WORKS.
Duty of, as to wood cars for supplying Richmond and Petersburg, 28

BONDS.
To be given by agents appointed to sell salt, 4
Penalty and condition of such bonds, 5
To be given before license to manufacture alcohol, 18
Condition of bond, 19

CANALS.
See Rail roads and canals.

CHANGES IN CODE.
Section 2, chapter 22, amended, 9
Exemptions from military service, 9
Section 1, chapter 99, repealed, as to certain counties, 20
Fence law repealed as to those counties, 20
County courts may dispense with it in others, 21
Repeal as to some counties limited in duration, 21
Section 17, chapter 36, amended, 22
Mode of making returns of delinquents changed, 22

CITIES.
See Counties and towns.

CITIZENS OF VIRGINIA.
See Redress of loyal citizens.
See Usurped government.

CITY OFFICERS.
What officers may be exempted from military service, and how,	9–10
When such exempts remanded to service,	10
And failing to obey, accounted deserters,	10

CLERKS.
Copies of requisition for slaves to be filed with clerks of counties, &c.	6
Clerks to summon the justices,	6
To attend sessions of the courts held under such requisition,	7
Clerk of court to be clerk of board of exemption,	10
Claims for exemption to be filed with him,	11
Clerk to report exempts to adjutant general,	11
Penalty for failure to discharge duty as clerk of board,	11
How, as to marriage licenses, when office of clerk of county vacant,	28
Or when, by reason of invasion, clerk absent,	29
What to be done on clerk's return,	29

CODE.
See Changes in Code.

COMMISSIONERS OF REVENUE.
To assist courts when requisition made for slaves,	7
To aid governor when courts fail to act,	7
What oath commissioner must require before issuing a license,	15
With what exception,	15
To assess taxes on manufacturers of alcohol,	18

CONFEDERATE STATES.
Contracts with, for salt, to be respected,	3
Slaves to be called into service of,	6
When value of such slaves to be paid by,	6
And compensation for injury to slaves,	6
Burden of proof to be on confederate authorities as to proper care,	6
President's request for slaves is an acceptance of the act by Confederate States,	8
Contracts to make whiskey, &c. may be made with C. S. medical purveyor,	19

CONTRACTS.
What, to be respected in carrying out act for procuring supply of salt,	3–4
In what case contracts with other states may be disregarded,	4

COUNTIES AND TOWNS.
What city officers may be exempted from military service,	9–10
Orange and Culpeper occupied by public enemy,	16
Sheriffs elect allowed further time to qualify,	16
Similar provision as to officers of other counties, &c.	16
Fence law repealed as to certain counties,	20
And may be dispensed with by county courts in others,	21
Limitation of time as to some of the counties,	21
Certain records, &c. of Essex county court legalized,	22
Acts of the court declared legal,	23
Charter of Danville amended,	24
As to jurisdiction and powers of hustings court,	25
Supply of wood for Richmond and Petersburg,	28
Rail road companies to furnish wood cars,	28
If companies object, burden to be apportioned,	28
When office of county clerk vacant, how, as to marriage licenses,	28
Or when clerk absent by reason of invasion,	29
What, when clerk returns,	29
For requisition on counties, &c. for slaves, see Slaves.	

COURTS.
Contracts with county courts for salt, to be respected,	3
Appeals from assessments under salt act to circuit court of Richmond city,	5
County and corporation courts to carry into effect requisition for slaves,	6
Specific duties of the courts under requisition,	6–7
Failing the courts, governor may impress slaves,	7
Before granting license what oath courts to require,	15
With what exception,	15
Courts of certain counties may dispense with fence law,	21
Essex county court, certain records, &c. legalized,	22
Acts of the court declared valid,	23

CULPEPER AND ORANGE.
Occupied by public enemy,	16
Sheriffs elect allowed time to qualify,	16

DAMAGES.
For use, &c. of property taken under salt act, see Assessment.
For cattle entering grounds where fence law is repealed, see Fence law.

DANVILLE.
Act to amend charter,	24
Jurisdiction of hustings court,	24
Compensation of aldermen,	25
Classification of aldermen,	25
Powers of hustings court,	25

DEFENCE.
See Public defence.

DELINQUENTS.
Mode of making returns of, changed,	22
List, how arranged,	22

Oath of returning officer, 22

DESERTERS.
In what case exempted city officers, &c. to be treated as deserters, 10

DISLOYALTY.
See Treason or disloyalty.

DISTILLATION.
See Alcohol.
See Spirituous and malt liquors.

ENGINES.
Necessary for production of salt, may be seized, 3

ESSEX.
Certain records, &c. of county court legalized, 22

ESTATES.
Persons connected with usurped government incapable of conveying real estate, 11
Their estates devoted to redress loyal citizens, 12
What liens on such estates not impaired, 12
Lien on estate of person acting under U. S. confiscation and emancipation acts, 15

EXCHANGE BANK OF VIRGINIA.
Branch at Richmond to declare dividend, 28

EXEMPTIONS FROM MILITARY DUTY.
Act changing provisions of Code, amended; general exemptions, 9
Agent of quartermaster or commissary not exempt: nor militia officers, 9
What additional officers of a city may be exempted, and how, 9–10
Officers, &c. of what companies may be exempted, 10
When exempts remanded to service, 10
Failing to return to service, deserters, 10
How places of exempts to be filled, 10
Persons leaving the service for which exempted, to be reported, 10
Boards of exemption, how constituted, 10
Who to act as clerk of board, 10
Powers of board, 10
Discharges for physical infirmity, 11
Claims for exemption, how tried, 11
Names of exempts, to whom reported, 11
Penalties for failure of duty in board and clerk, 11

FAITH OF COMMONWEALTH.
May be pledged by governor to contracts necessary for procuring salt, 3

FEES.
Fee of gauger for inspecting alcohol, 17
Jailors' fees for keeping prisoners, increased, 21
County courts may establish different rate, 21
When act to expire; former law revived, 21

FENCE LAW.
Loss of fencing, &c. in invaded counties, 20
Repealed as to certain counties, 20
And may be dispensed with by county courts in others, 21

Damages for entry of animals, &c. 21
Repeal limited in duration as to some of the counties, 21

FINES.
What fine for selling salt at higher than regulation price, 4
Or for other violations of rules for sale, 4
On board of exemptions and clerk for failures in duty, 11
For removal of gauger's mark on cask of alcohol, 18
For selling alcohol as a beverage, 18

FIRE DEPARTMENT.
Officers of, how exempted from military service; when remanded to service, 10

FORTIFICATIONS.
Act for calling out slaves to work on, 6
For particulars of this act, see Slaves.

GAS WORKS.
Officers of, how exempted from military service, 10
When remanded to service, 10

GAUGERS.
Of alcohol to be appointed; their fees, 17
Cask not to be sold without gauger's mark, 17
To condemn alcohol below standard, 17
Fine for removal of gauger's mark, 18

GENERAL ASSEMBLY.
Communications to, as to militia officers removed for treason or disloyalty, 8
Resolution as to adjournment, 29

GOVERNOR.
Powers for procuring supply of salt, 3–5
Under president's call for slaves, 6–7
For removal of militia officers for treason, &c. 8
As to exemptions from military service, 10
To appoint gaugers for inspection of alcohol, 17
And assessor under salt act when a vacancy, 29

GRIFFIN, MRS. JANE A.
Her agent's account for rations of public guard to be settled, 24
Actual loss under contract to be paid, 24

HUSTINGS COURT.
See Courts.

INVASION.
Of Orange and Culpeper, 15
Sheriffs allowed further time to qualify, 16
Similar provision as to officers of other counties and towns, 16
Persons charged with felony in such counties, &c. to be removed for trial, 16–17
Fencing, &c. destroyed in parts of the state, 20
Fence law repealed in certain counties, 20
Repealable in others, 21
Repeal limited in duration as to some counties, 21
Exchange Bank at Norfolk within enemy's line, 28

INDEX.

Richmond branch may declare dividend, 28
Provision for marriage licenses when by reason of invasion clerk of county absent, 29
What to be done when clerk returns, 29

JAILORS' FEES.
See Fees.

JONES, SAMPSON.
His account as agent of Mrs. Griffin to be settled, 24
Loss under contract to be paid him, 24

JUSTICES OF THE PEACE.
In counties where office of clerk vacant, may issue marriage licenses, 28
Or when clerk absent by reason of invasion, 29
What, when clerk returns, 29

KANAWHA SALT WORKS.
Not to be purchased by governor, 3

LICENSES.
Before any license granted, what oath as to circulating notes, 15
To what persons this does not apply, 15
License to make alcohol to be obtained of governor, 17
And is revocable at his discretion, 18
What oath applicant must take, 18
Applicant must also give bond, 19
Must be recommended by court, 19
License to distill ardent spirits from fruit, &c.; act amended, 20
Tax on such license, 20
Penalty for failure to get license, 20
Proviso as to quantity to be distilled without license, 20
Marriage licenses, by whom issued when office of county clerk vacant, 28
Or when clerk absent by reason of invasion; what, when clerk returns, 29

LIENS.
See Estates.

LOYAL CITIZENS.
See Redress of loyal citizens.
See Usurped government.

MACHINERY.
Necessary for production of salt, may be seized, 3

MARRIAGE LICENSES.
By whom issued when office of county clerk vacant, 28
Or when by reason of invasion clerk absent, 29
What to be done when clerk returns, 29

MEDICAL DIRECTOR.
Of Virginia state line may contract for whiskey, &c. 19

MEDICAL PURVEYOR.
Of Confederate States may contract for whiskey, &c. 19

MILITIA.
Officers may be removed by governor for treason or disloyalty, 8
Senate may reverse governor's action, 8
Governor not to remove when arrests can be made and charges preferred, 8
To assign his reasons for removals, 8
Militia officers not exempt from draft, 9
When drafted, their commissions vacated, 9

NORTHWESTERN VIRGINIA.
Rail road connection between that section and the seaboard guaranteed, 27

ORANGE AND CULPEPER.
Occupied by public enemy, 16
Sheriffs elect allowed time to qualify, 16

OVERSEERS.
Of slaves furnished under requisition, see Slaves.

POLICE OFFICERS.
How exempted from military service, 10
When remanded to service, 10

PRESIDENT OF CONFEDERATE STATES.
Slaves to be called out at his request,
President's request accepts provisions of act, 8

PRICE OF SALT.
What publication of, required, 4
Fine for selling at higher price, 4

PRISONERS.
Jailors' fees for keeping, increased, 21
For what time increased, 21

PUBLIC DEFENCE.
Act further to provide for, 6
Authorizes governor to call out slaves, 6
For particulars of this act, see Slaves.

PUBLIC GUARD.
Account of Sampson Jones for rations, to be settled, 24
Loss under contract to be paid, 24

QUALIFICATION OF OFFICERS.
Sheriffs of Culpeper and Orange allowed time to qualify, 16
Similar provision as to officers of other invaded counties, &c. 16

RAIL ROADS AND CANALS.
May be controlled for transportation of salt, &c. 4
Officers, &c. how exempted from military service, 10
When their service again due, 10
Presidents to report such to governor, 10
Rail road connection between northwest and seaboard guaranteed, 27
Rail roads terminating in Richmond and Petersburg to furnish wood cars, 28
If companies opposed, burden to be apportioned, 28

REDRESS OF LOYAL CITIZENS.

Act for relief of those injured by usurped power,	11
What estates devoted to their relief,	12
Act to protect and indemnify citizens of Virginia,	12
Who liable for confiscating property,	12
Purchasers liable,	12
Judgment, how obtained,	13
Right to recover otherwise,	13
Recovery otherwise not to impair remedy given by act,	13
Who liable for leasing property of citizens,	13
How liability enforced,	13
Jury may be summoned,	13
Similar liabilities and proceedings for emancipating slaves,	13
Liabilities of other persons assisting in such confiscation, &c.	14
Liabilities for prosecuting suits before judges, &c. of usurped government or of U. States,	14
Who liable for exposing property of citizens to sale or confiscation,	14
Purchasers also liable,	15
Judgment, how obtained,	15
As additional remedy, property may be retaken,	15
Lien on estates of persons liable for such offences,	15

RESOLUTIONS.

Resolution guaranteeing rail road between Northwestern Virginia and the seaboard,	27
Increased facilities for travel, &c. required,	27
Assurance given of a rail road connection,	27
When surveys should be made,	27
Resolution as to dividend by Richmond branch of Exchange Bank,	28
Amount of dividend,	28
Resolution to require wood cars for supplying Richmond and Petersburg,	28
Duty of board of public works,	28
If rail road companies opposed, burden to be apportioned,	28
Resolution as to marriage licenses in certain cases,	28
When office of clerk vacant,	28
Or when clerk absent by reason of invasion,	29
Duty of justices on clerk's return,	29
Resolution as to vacancy in office of assessor under salt act,	29
Governor to fill vacancy,	29
Resolution as to adjournment of general assembly,	29

SALT.

Act for production, distribution and sale of; general powers of governor,	3
May pledge faith of commonwealth,	3
His power over property and franchises,	3
Salt works not to be purchased,	3
What property may be seized,	3
What contracts to be respected,	3-4
When contracts with other states to be disregarded,	4
When other states to be furnished,	4
Right to manufacture and sell, after uses of state are supplied,	4
Powers over rail roads and canals for transportation,	4
Places of distribution to be designated,	4
Rules and regulations for sale,	4
Publication of prices,	4
After publication, sale at higher price a misdemeanor,	4
Violation of rules a misdemeanor,	4
Upon conviction, what fine,	4
Agents for sales,	4
Agents to give bond,	4
Penalty and condition of bond,	5
Amount appropriated to carry out the act,	5
Payments out of treasury, how to be made,	5
Board of assessors, how composed and appointed,	5
What assessments board to make,	5
How assessment to be certified and paid,	5
Certificate to be filed with secretary of state,	5
Secretary to forward copy to person entitled,	5
When assessment final,	5
When appeal allowed, and to what court,	5
Proceedings on the appeal,	5
Injunction not to be granted against governor,	5
How board of assessors to be convened and paid,	5
Vacancy in office of assessor, how filled,	29

SEIZURE OF PROPERTY.

Authorized, if necessary, for procuring supply of salt,	3

SENATE.

May restore militia officers removed for treason or disloyalty,	8

SHERIFFS AND SERGEANTS.

To execute summons for justices under requisition for slaves,	6
When slaves to be delivered to them,	7
To seize slaves not delivered,	7
To attend sessions of courts under requisition,	7
Sheriffs of Orange and Culpeper allowed time to qualify,	16
Similar provision as to officers of other invaded counties, &c.	16

SLAVES.

May be called out for work on fortifications, &c.	6
Call to be made upon request of president,	6
Time for which they may be called out,	6
Number limited,	6
Requisition to be apportioned ratably,	6
Compensation for services of slaves,	6
Value of slaves, when to be paid,	6
When compensation for injury to slaves,	6
Hired slaves to be regarded as in possession of their owners,	6
Notice of call, how given to counties, &c.	6

Upon such notice, clerks to summon justices, 6
Summons, how directed, 6
Duty of county and corporation courts thereupon, 6
Commissioners of revenue to assist, 7
How requisitions apportioned, 7
When slaves to be taken ascertained by lot, 7
What slaves of soldiers in army exempt, 7
When slaves to be delivered to sheriff, 7
Sheriff to deliver to confederate officer or agent, 7
When slaves so delivered must be returned, 7
Slaves not delivered to be seized by sheriff, 7
Duty of confederate officer in such cases, 7
Term of service of slaves so seized, 7
If court fails to act, clerk to notify governor, 7
Governor then to impress slaves, 7
Mode of impressment, 7
Term of service for impressed slaves, 7
Burden to be equalized among counties and towns, 7
Slaves before furnished to be considered, 8
When owners may select overseers, 8
Where overseer to deliver slaves, 8
If a fit person, overseer to have charge during service, 8
How as to subsistence of slaves by owner, 8
Slaves sent voluntarily, how regarded, 8
President's request for slaves an acceptance of the act, 8
Slaves emancipated by U. S. authority, 13
Who liable, and what proceedings, 13

SMYTH AND WASHINGTON SALT WORKS.
Not to be purchased by governor, 3

SOLDIERS IN ARMY.
When their slaves exempt from requisition, 7

SPIRITUOUS AND MALT LIQUORS.
Act of 1861-2 amended, 19
Distillation prohibited, 19
Exceptions, 19
Violation of this act a misdemeanor, 19
Penalty, 19
Act concerning license to distill from fruit, &c. amended, 20
Tax on such license, 20
What quantity may be distilled without license, 20
See Alcohol.

STATES.
Contracts with other states for salt to be respected, 3
In what case contracts may be disregarded, 4
When other states to be furnished with salt, 4

SUBSISTENCE.
For slaves in confederate service, owners may furnish, 8

TAXES.
On alcohol, 18
On spirits distilled from fruit, &c. 20

THOMPSON, JUDGE GEORGE W.
Ordinance suspending his salary, repealed, 23

TOWNS.
See Counties and towns.

TREASON OR DISLOYALTY.
Militia officers may be removed by governor for treason or disloyalty, 8
But senate may reverse governor's action, 8
No removals when arrests can be made and charges preferred, 8
Governor to give reasons for removal to general assembly, 8
See Redress of loyal citizens.
See United States government.
See Usurped government.

TRIALS.
Of felonies charged in invaded counties, &c. how provided for, 17

UNITED STATES GOVERNMENT.
Persons holding office under or aiding, subjected to further liabilities, 13-14
Also those acting under U. S. confiscation and emancipation laws, 14-15
Record evidence of official position not required, 14

USURPED GOVERNMENT.
Established within this commonwealth, 11
Persons establishing, or holding office under, incapable of conveying real estate, 11-12
Their estates devoted to redress of loyal citizens, 12
What liens on such estates not impaired, 12
Other liabilities of officers, &c. of usurped government, 14

VIRGINIA STATE LINE.
Medical director of, may contract for spirituous liquors, 19

WASHINGTON AND SMYTH SALT WORKS.
Not to be purchased by governor, 3

WATER WORKS.
Officers of, how exempted from military service; when remanded to service, 10

WHISKEY.
See Spirituous and malt liquors.

WOOD.
Cars to supply Richmond and Petersburg to be furnished by rail road companies, 28
If companies opposed, burden to be apportioned, 28

ACTS

OF THE

GENERAL ASSEMBLY

OF THE

STATE OF VIRGINIA,

PASSED AT ADJOURNED SESSION, 1863,

IN THE

EIGHTY-SEVENTH YEAR OF THE COMMONWEALTH.

RICHMOND:
WILLIAM F. RITCHIE, PUBLIC PRINTER.
1863.

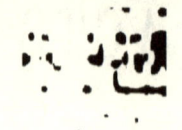

PUBLIC OR GENERAL ACTS.

CHAP. 1.—An ACT imposing Taxes for the Support of Government.

Passed March 28, 1863.

Be it enacted by the general assembly, that the taxes on the persons and subjects in this chapter mentioned, or required by law to be listed or assessed, shall, for the year commencing on the first day of February eighteen hundred and sixty-three, and thereafter, be yearly as follows:

Taxes on lands and lots.

1. On tracts of lands and lots belonging to any person, firm, company or corporation, with the improvements thereon, not exempt from taxation, one per centum on the assessed value thereof. Tax on lands

Personal property.

2. On all the personal property (except property owned and not hired or impressed by the confederate government), moneys and solvent credits, as defined in this section, including all capital, personal property and moneys of incorporated joint stock companies (other than rail road, canal or turnpike companies), and all capital invested, used or employed in any manufacturing, trade or other business, one per centum on the assessed value thereof. But property otherwise taxed, and property from which any income is derived, or on the capital invested in any trade or business, in respect to which a license so taxed is issued, certificates of stock, moneys and personal property that constitute part of the capital of any bank, savings institutions and insurance companies shall not be listed under the provisions of this section. The word "moneys" shall be construed to include not only gold, silver and copper coin, but bullion and bank notes, and confederate and state treasury notes, and county and corporation notes. The word "credits" shall be construed to mean all bank, state or corporation stocks, claims or demands owing or coming to any person, whether due or not, and whether payable in money or other thing, after deducting therefrom all bona fide debts due by such person as principal debtor. Money and credits in any state of the Confederate States, or in any other country, owned by any resident of this state, shall be listed by such resident, and taxed to him at the rate prescribed by this act. In ascertaining the value of such money or credits, the commissioner shall examine the person on oath, if to be found; if not found, shall assess the same upon the best informa-

On personal property, moneys and credits

What exempted

Moneys, what included in

Credits, how construed

Moneys and credits in other states, by whom listed

How value ascertained

tion he can obtain, and shall add to, or deduct the exchange on the value of such money or credit between this state and such state or country where such moneys or credits may be, to be computed as of the first of February next preceding.

Free negroes.

Free negroes 3. On every male free negro who has attained the age of twenty-one years, two dollars; but no tax shall hereafter be assessed or collected on such free negro under the act of the sixth of April eighteen hundred and fifty-three, establishing a colonization board.

White males.

White males 4. On every white male inhabitant who has attained the age of twenty-one years, not exempt from taxation by order of the court, in consequence of bodily infirmity, two dollars.

Public bonds.

Interest on public bonds 5. On the interest or profit which may have accrued, and is solvent, or which may have been received by any person, or converted into principal so as to become an interest bearing subject, or otherwise appropriated, within the year next preceding the first day of February of each year, arising from bonds, interest bearing treasury notes, or other certificates of debt of the Confederate States, or of this or any other state or country, or any corporation created by this or any other state, whether the stock of such company be exempt from taxation or not, seventeen per centum. But such interest or profits derived from bank stock or shares of savings institutions and insurance companies which pay taxes thereon into the treasury, shall not be included herein, unless invested or otherwise appropriated; and if so invested or otherwise appropriated, the tax thereon shall be at the rate of one per centum on the assessed value thereof. If no interest shall have been received within the year preceding the first day of February, then the value of the principal of such bonds shall be assessed and taxed as other property, and as prescribed by law.

Bank dividends.

On bank dividends 6. On the dividends declared by any bank incorporated by this state, the tax shall be seventeen per centum upon the amount thereof; to be paid into the treasury by the bank. If the dividend be that of a bank incorporated elsewhere, the tax shall be seventeen per centum upon the amount thereof; to be assessed and collected as other taxes.

Dividends of steam boat and such like companies.

On dividends of steam boat and similar companies 7. On the dividends declared within the year next preceding the first day of February, if the same be equal to or over six per centum on its capital, by steam boat and companies of similar character, not specially named for taxation, whether incorporated by this or any other state, or whether operating with or without a charter, seventeen per centum. If there be no dividend, or such dividend be not equal to six per centum of such capital, then such company shall pay a tax on its capital at the rate of one per centum on such capital. For this purpose, capital shall be held to consist of stock subscribed, money deposited, and bonds, certificates and other evidences of debt held or owned by such companies.

Savings banks and insurance companies.

8. Savings banks and insurance companies, whether incorporated by this state, or operating without a charter granted therein, shall, in June and December of each year, either declare a dividend of profits arising out of the operations of such savings banks and insurance companies, for the six months ending on the first day of June and December next preceding, or determine their inability to do so. If a dividend be declared of as much as three per centum of its capital, as herein defined, the said institution and company shall cause a tax, at the rate of seventeen per centum per annum, to be paid into the treasury, and the same shall be retained from the dividend on which it is payable. If there be no dividend, or if such dividend be not as much as three per centum of such capital, as herein defined, then such institution and such company shall pay into the treasury a tax on its capital at the rate of fifty cents on every hundred dollars of such capital. For this purpose, the capital stock shall be held to consist of stock subscribed, money deposited, and bonds, certificates and other evidences of debt held or owned by such institution and company. Between the first and fifteenth of June and December of each year, such institution and company shall certify, on the oath of its chief accounting officer, the amount of the dividend declared, if any, and of its capital, where no dividend has been declared, and shall pay the tax herein imposed into the treasury. If any such institution or company fail to make such report and pay such tax, it shall be liable for the same, and forfeit not less than five hundred dollars nor more than two thousand dollars.

On savings banks and insurance companies

Dividends of companies not incorporated by this state.

9. On dividends of rail road or other like companies not incorporated by this state, the tax shall be seventeen per centum upon the amount thereof; to be listed and charged to the recipient of such dividends, or those entitled to receive the same. If such dividend be not equal to six per centum of such capital, the stock so held shall be listed and taxed as other property, and no tax shall be imposed on the dividends of such companies.

On companies not incorporated by the state.

Income.

10. On the income, salary, compensation or fees received during the year ending the first day of February of each year, in consideration of the discharge of any office or employment in the service of

On income or fees

the state, or in consideration of the discharge of any office or employment in the service of any corporation, or in the service of any company, firm or person, except where the service is exclusively that of a minister of the gospel, two and one-half per centum upon so much thereof as exceeds five hundred dollars. The tax on a salary, payable under this section by an officer of government, receiving the same out of the treasury, shall be deducted at the rate chargeable on the annual salary, on the amount drawn from the treasury at the time the salary is audited and paid; and fees or other income of such officer shall be listed and assessed by the commissioners as in other cases, and at the rates prescribed thereon.

Exception

Taxes of officers of government, how paid

Profits.

On profits

11. The commissioner of the revenue shall ascertain from, and assess for taxation against, every person in his district, the net income of such person, received or realized, though not received, during the year next preceding the first day of February of each year, derived in any of the modes following, set:

First—All profits from any licensed trade, business or occupation.

Second—All profits from the use of money by another, for the benefit of the owner thereof.

Third—All profits from buying and selling, or from the exchange of real or personal property, or from buying and selling, or from the exchange of bonds, public and private, stocks and other choses in action, and all profits from any other trading or speculating: provided, however, that this section shall not be construed to embrace the agricultural products, when sold by the producer, or the personal property used in raising said products, nor cattle or other live stock, when sold by the person assessed with the tax on said cattle or other live stock; nor cattle or other live stock sold by the person who has grazed or fed the same for a period not less than three months prior to such sale; nor a sale of real or personal property, purchased by the vendor for his own individual use, and not for resale by him; nor any income, salary, compensation or fees received from the discharge of any office or employment mentioned and taxed under the provisions of the next preceding section. The auditor of public accounts shall make such rules and regulations for the guidance of the commissioner under this section, as he shall deem proper; and shall, for that purpose, direct the examination on oath of any party concerned, and of any other person whose evidence may aid the commissioner in the performance of his duty.

What exempted

Erroneous assessment, how redressed

12. Redress for any alleged erroneous assessment, and all proceedings thereon, shall be regulated by the laws in force in other cases.

Rate of tax

13. The tax under this section shall be ten per centum upon so much of the net income, assessed as herein before provided, as ex-

ceeds the sum of three thousand dollars: provided, that all licenses, taxes or per centage taxes paid for the year preceding the first day of February eighteen hundred and sixty-three, by persons who may have obtained a license, shall be abated from the gross incomes, in order to ascertain the net incomes taxed under this section; and all other expenses incurred in carrying on the business which may have produced such income for said year, and all county, city and corporation taxes for the privilege of carrying on said business for said year, shall be abated from the gross income. *What deducted from gross income.*

Toll bridges.

14. On the yearly rent or annual value of toll bridges and ferries, whether authorized by law or not, other than those toll bridges and ferries exempt by their charter from taxation, seventeen per centum. *On toll bridges and ferries*

Collateral inheritances.

15. On the estate of a decedent, which passes under his will or by descent to any other person, or for any other use than to or for the use of the father, mother, husband, wife, brother, sister, nephew, niece, or lineal descendant of such decedent, there shall be a tax of three per centum of such estate. *On collateral inheritances*

Estates passing under sequestration acts.

16. On all estate, which, under the effect or by the provisions of the sequestration act of the confederate congress, or any act amendatory thereof, may legally pass, otherwise than by purchase, to any person, there shall be a tax of ten per centum on the value thereof. *On estates under sequestration act*

Internal improvement companies.

17. On every passenger transported on any rail road or canal in this state, for and on behalf of this state or of the Confederate States, one and a half mill for every mile of transportation; and on all freight so transported, three-fourths of one per centum of the gross amount received by the company controlling such rail road or canal, for the transportation of such freight, or for tolls thereon, or for privileges granted thereby; and on every passenger transported on any rail road or canal in this state, other than those above mentioned, two and a half mills for every mile of transportation; and on all freight so transported, other than that above mentioned, one and a quarter per centum of the gross amount received by the company controlling such rail road or canal, for the transportation of such freight or tolls thereon, or for privileges granted thereby. And it shall be the duty of every such company to collect for the state the tax herein imposed; and every rail road company or canal company, whether exempted from taxation by its charter or not, shall hereafter report quarterly, on the fifteenth day of March, June, September and December in each year, to the auditor of public accounts, the number of passengers transported, and the aggregate number of *On internal improvement companies. When and what to report to auditor*

miles traveled by them within this commonwealth, and the gross amount received by such company for the transportation of freight over such road or canal, or any part thereof, or water or other improvement owned or connected therewith, during the quarter of the year next preceding the first day of the month in which such report *When only partly in the state* is to be made. Such company, whose road or canal is only in part within the commonwealth, shall report as aforesaid such portion only of such amount received for passengers and for transportation of freight, as the part of the said road or canal which is within this *Tolls, how to be construed* commonwealth bears to the whole of such road or canal. If the profits of such road or canal consist in whole or in part of tolls, the gross amount thereof shall, for the purposes of this act, be construed to be a part of the gross amount received for the transportation of *Exemptions annulled* freight. It is the intention of this act to abrogate and annul all exemptions from taxation of any such company, contained in its charter, during the existing war, and to subject such company to the uniform rate of taxation prescribed by law, so far as the general assembly has power to do so. The property of such company, over and above the property they are authorized by its charter to hold, shall be taxed as other property.

Statement of rail road officers.

Report made on oath   18. Such statement shall be verified by the oaths of the president and the superintendent of transportation, or other proper officer. *Penalty for failure* Every company failing to make such report, shall be fined five hundred dollars; and any company having a subordinate board, or any board managing any part of its works, may by its by-laws create and enforce such penalties as will secure proper reports of such compa- *When taxes to be paid into the treasury* nies. At the time of making such reports, such company shall pay into the treasury the taxes imposed on passengers, freight, tolls and privileges, as in this act provided. Every such company paying such taxes, shall not be assessed with any tax on its lands, buildings, cars, boats or other property (owned but not hired) which they are *When liable to pay taxes on lands and other property* authorized by law to hold or have. But if any such company fail to pay such taxes at either of the times specified therefor, then its lands, buildings, cars, boats and other property shall be immediately assessed, under the direction of the auditor of public accounts, by any person appointed by him for the purpose, at its full value, and a tax shall at once be levied thereon as on real estate and other property; at twenty-five cents on every hundred dollars value thereof, on account of each quarterly default; to be collected by any sheriff whom the auditor may direct; and such sheriff shall distrain and sell any personal property of such company, and pay such taxes into the treasury within three months from the time when such assessment is furnished to him.

Express companies.

Express companies to report   19. Every express company shall make return to the auditor of

FINANCIAL.—TAXES.

public accounts, on or before the fifteenth day of March, June, September and December of each year, of the gross receipts of such company, on account of any transactions, profits or charges within the state of Virginia, within the three months next preceding the first day of March, June, September and December of each year. If the auditor of public accounts shall have prescribed a form for such return, the said report shall be in the form prescribed. If no such form shall have been prescribed, the report shall be in such form as will best disclose the operations of such company. The report of such company shall be verified by the oaths of the agents and chief officers of such company, at its principal office in this state. The report shall show the gross receipts and charges of such company for business done in this state, whether collected in or out of the state. Such express company shall be the collector for the state of the taxes herein imposed, and shall, on or before the fifteenth day of March, June, September and December, pay, on the total receipts so reported, a tax of two and one-half per centum. For a failure to make such report or pay such tax, a penalty of not less than one thousand nor more than five thousand dollars shall be imposed upon the company so failing. For the payment of the tax and of such penalty, the stockholders and members of such company shall be personally liable, and judgment may be rendered against them, or any of them, personally, in the circuit court of the city of Richmond, in the mode prescribed by law. Such company and its officers and agents are hereby prohibited from doing any business appertaining to the business of a broker or merchant, unless licensed as broker or merchant. Such principal officer shall require from the several agents employed by such company, a report of their transactions on oath; which report, so sworn to, shall accompany the report of the chief officer to the auditor of public accounts. All reports made after the first day of December eighteen hundred and sixty-two, shall be made under the provisions and in pursuance of this act. Such company, its officers and agents, doing business as broker or merchant, without a license, shall forfeit not less than two hundred nor more than two thousand dollars.

quarterly to auditor.
Form of report
Penalty for failure to report
Stockholders and members liable for tax and penalty
Not to do brokerage business
Penalty for doing business of broker or merchant

Suits.

20. When any original suit, ejectment, attachment (other than on a summons to answer a suggestion, sued out under the provisions of the eleventh section of chapter one hundred and eighty-eight of the Code) or other action is commenced in a circuit, county or corporation court, there shall be a tax of one dollar and seventy cents; if it be an appeal, writ of error or supersedeas in a circuit court, there shall be a tax of three dollars and forty cents; if it be an appeal, writ of error or supersedeas in a district court, eight dollars and fifty cents; and if in the court of appeals, eight dollars and fifty cents.

Original suits
Appeals

Seals.

21. When the seal of a court, of a notary public or the seal of

On seals

FINANCIAL.—TAXES.

the state is annexed to any paper except in those cases exempted by law, the taxes shall be as follows: For the seal of the state, five dollars; for any other seal, two dollars and fifty cents; and herein shall be included a tax on a scroll annexed to a paper in lieu of an official seal. But this section shall not apply to seals of courts affixed to bonds of any county, executed for money raised to aid in equipping soldiers of such county, or to aid in the support of the families of such soldiers; nor shall the tax provided in this section apply to any seal of a court affixed to any papers required in order to receive the arrearages of pay or allowances due to a deceased soldier, either from this state or the Confederate States.

What exempted

Transfer of state stock.

22. For the transfer of all state stock to be registered in the office of the second auditor, for each certificate of stock, there shall be a tax of ten cents for every hundred dollars. It shall be the duty of the second auditor to collect said tax before the delivery of such certificate of transferred stock, and render an account of receipts for each preceding quarter of a year, and pay the same into the treasury, at the end of each quarter, to the credit of the commonwealth, deducting five per centum thereupon as his compensation.

On transfer of state stocks
How tax collected
Compensation of second auditor

Wills and administrations.

23. On the probate of every will or grant of administration not now exempt by law, there shall be a tax of two dollars and fifty cents.

On wills and administrations

Deeds.

24. On every deed admitted to record, whether the same has been recorded before or not, and on every contract relating to real estate, whether it be a deed or not, which is admitted to record, there shall be a tax of two dollars and fifty cents.

On deeds

Bank corporations.

25. On every law incorporating or chartering or rechartering any bank, with a capital not exceeding two hundred thousand dollars, there shall be a tax of one hundred and twenty-five dollars; with a capital of over two hundred thousand dollars and not exceeding four hundred thousand dollars, there shall be a tax of two hundred and fifty dollars; with a capital of over four hundred thousand dollars and not exceeding six hundred thousand dollars, there shall be a tax of three hundred and seventy-five dollars; with a capital of over six hundred thousand dollars and not exceeding eight hundred thousand dollars, there shall be a tax of five hundred dollars; and with a capital of over eight hundred thousand dollars, there shall be a tax of six hundred and twenty-five dollars.

Bank charters

Manufacturing companies.

26. On every law incorporating or rechartering any oil, iron, coal

Charters of ma-

or manufacturing company, if the maximum capital is one hundred thousand dollars or less, there shall be a tax of one hundred and twenty-five dollars; and if it exceed that amount, there shall be a tax of two hundred and fifty dollars.

nufacturing companies

Gas light and other companies.

27. On every law for the incorporation of any canal, rail road, insurance, gas light, express or telegraph company, if the maximum capital is one hundred thousand dollars or less, there shall be a tax of one hundred and twenty-five dollars; and if it exceed that amount, there shall be a tax of two hundred and fifty dollars: provided, that the tax imposed by this section shall not apply to the Virginia canal company.

Charters of gas light and other companies

Savings institutions.

28. On every law chartering, renewing or extending the charter of any savings institution, if the maximum capital is one hundred thousand dollars or less, there shall be a tax of one hundred and twenty-five dollars; and if it exceed that amount, there shall be a tax of two hundred and fifty dollars.

Charters of savings institutions

Private corporations.

29. On every law chartering, renewing or extending the charter of any private corporation, other than those herein before mentioned, and other than acts for the incorporation of a college, academy, seminary of learning, or literary or charitable institution or cemetery, if the maximum capital is one hundred thousand dollars or less, there shall be a tax of one hundred and twenty-five dollars; and if it exceed that amount, there shall be a tax of two hundred and fifty dollars.

Private charters

Unorganized companies, how taxed.

30. All the acts of assembly creating or continuing corporations mentioned in this act, which, since the third day of April eighteen hundred and sixty-one, have not been organized, by accepting the charter granted to the corporators, and paid the taxes thereon, according to the provisions of the act entitled an act imposing taxes for the support of government, passed April the third, eighteen hundred and sixty-one, shall hereafter, upon being organized, or upon accepting the charter, return a statement, verified by the oath of the president or other proper officer, to the auditor of public accounts, showing the amount of the capital of the company or corporation of which he is president, on or before the first day of July, eighteen hundred and sixty-three; and those corporators omitting so to accept the charter, and to return by that time, and afterwards accepting, shall, on or before the first day of July in the year next after such acceptance, make such report, and at the same time pay into the treasury the amount of tax imposed by this act.

Unorganized companies

When to make report to auditor

ON LICENSES.

Ordinaries.

Ordinaries and public entertainment

31. The taxes on licenses shall be as follows: On a license to keep an ordinary or house of public entertainment, one hundred dollars; and if the yearly value of such house and furniture, whether rented or kept by the proprietor, exceed one hundred dollars, and is less than two hundred dollars, the tax shall be one hundred and twenty-five dollars; and if the yearly value thereof exceed two hundred dollars, there shall be added to the last mentioned sum thirty-four per centum on so much thereof as exceeds two hundred dollars; *License to sell ardent spirits* and if the license grants the privilege of retailing ardent spirits, porter, ale or beer, to be drank elsewhere than at such ordinary, there shall be added to said license a tax of one hundred and twenty-five dollars, in addition to the amount otherwise imposed; and if the business be continued, there shall also be a tax of two and a half per centum upon the amount of such sales for the preceding year, in *Not to include sale of other things* addition to the specific tax. But the privilege to sell ardent spirits hereby authorized, shall not be construed to authorize the sale of any other thing under cover of a license to keep an ordinary; and any sales not authorized at such ordinary, shall be deemed to be sales *What houses deemed ordinaries* made by the ordinary keeper without license. All houses at any time heretofore kept as hotels or licensed ordinaries, shall be deemed to be houses of public entertainment; and if licensed, shall be licensed as such, with or without the privilege of selling ardent spirits.

Private entertainment.

Private entertainment and boarding houses

32. On a license to keep a house of private entertainment or a private boarding house, twenty dollars. If the yearly value thereof and furniture exceed one hundred dollars, there shall be added to the last mentioned sum twenty-five per centum on so much thereof as exceeds one hundred dollars. But no house shall be deemed a private boarding house, with less than five boarders.

Cook shops and eating houses.

Cook shops and eating houses

33. On every license to keep a cook shop or eating house, fifty dollars; and in addition thereto, fifty per centum on so much of the yearly value thereof as exceeds one hundred dollars.

Bowling alleys.

Bowling alleys

34. On every license permitting a bowling alley or saloon to be kept for a year, one hundred and twenty-five dollars; but if there be more than one such alley kept in any one room, forty dollars each shall be charged for the excess over one.

Billiard tables.

Billiard tables

35. On every license permitting a billiard table to be kept for a

year, two hundred and fifty dollars; but if there be more than one such table kept in any one room, one hundred and twenty-five dollars each shall be charged for the excess over one table.

Bagatelle tables.

36. On every license permitting a bagatelle or other like table to be kept for one year or any less time, fifty dollars for the first, and if more than one, thirty dollars for each additional table. *Bagatelle tables*

Livery stables.

37. On every license to a keeper of a livery stable, two dollars and a half for each stall thereof; and herein shall be included as stalls, such space as may be necessary for a horse to stand, and in which a horse is or may be kept at livery otherwise than for the purpose of feeding horses by one day only; and no exemption from this license shall be allowed to any person in consequence of such person being licensed to keep an ordinary or house of private entertainment, if any horses be kept, fed or hired for compensation by the proprietor thereof, except that no tax shall be required on such stalls as are kept exclusively and used for horses belonging to travelers or guests stopping at such house. *Livery stables* *What included as stalls* *Ordinary keepers not exempt*

License to distill or rectify ardent spirits.

38. On every license to distill or rectify ardent spirits, if the machinery be propelled by steam power, the tax shall be two hundred and fifty dollars; if the machinery be not so propelled, the tax shall be one hundred and twenty-five dollars; and if the distillery is for the manufacture of ardent spirits from fruit, vegetables, syrup, molasses, sugar cane or sugars only, the tax shall be twenty dollars, and no deduction shall be allowed if the privilege be exercised for less than a year. In either case, there shall be a tax of fifty cents per gallon on the quantity of ardent spirits to be manufactured, which shall be stated in the license; and when the quantity so stated shall have been made, the license thereafter shall be void; and any person continuing the manufacture, after the quantity named in the license shall have been made, shall be liable to all penalties of a person distilling without a license. If the person desiring such license make application therefor, he shall state on oath the probable quantity which in his opinion he will distill during the time the license is to continue, and the tax shall be assessed as well for the specific amount as upon the quantity to be produced. If the application shall not be made to the commissioner for an assessment, the commissioner shall assess the specific tax as in other cases of default, and shall ascertain, upon the best information he can obtain, the probable quantity which the distillery will produce during the time the license will continue, and shall therefrom assess the actual rate per gallon provided for in this act. If the quantity to be manufactured under such license shall have been made, and the person desires an enlargement *Distilling or rectifying ardent spirits* *Additional tax per gallon* *How quantity to be ascertained*

FINANCIAL.—TAXES.

When this section to commence

of the quantity, he may apply for a new assessment and new license for the additional quantity desired, which shall be granted upon the payment of the tax on the gallon, without the specific tax to rectify or distill. This section of this act shall be in force from the passage thereof, so far as to impose the tax for the manufacture of ardent spirits from fruit, vegetables, syrups, molasses, sugar cane or sugars; for the manufacture of ardent spirits for the confederate government, or under any contract or agreement therewith; and shall be in force, as to the manufacture of liquors generally, from and after the time the act entitled an act to prevent the unnecessary consumption of grain by distillers and other manufacturers of spirituous or malt liquors, passed March twelfth, eighteen hundred and sixty-two, shall expire: provided no license or tax shall be required of any person for manufacturing thirty-three gallons, in one year, out of the fruit, vegetables, syrups, molasses, sugar cane or sugars of his own production, for his own use.

Merchants.

Merchant's specific tax. Tax, when proportioned to sales.

39. On every license to a merchant or mercantile firm, where a specific tax is to be paid, one hundred and fifty dollars; and where the tax is in proportion to the sales, if the taxable sales shall be under one thousand dollars, the tax shall be fifty dollars; if one thousand dollars and under fifteen hundred dollars, sixty dollars; if fifteen hundred dollars and under twenty-five hundred dollars, eighty dollars; if twenty-five hundred dollars and under five thousand dollars, one hundred and twenty dollars; if five thousand dollars and under ten thousand dollars, one hundred and ninety dollars; if ten thousand dollars and under fifteen thousand dollars, two hundred and forty dollars; if fifteen thousand dollars and under twenty thousand dollars, two hundred and eighty dollars; if twenty thousand dollars and under thirty thousand dollars, three hundred and fifty dollars; if thirty thousand dollars and under fifty thousand dollars, five hundred and twenty dollars; and if over fifty thousand dollars, twenty-five dollars for every ten thousand dollars excess over the said sum

License tax to be had for selling articles for others

of fifty thousand dollars. In addition to the amount herein required to be paid upon taxable sales, there shall also be paid a license tax of three-tenths of one per centum upon the amount of all articles sold by said merchant for others, whether such goods be agricultural productions, or other articles exempted in the hands of the producer

Not to sell at auction except to close business

or owner from taxation or otherwise. If any merchant is about to close out and discontinue his business, he may sell the same by auction; but under no other circumstances shall he sell by auction, unless he obtain a license as auctioneer. But nothing contained in this section shall be construed to authorize any such person to sell wine, ardent spirits, or a mixture thereof.

Merchants' permission to sell ardent spirits.

Merchants'

40. In every case in which the license to a merchant or mercan-

tile firm includes permission to sell wine, ardent spirits, or a mixture License to sell thereof, porter, ale or beer, by wholesale and retail, or by retail only, ardent spirits if such merchant or firm sell by wholesale and retail, or by wholesale only, an additional tax of two hundred and fifty dollars; and on the Tax on sales of amount of such sales within the year next preceding, there shall be preceding year a tax of two and one-half per centum on the amount of such sales for the year next preceding the time of obtaining said license, in addition to the specific tax imposed as aforesaid; but said sales shall not be estimated in ascertaining the amount of a merchant's license, except where such merchant fails to take out a license to sell ardent spirits; in which case, the sales of liquors for the preceding year shall be estimated as part of the sales of merchandise, whether such liquors were sold under a license or not, and on such part of his sales there shall be an additional tax of ten and one-half per centum.

Merchant tailors and others.

41. Merchant tailors, lumber merchants and dealers in coal or Merchant wood, shall obtain license as merchants, and be assessed and taxed tailors, &c thereon as other merchants are by the preceding sections of this act, and shall be subject to like penalties for conducting such business without a merchant's license, except that any captain or other person having the command or control of any vessel, shall not be required to take out a license to sell wood by retail from such vessel.

Commission merchants.

42. The tax on every license to a commission merchant, forward- Commission ing merchant or ship broker, shall be one hundred dollars each for merchants commencing business; and if to continue such business after the Additional tax same has been carried on for one year, the tax on such license shall for continuing business be five per centum on the amount of all commissions of every kind received; and this tax shall be in addition to such tax as may be imposed on a license to such merchant or firm to sell goods, wares or merchandise. All goods consigned to any such commission merchant or forwarding merchant, whether such goods be agricultural productions, or other articles exempted in the hands of the producer or owner from taxation, shall be included as subjects of taxation, under the provisions of this section.

General auctioneers.

43. On every license to an auctioneer or vendue master to sell General auc- goods, wares and merchandise at public auction, sixty-five dollars; tioneers and if the place of business be in a town containing, when assessed, a population of three thousand inhabitants, eighty dollars; if the population exceed three thousand, an additional tax of forty dollars for every thousand persons above that number, and at that rate for any fractional excess less than one thousand; but such license shall not authorize the sale of slaves or real estate at auction. On every For continuing business

FINANCIAL.—TAXES.

license to an auctioneer or vendue master in this section mentioned, to continue the business after the same has been carried on for a year, there shall be an additional tax of five-eighths of one per centum on the amount of taxable sales of such auctioneer or vendue master for the preceding twelve months. But no sale shall be made at any place other than the house named in the license as the place of business, or at such other place as the person owning the property is authorized to sell the same; but this prohibition shall not apply to cargo sales, or the property of persons closing out business for which they have a license; and no goods shall be consigned to such auctioneer for sale, unless the owner thereof has obtained a merchant's license for a period as long as one whole year.

_{Where sales to be made}

Negro auctioneers.

_{Negro auctioneers} 44. On every license to an auctioneer or vendue master to sell slaves at public auction, sixty-five dollars; and if the place of business be in a town containing a population of three thousand inhabitants, eighty dollars; if the population exceed three thousand, an additional tax of forty dollars for every thousand persons above that number, at the time of making the assessment, and at that rate for any fractional excess less than one thousand. On every license to an auctioneer or vendue master, in this section mentioned, to continue the business after the same has been carried on for a year, an additional tax of one-half of one per centum on the amount of taxable sales of such auctioneer or vendue master.

Real estate auctioneers.

_{Real estate} 45. On every license to an auctioneer or vendue master who deals exclusively in real estate, sixty-five dollars; and if the place of business be in a town containing a population of three thousand inhabitants, eighty dollars; if the population exceed three thousand, an additional tax of forty dollars for every thousand persons above that number, and at that rate for any fractional excess less than one thousand. On every license to an auctioneer or vendue master in this section mentioned, to continue the business after the same has been carried on for a year, an additional tax of one-half of one per centum on the amount of taxable sales of such auctioneer or vendue master. _{Taxable sales, how construed} "Taxable sales," in this and the two preceding sections, shall be construed to embrace all sales made by such auctioneers or vendue masters, whether such sales be public or private: provided, that such tax on private sales shall not apply to cases where the merchant's tax is payable on said sales.

Common crier.

_{Common crier} 46. On every license to a common crier, if in a town of more than one thousand inhabitants, twenty-five dollars; but he shall not be authorized to act in the sale of any property belonging to any person,

FINANCIAL.—TAXES.

unless such owner is authorized to sell such property without a license, or has obtained license to do so.

Sample merchants.

47. On every license to sell goods by sample, card or other representation, five hundred dollars.

Telegraph companies.

48. On every license to a telegraph company to operate within this state, one hundred and sixty-five dollars; and on the business of the preceding year, an additional tax of two and a half per centum on the gross receipts received or contracted to be received by such company for business done within the year next preceding the time of obtaining license.

Patent rights.

49. On every license to sell or barter the right to manufacture or use any machinery or other thing patented to any person or company, under the laws of the Confederate States, twenty-five dollars in each county; and no merchant shall sell the same without an additional license and the payment of the tax prescribed by this section. But patentees who are citizens of Virginia shall not be subject to the tax imposed by this section.

Medicines.

50. On every license to sell medicines, if by retail, sixty-five dollars; and if by wholesale, one hundred and twenty-five dollars. A person having a merchant's license may sell medicines without any additional license, unless the same be sold on a commission; in which case, the additional license and tax shall be imposed. Such license shall continue to be construed not to authorize the sale of ardent spirits by prescription or otherwise.

Book agents.

51. On every license to a person obtaining subscriptions to books, maps, prints, pamphlets or periodicals, sixty-five dollars for each county, city or town. On every license to sell or in any manner furnish the same, sixty-five dollars. If the person obtaining such license has not been a resident of the Confederate States two years, the tax shall be in each case five hundred dollars. But any person who has been a resident of the Confederate States for two years, desiring to distribute or sell any religious books, newspapers or pamphlets, may apply to the county or corporation court of each county, city or town in which he may desire to distribute or sell the same; and such court, upon being satisfied that such person is a proper person for such duty, may grant him a license without the imposition of any tax for the privilege; but this section shall not apply to books, newspapers or pamphlets written by citizens of, or published in the Confederate States.

Agents for renting houses.

Agents for renting houses.   52. On every license to a person engaged as agent for the renting of houses, one hundred and twenty-five dollars.

Agents for hiring negroes.

Agents for hiring negroes   53. On every license to a person engaged as agent for the hiring of negroes, one hundred and twenty-five dollars.

Stallions.

Stallions   54. On every license to the owner of a jackass or stallion, for services of which compensation is received, three times the amount of such compensation, when the charge is for such service by the season; and when such services are for less than a season, then three times what a commissioner may judge to be a reasonable charge therefor; the tax, however, in no case to be less than fifteen dollars. Such license shall authorize the performance of such services in any part of the commonwealth.

Theatrical performances.

Theatres   55. On every license permitting the proprietor or occupier of a public theatre, or rooms fitted for public exhibitions, to use the same for the year, if such room be in a town or city of more than five thousand inhabitants and less than ten thousand inhabitants, fifty dollars; and in all towns containing more than ten thousand inhabitants, one hundred and fifty dollars; and it shall not be lawful to exhibit such performances in any other than a licensed house in such Tax for twenty-four hours   towns; and on every license permitting theatrical performances therein for twenty-four hours, fifteen dollars; but a license may be granted permitting theatrical performances for the term of one week; in which case, the tax shall be twenty dollars during said last mentioned time; and on a license to continue such performances in such houses, there shall be an additional tax of ten cents on each person who shall have attended the exhibitions during the time the last preceding license continued; but if the commissioner shall apprehend that the license will not be renewed at the end of the week, he may refuse the license for a longer period than twenty-four hours.

Refreshments in theatres.

Refreshments in theatres   56. On every license permitting the sale of refreshments in a theatre during such performances, eighty-four dollars for each place of sale, and no abatement shall be made, if the privilege be exercised for a period less than one year. But such license shall not include the privilege of selling wine, ardent spirits, or a mixture thereof.

Sales of ardent spirits in a theatre.

Sale of ardent   57. On every license permitting the sale of wine, ardent spirits,

or a mixture thereof, porter, ale or beer, at a theatre, to be drank at *spirits in theatres*
the place where sold, two hundred and fifty dollars for each place of
sale; and no abatement shall be made, if the privilege be exercised
for a period less than one year.

Public shows, circuses and menageries.

58. On every license permitting any public show, exhibition or *Shows* performance other than the drama, whether in a licensed house or not, if in a corporate town, or within five miles thereof, for each time of performance, twenty-five dollars; if elsewhere, fourteen dollars; and for every exhibition of a circus, if within a corporate town, or *Circuses* within five miles thereof, one hundred dollars; if elsewhere, fifty dollars; and for every exhibition of a menagerie, if within a corporate *Menageries* town, or within five miles thereof, one hundred dollars; if elsewhere, fifty dollars. All such shows, exhibitions and performances, whether under the same canvas or not, shall be construed to require separate licenses therefor, whether exhibited for compensation or not; and upon any such shows, exhibitions and performances being concluded, so that an additional fee for admission be charged, in lieu of a return check authorizing the holder to re-enter without charge, such additional admission fee shall be construed to require an additional license therefor.

Manufacturers of porter, ale and beer.

59. On every license to manufacture porter, ale and beer, or either *Manufacture of porter, ale and beer* of them, one hundred and twenty-five dollars.

Sale of porter, ale and beer.

60. On every license to sell porter, ale or beer, by wholesale or *Sale of porter, ale and beer* retail, except in towns whose population exceeds five thousand, one hundred dollars; in towns whose population does not exceed five thousand, and elsewhere, fifty dollars; and if the business be continued for more than one year, an additional tax of five per centum on the amount of sales of the previous year. But if the license be to retail, to be drank where sold, it shall be granted upon the certificate of the county or corporation court, in every respect as certificates are granted to ordinary keepers and merchants to retail ardent spirits.

Brokers.

61. On every license to a broker who deals in stocks, bank notes, *Brokers* gold or silver coin, foreign or domestic exchange, or in securities of any kind, one thousand seven hundred dollars. A broker shall have the right to sell stocks at auction or otherwise; and any person who may sell stocks, gold or silver coin, bank notes, treasury notes, foreign or domestic exchange, shares in any corporation or chartered company, certificates of debt due by the Confederate States, or by any state or corporation or chartered company, or securities of any kind, on commission, shall be regarded as a broker.

Insurance companies.

Insurance companies

62. On every license to an agent or sub-agent of any insurance company, not chartered by this state, sixty-four dollars.

Physicians and others.

Physicians, dentists and attorneys

63. On every license to a physician, surgeon or dentist, fourteen dollars each; and on every license to an attorney at law, fourteen dollars. If the yearly income derived from the practice of any such callings or professions, during the year next preceding the time of obtaining such license, shall exceed five hundred dollars, there shall be an additional tax on the excess of two and a half per centum; and this income shall be included in the license tax. A license to any such person shall confer on him the privilege of practicing such profession in any part of the commonwealth.

Daguerreian artists.

Daguerreian artists

64. On every license to exercise the daguerreian art, or such like profession or performance, by whatever name it may be known or called, if in a city or incorporated town of less than five thousand inhabitants, fifty dollars; if more than five thousand inhabitants, one hundred dollars; if elsewhere, twenty-five dollars. And if the yearly income derived from the practice of said art exceed five hundred dollars in any county, city or town, an additional tax of two and a half per centum on such excess for the year next preceding the time of obtaining such license; and such tax shall be imposed, whether an artist perform in a gallery or not. If more than one person be engaged in the joint exercise of such profession or performance in the same gallery, the tax shall not be imposed upon each artist, but upon the gallery.

Horses, mules, &c. sold for profit.

Selling horses, mules, &c. for profit

65. On every license to sell for others, on commission or for profit, horses, mules, asses, jennets, cattle, sheep and hogs, or either of them, fifty dollars; and the sale may be made under such license in any county or corporation.

Carriages, buggies and other vehicles.

Carriages, buggies, &c. manufactured out of state

66. On every license to sell carriages, buggies, barouches, gigs, and such like vehicles, manufactured out of this state, one hundred and twenty-five dollars in each county or corporation. If the business be continued after the same has been carried on for a year, the tax shall be on the amount of sales, in addition to the specific tax, as on merchants' licenses. But this section shall not be so construed as to exempt persons from taxation who may put together the principal parts of such vehicles as may be manufactured out of this state.

Slaves bought or sold for profit.

67. On every license to buy or sell slaves on commission or for profit, other than at public auction, thirty-five dollars in each county; and on the yearly income of such business in all the counties (to be taxed but once), an additional tax of two and a half per centum on such income. If the sale be made by an auctioneer, no additional license from him shall be required for that purpose. Slaves bought or sold for profit

Barbers.

68. On every license to keep a barber's shop, twenty dollars; and for every person above one engaged or employed therein, ten dollars. The number to be engaged or employed shall be specified in the license. For any violation of this section, the person licensed and so offending, shall forfeit twenty dollars for each offence. Barbers

Hawkers and peddlers.

69. On every license to a hawker or peddler to deal in goods, wares and merchandise, two hundred and fifty dollars: provided, however, the hawker and peddler to be taxed under this section, shall first obtain from the county or corporation court, within whose jurisdiction the said license is intended to be used, a certificate that the applicant is a loyal citizen of some one of the Confederate States, and has been a resident of this state for two years, and of the county, city or town for one year next preceding the granting of said certificate. Hawkers and peddlers

To whom not to be issued.

70. No license shall be granted to a married woman, unless she shall be living separate and apart from her husband, or unless her husband would be entitled to take out a license in his own name. When married women may be licensed

Licenses to miners and manufacturers.

71. The commissioners of the revenue shall, on or before the thirtieth day of April eighteen hundred and sixty-three, and on or before the thirty-first day of January in each succeeding year, deliver a certificate of a license, and the tax to be paid therefor, to every person, firm, company or corporation, for the privilege of carrying on any of the occupations following, viz: Miners and manufacturers

Mining for coal, iron, or other ores and minerals, and the sale of the products thereof. Coal, iron, &c

The manufacture and sale of salt, iron and other metals, and the sale of salt water and copperas. Salt, &c

The manufacture and sale of cotton and woolen fabrics made by the use of machinery worked by steam or water power. Cotton and woolen fabrics

The manufacture and sale of paper of all kinds. Paper

The manufacture and sale of leather. Leather

Boots, shoes, &c	The manufacture and sale of boots, shoes and the like.
Flour	The manufacture and sale of flour from grain not raised nor received as toll for grinding by the miller.
When licenses terminate	The said licenses shall terminate on the thirty-first day of January eighteen hundred and sixty-four.
Penalty for failure to obtain license	72. Any person, firm, company or corporation carrying on any such occupation after the thirtieth day of April eighteen hundred and sixty-three, without having first obtained a license therefor, shall forfeit, for each day it may be done, not less than fifty dollars nor more than five hundred dollars; to be recovered by motion in the circuit court of the county wherein the offence shall be committed, or in the circuit court of the city of Richmond: provided, that a mechanic who manufactures boots and shoes, and sells the articles of his manufacture only to persons for their own use and consumption, shall not be required to obtain a license under this act.
Tax on business of preceding year	73. When the business for which a license issues under this section shall have been carried on during the year ending on the thirty-first of January eighteen hundred and sixty-three, by the person, firm, company or corporation obtaining it, or by any other person, firm, company or corporation, at the place or on the property where it shall be licensed for the coming year, the commissioner of the revenue shall assess the tax upon such license at ten per centum upon so much of the net profits of the business during the year so ending on the thirty-first of January eighteen hundred and sixty-three, as exceeds three thousand dollars; and if the business has only been carried on for a part of the year preceding the said thirty-first day of January eighteen hundred and sixty-three, then the commissioner shall ascertain the taxable products, by adopting the same for such part of the year as a basis for ascertaining the same for the entire year.
Tax on persons commencing business	74. When the person, firm, company or corporation, obtaining a license under this section, is commencing business, and no other person, firm, company or corporation has carried on business for the year ending January thirty-first, eighteen hundred and sixty-three, as aforesaid, the commissioner of the revenue shall assess the tax on such license at one per centum upon the present value of the real and personal property, including capital employed in the business so
Beginners to give bond for amount of tax	to be commenced, and shall take an obligation from the licensed person, firm, company or corporation, with approved security, covenanting to pay into the treasury, at the end of the license year, ten per centum upon the net profits of the business during the said license year, less the tax of one per centum to be assessed as aforesaid at the time of, and to be paid before the granting of said license: but any tax on the capital invested in the trade or business in respect to which any license is required by this section, shall be deducted from the amount of tax imposed by this section, and the residue shall
Bonds to be re-	be the tax assessed upon such license. The commissioner of the

revenue shall return all such obligations to the auditor of public accounts, within thirty days after they may be executed, and for failure so to do, shall forfeit the sum of five hundred dollars. *turned to auditor*

75. At the close of the license year the auditor shall proceed against the parties to said obligations, in the circuit court of Richmond city, in the same manner as provided for against defaulting collectors of the public revenue, and shall be entitled to recover the amount of the tax thereby covenanted to be paid into the treasury as aforesaid. *How forfeiture recovered*

76. The certificate by the commissioner of the revenue of the tax to be paid, and that the obligation required in the cases aforesaid has been duly executed, with the receipt of the tax by the collecting officer, shall be deemed to constitute a license under this section. *What constitutes a license*

77. If any person, firm, company or corporation shall, without obtaining the license hereby required, carry on any business herein mentioned, the commissioner of the revenue shall, as in other cases, assess four times the tax prescribed by this section against such person, firm, company or corporation. *Penalty for failing to obtain license*

78. The auditor shall, for good cause to him shown, have full power to reform any assessment under this section, and to require a new obligation, with additional security, where the original is deemed insufficient, and may appoint a special agent to make a new assessment and take a new obligation; and thereupon the original assessment shall be set aside, and the license granted shall cease. *Auditor to reform assessments*

79. If the commissioner of the revenue shall make a false certificate, or take an insufficient obligation in the cases required, he and his sureties shall be liable for all loss and damage therefrom on his official bond, and the recovery against him shall not be limited by the penalty thereof: provided, that no person, firm, company or corporation engaged in any business, trade or calling embraced in this section, shall be taxed under the section of this act imposing a tax of ten per centum upon net income. *Penalty for false certificate by commissioner*

GENERAL PROVISIONS.

Tax on corporations.

80. No private act of assembly on which a tax is imposed, shall be published, nor any copy thereof furnished to any person, until the party asking and requiring the same shall have paid into the treasury of the commonwealth the taxes prescribed by law; and it shall be the duty of the keeper of the rolls to publish, with the acts of assembly of each session, all acts upon which the tax prescribed by law has been paid into the treasury since the last publication thereof. *Tax on corporations*

FINANCIAL.—TAXES.

When tax tickets to be made out by commissioners.

Tax tickets, when made out

81. After the first day of February and until the first day of July, in each year, and until the delivery of the commissioner's books to the sheriff or collector of any county, if the same be delivered after the first day of July, it shall be lawful and the duty of every commissioner of the revenue to make out tickets showing the amount of taxes which will be chargeable on his books when completed, against any person whom he has reasonable ground to suspect is about to depart from his county before the first day of July, or before the delivery of said books to said sheriff or collector. Upon the delivery of such tickets, the sheriff or collector shall be authorized to make immediate distress for the taxes therein specified, and to use all the remedies for the collection of such taxes, as are now given, after the first day of July, upon the delivery of the commissioner's books.

Penalty for failure to obtain license.

Penalty for failing to obtain license

82. Whenever a tax is imposed by law on a license to engage in any business, calling or profession, it shall be lawful to obtain a license as in similar cases; and it shall be unlawful to engage in such business, calling or profession without obtaining a license therefor. Any person who shall in any manner violate this section, or any section of this act for which no specific fine is imposed, shall pay a fine of not less than twenty nor more than one thousand dollars for each offence.

Limitation of license.

Limitation of license

83. No license shall be construed to grant any privilege beyond the county or corporation wherein it is granted, unless it be expressly authorized.

Where licensed privilege to be exercised.

Where license to be exercised

84. Every license granting authority to sell, unless the license be specially authorized by law for a county or corporation, shall be at some specified house or place within such county or corporation.

When forms for tax payers to be furnished.

When forms furnished tax payers

85. If a commissioner of the revenue shall have been furnished with forms for tax payers, he shall distribute the same, or as many as may be furnished, amongst the tax payers to be found in his district, as prescribed by the sixty-fifth section of chapter thirty-five of the Code. He shall require answers according to said section, and with his books shall transmit said forms to the auditor of public accounts, if required by him; and the auditor may furnish as many such forms as he may think necessary.

Market value of stocks to be taxed.

Stocks taxed at market value

86. In all cases where this act imposes a tax on any public bond,

including the bonds of incorporated companies, or on any stock, in lieu of a tax on the interest or profits thereof, the commissioner shall assess the cash market value of such bond or stock.

When double tax to be imposed.

87. Any person continuing business after any license obtained by him shall have expired, without obtaining, on or before the day his former license so expired, a license for the succeeding term, shall be assessed with twice the amount of tax otherwise imposed on such license. [*When double tax to be imposed*]

Deduction from commissioner's compensation.

88. If a commissioner shall, in his list of licenses to be furnished to the auditor of public accounts, charge or extend in any case a tax less than the law requires, the auditor of public accounts shall deduct the amount omitted to be charged or extended, from the compensation of the commissioner; and to enable the auditor to make an examination of such lists, the commissioner shall return to him with his return of licenses, all interrogatories which may have been propounded by him, under the direction of the auditor of public accounts, and answered. [*When deductions from commissioner's compensation to be made*]

Slaves and similar subjects, how taxed.

89. The number of slaves and the value thereof shall be listed by the commissioners, and taxed according to their value, to the hirer or person in possession thereof on the first day of February. But taxes on slaves carried away or escaping from the owner or hirer to the public enemy, and not recovered, may be exonerated in the same manner that taxes erroneously assessed may be exonerated; and an order of exoneration shall have the same effect, in all respects, as if it had been made exonerating or refunding taxes erroneously assessed; and all subjects of taxation required to be listed under the provisions of the thirty-fifth and thirty-eighth chapters of the Code, and not specially taxed herein, shall be listed and taxed as similar subjects, according to the forms furnished by the auditor of public accounts. [*Slaves, &c. how taxed*]

Value of lands and lots generally not to be changed.

90. The value of lands and lots, as ascertained by the assessment made under the tenth chapter of the Acts of eighteen hundred and fifty-five and eighteen hundred and fifty-six, passed March tenth, eighteen hundred and fifty-six, under special acts, and under the thirty-fifth chapter of the Code, in respect to new grants, shall be permanent and not be changed, except under the provisions of the said thirty-fifth chapter, in case of a partition or conveyance, and except as provided by this act; and the auditor of public accounts may so far change the form of the commissioner's land book as to show in one column the value of lands and lots, exclusive of buildings. [*Value of lands and lots under certain assessments, not to be changed*]

When the value of lands and lots may be changed.

Commissioner to make new assessment in counties wasted by war

91. And inasmuch as many tracts of land and lots, with improvements thereon, situate in counties invaded by the public enemy, have been permanently diminished in value by said invasion, and despoiled and reduced in value by military occupation, and by the waste and violence incident to war, it shall be the duty of the commissioners of the revenue for such counties, upon the requisition of the owner of any real property situate in such counties, or of his agent, to make a new assessment of such real property, upon the following basis and

Basis of new assessment

mode of valuation, viz: The commissioner shall deduct from the amount at which such property stands assessed at its last assessment, such sum as is equal to a fair estimate of the permanent diminution in the value thereof, caused by the invasion of such county, and of the permanent injury and damage inflicted upon such property by military occupation thereof, and the waste and violence incident to war. In making which estimate, he shall appraise and fix the amount of such permanent diminution, injury and damage, according to what would have been the standard and rate of valuation thereof, if such permanent diminution, injury and damage had been estimated during the year eighteen hundred and fifty-six; and the remainder left, after deducting the diminution, damage and injury thus estimated, shall be the valuation at which such property shall be assessed by the commissioner.

Redress against new assessments.

Redress against errors in new assessment.

92. Any person feeling himself aggrieved by such new assessment, may apply to the court of the county or corporation in which such property is situate, for a review of such assessment, at the June or July term of said court succeeding the period of said assessment: provided ten days' previous notice of such application be given to

Case may be continued for three terms

the commissioner; and if from any cause the court cannot, in justice to the commonwealth or to the applicant, adjudge the matter of complaint during the first term at which such application is made, the same may be continued for a period not exceeding the three terms next occurring. If the court, upon considering such application, and the evidence adduced by the applicant or commissioner, shall deem the assessment made to be erroneous, it may declare what will be a

How commissioner to correct his books.

just assessment upon the mode of valuation above prescribed; and the commissioner shall thereupon correct the assessment made by him, and assess such property on his books at the valuation so adjudged by the court.

When agricultural productions are to be taxed.

When agricultural products and provisions exempt from tax

93. Agricultural productions of this state, and provisions in the hands of the producer, including pork, bacon, beef, poultry, fish, and all other meats, butter, lard, eggs and such like marketing, and in the hands of those who have purchased the same for the use of their

FINANCIAL.—TAXES.   27

own household, and not for sale, and goods and materials manufactured in this state, except ardent spirits, porter, ale and beer, shall be exempt from taxation as property while remaining in the hands of the producer or manufacturer, and while such agricultural productions and provisions, specified as aforesaid, are held as aforesaid. Such production, provisions and manufactured articles may also be sold by the producer or manufacturer without a license tax; but when once sold (with the exception named in this section) they shall be subject to a tax as other property, and to a license tax when thereafter sold. To give effect to this section, chapter first, entitled an act for the assessment of taxes on persons and property, passed March thirtieth, eighteen hundred and sixty, and chapter second, entitled an act making general regulations concerning licenses, passed March thirtieth, eighteen hundred and sixty, in cases where said chapters might be otherwise construed, shall be construed according to the provisions of this section: provided, that no person shall be required to take out a license or pay any tax for the privilege of buying his neighbor's produce to take out of the county in his own vessel or other conveyance, to market, or for selling the same. <small>When subject to license tax</small> <small>Revenue and license acts construed</small>

Domestic manufactures, how taxed.

94. Merchant tailors and all other persons manufacturing any production or material, except ardent spirits, porter, ale and beer, the sale of which material would be prohibited without a license, shall only be charged so much tax on the sales as the value of the material sold would bear to the whole value of the manufactured articles; to be ascertained upon the oath of the person, as in other cases. <small>How tax on sales of merchant tailors and others ascertained</small>

Licenses, how granted ; prohibition of the sale of ardent spirits, &c.

95. A license to manufacture porter, ale and beer, or either of them, may be granted by the commissioner of the revenue, as in other cases, without any previous certificate or order of the court; but a license to sell the same, or any of them, and the privilege of selling ardent spirits, shall only be granted upon the certificate of the county or corporation court, that the person to be licensed is sober and of good character. But if the person shall have commenced or continued the sale of ardent spirits, without making application for such license: in the former case, he shall be assessed four times, and in the latter, twice the amount of taxes otherwise imposed for a year; which shall in no case be refunded to him, unless under proceedings provided for by chapter twenty-nine of the Acts of eighteen hundred and sixty-one, such assessment is pronounced erroneous by the court. <small>How license to make and sell malt liquors granted</small> <small>Liability of persons selling without license</small>

Effect of the change of the name of a firm.

96. No change in the name of any firm of merchants, commission merchants, sample merchants, merchant tailors, auctioneers, or any other persons who are taxed upon the amount of business or sales of the preceding year, nor the taking into the firm of a new <small>What not considered commencing business</small>

partner, nor the withdrawal of one or more of the firm, shall be considered as commencing, so as to allow, on that account, the payment only of the specific tax imposed by law for the privilege granted; but if any one of the parties remain in the firm, either as a general or special partner, or otherwise, in interest, to be ascertained upon the oath of the party to whom the license is granted, the business shall be regarded as continuing.

Insolvents, how collected.

<small>List of insolvents, how sent out for collection</small>

97. A copy of every list of insolvents, whether of persons, personal property, licenses or militia fines, whether allowed by any court or board, or by the auditor of public accounts, under ordinance number seventy-two of the convention, entitled an ordinance for the relief of sheriffs of certain counties, passed June twenty-eighth, eighteen hundred and sixty-one, shall in his discretion, as soon as practicable, be placed by the auditor of public accounts in the hands of any sheriff, collector or constable of any county or corporation for collection. Such sheriff, collector or constable shall receive and receipt for the same, and shall make return of delinquents thereon within one year from their receipt, in the same manner and under the same regulations as are prescribed for the return of other delinquent taxes. The amount appearing due after such return of delinquents, and the allowance of such commissions as may have been prescribed by the governor, shall be paid into the treasury within one year from the time such copy of such delinquents may have been received by such sheriff or other officer. When such copies are received by such officer, he shall have the same powers of distress and other remedies for the collection of the amount appearing due thereby, as are allowed to sheriffs for the collection of taxes. Any officer failing or refusing to receive and execute a proper receipt for any such copy of delinquents, shall forfeit not less than one hundred nor more than five hundred dollars.

<small>Commissions for collection, how allowed</small>

<small>Penalty on officers for failing to receive and receipt</small>

License to a sutler or other person to sell goods, &c., within or near to a military encampment.

<small>License to sutlers</small>

98. No license shall be granted to a sutler or other person to sell goods, wares and merchandise or other thing, within or near to a military post or encampment, unless the person desiring such license shall produce to the court or to the commissioner of the revenue, as may be required by law, a certificate of the commander of such post or encampment, approving of the issuing of a license to such sutler or other person; and any sutler or other person so selling without a license at such places, shall be subject to all the penalties and liabilities imposed upon merchants and other persons selling without a license: provided, however, that no license shall be required of persons selling provisions only to the army.

License to a merchant who is a beginner.

<small>When license to</small>

99. A license to a merchant who is a beginner, shall specify the

value of goods to be sold by such merchant; and when goods to the *merchants who are beginners,* value specified have been sold, the license thereafter shall be deemed *void* to be void; and if such merchant fail to apply to a commissioner of the revenue for a new assessment and new license, and continue in business after his license is deemed to be void as aforesaid, he shall forfeit to the commonwealth, for the benefit of the general treasury, not less than one hundred nor more than two thousand dollars.

Population of counties, cities and towns, how estimated.

100. In all cases where the population of any county, city or town *How population of counties, &c. to be estimated* is a data for estimating the taxes imposed by law for the exercise of any privilege therein, or for any other purpose, the commissioner, after ascertaining the actual number of slaves assessed, shall assume that the white and free negro population is five and a half times the number of white persons and free negroes of and over the age of twenty-one years. The actual number of slaves as ascertained, and the estimate of the white and free negro population, made as aforesaid, shall constitute the population for the purposes aforesaid.

Banks, insurance and other companies, when and what to report to auditor of public accounts.

101. Banks, savings banks, insurance companies, express compa- *Banks, insurance companies, &c. when and what to report to auditor* nies, rail road companies, and all other companies which by law are required to make a report to the auditor of public accounts, and also all such companies, firms and persons engaged in manufacturing or working in cotton, woolen or iron, or any other agricultural or mineral products, shall, as soon after the first day of July in each year as may be, make report to the said auditor of the amount of capital employed by such company; the capital stock actually paid in, if an incorporated company; the gross income received and contracted to be received during the preceding year ending on the thirtieth day of June; the salaries and other compensation paid to the officers and employees receiving compensation in the nature of a salary, together with their names; the number of persons employed as laborers; the slaves, and the aggregate amount of hire paid therefor, assuming the total number to be equal to the average number in the year. If the company be a work of internal improvement, the report shall also show the length of the work and the cost of construction. From such reports the auditor shall condense the same into a report to the general assembly. Any such bank, company or firm failing for one *Penalty for failing to report.* month to make such report, shall forfeit not less than five hundred dollars nor more than five thousand dollars; to be recovered in the circuit court of the city of Richmond, upon the motion of the auditor of public accounts.

Personal property exempt from taxation.

•102. The forty-third section of chapter thirty-five of the Code (edition of eighteen hundred and sixty) is hereby amended and re-enacted so as to read as follows:

Personal property exempt from taxation

"§ 43. All personal property described in this section, and to the extent herein limited, shall be exempt from taxation, that is to say:

The household and kitchen furniture used in a licensed ordinary, house of entertainment or private boarding house, and belonging to the keeper thereof, the value whereof has been included in such license tax.

All books, apparatus and furniture belonging to colleges, free schools and incorporated academies, and used for college or school purposes; to the university of Virginia; to the Virginia military institute; to the institution for the education of the deaf and dumb and the blind; and to the lunatic asylums.

And all personal property belonging to orphan asylums, overseers of the poor, and exclusively to the commonwealth.

All fire engines or other implements for the extinguishment of fires.

All books, family portraits and pictures, and the wearing apparel of every person and family, except watches and jewelry.

All agricultural productions of this state in the hands of the producer.

All mineral productions of this state in the hands of the producer or miner.

All felled wood or timber in the hands of the person owning, renting or leasing the land where the same was grown.

All plantations of oysters and fisheries.

All capital invested in any trade or business for the prosecution of which a license is required.

All farming implements actually used for farming purposes, except road wagons, or wagons used principally for other than farming purposes.

All mechanics' tools used on any farm, or by any person actually engaged in any trade, occupation or profession."

Sheriffs' commissions on taxes other than license taxes.

103. The twenty-second section of chapter thirty-six of the Code (edition of eighteen hundred and sixty) is hereby amended and re-enacted so as to read as follows:

Commissions for collection of taxes

"§ 23. Every sheriff or collector shall be allowed a commission of two per centum on the amount of taxes, other than license taxes, with which he is chargeable; and if he shall punctually pay the same into the treasury within the time required by law, he shall be allowed an additional commission of three per centum. But when the taxes with which he is chargeable exceed sixty thousand dollars, and do not exceed one hundred thousand dollars, the commission on the excess shall be only one per centum; and if he shall punctually pay the same into the treasury within the time required by law, he shall be allowed an additional commission of two per centum on such excess; and if the taxes with which he is chargeable shall exceed one hundred thousand dollars, the commission on the excess over said sum shall be only one-half of one per centum; and if he shall punctually pay the same into the treasury within the time required by law, he shall be allowed an additional commission of one per centum on the excess over one hundred thousand dollars."

Commissioner's compensation other than fees.

104. The ninety-fifth section of chapter thirty-five of the Code (edition of eighteen hundred and sixty) is hereby amended and re-enacted so as to read as follows:

"§ 95. Every commissioner of the revenue shall be entitled to receive, in consideration of his services, to be paid on or before the first day of September, out of the treasury, upon the warrant of the auditor of public accounts, a commission of one and one-half per. centum on the amount of taxes lawfully assessed by him on persons and property within the preceding twelve months. But where the taxes on persons and property assessed in any district in a county exceed twenty thousand dollars, the commission allowed on the excess shall be only three-fourths of one per centum; and where the said taxes assessed in any district in a town or city exceed sixteen thousand dollars, the commission allowed on the excess shall be only one-half of one per centum." Commissions for assessing taxes

List for sheriffs, auditor and clerk of court; commissioner's fees, by whom payable.

105. The forty-seventh section of chapter thirty-eight of the Code (edition of eighteen hundred and sixty) is hereby amended and re-enacted so as to read as follows:

"§ 47. After the commissioner of the revenue shall have assessed all persons required by law to obtain licenses, he shall make a fair classified list thereof, as far as he may have progressed with the same, at intervals not exceeding fifteen days, and deliver such lists to the sheriff or other collector of the revenue, for his guide in collecting the taxes imposed by law on such licenses. He shall return to the auditor of public accounts and to the clerk of the court of the county or corporation a list of all such licenses; that is to say, a list of such as are granted on or after the first day of September and before the first day of May following, shall be returned on or before the tenth day of the said month of May; and a list of such as are granted on or after the first day of May and before the first day of September following, shall be returned immediately after the first day of September. Such lists shall specify the date of each license, for what it was granted, the name of the person to whom granted, the amount of the tax, to whom paid, and the data upon which the tax was assessed. For every certificate delivered by a commissioner to a person desiring, or who ought to obtain a license, the commissioner shall be entitled to a fee of one dollar for each license, unless such license Lists of licenses granted

When to be returned to auditor

Fee for certificate of license be refused by the court; which fees shall be paid to him by the person to whom the license shall be granted."

Commissions to sheriffs and collectors.

106. The fifty-sixth section of chapter thirty-eight of the Code (edition of eighteen hundred and sixty) is hereby amended and re-enacted so as to read as follows:

Commissions for collecting license tax.

"§ 56. Every sheriff, or person receiving taxes on licenses under this chapter, shall be allowed a commission of one per centum for their collection on the first five thousand dollars, and one-half of one per centum upon any excess over that sum; and if he shall punctually pay the same into the treasury within the time prescribed by law, he shall be allowed an additional compensation of one per centum on the first five thousand dollars, and one-half of one per centum on any excess over that sum."

Penalties, how recoverable.

107. The fifty-ninth section of chapter thirty-eight of the Code of Virginia (edition of eighteen hundred and sixty) is hereby amended and re-enacted so as to read as follows:

Suits to recover penalties, when and how instituted.

"§ 59. Such action of debt may be instituted at any time within five years after the offence was committed, and shall be for the maximum penalty prescribed, and for each violation of any of the laws and prohibitions contained in this act or the thirty-eighth chapter of the Code of Virginia (edition of eighteen hundred and sixty). In the action of debt, bail shall be required as a matter of right; and if deemed necessary, an attachment may issue without the affidavit and bond required in other cases, either before the institution of a suit or during the pendency of the same. A declaration shall be filed, but no orders or pleadings at rules shall be necessary, and no exceptions shall be allowed to the declaration for any defect or want of form. If the offence is not sufficiently stated, the court shall require, under such rules as it may adopt at any time before a verdict may be rendered thereon, a full and explicit statement of the offence. In all such proceedings the court shall render judgment according to the very right of the case. In case the defendant be arrested and in custody for want of bail, he may, at the time of arrest, or at any time before a judgment be rendered in the action, give bond with sufficient security, in a penalty equal to the penalty sued for, to the officer making the arrest, or to the clerk of the court wherein the action was instituted. Such bond shall be payable to the commonwealth, and shall be conditioned for the appearance of the party to answer the action, and to abide by and satisfy the judgment of the court. Upon the execution of such bond the defendant shall be discharged from custody. The bond shall be returned to and filed with the clerk in the papers of said action. No officer shall be entitled to the payment of any fees out of the treasury for services rendered in

Form of proceedings

When defendant in custody may give bond for his appearance

Where bond filed

any proceedings herein authorized. In all cases of conviction under this act, a fee of ten dollars to the commonwealth's attorney shall be taxed in the bill of costs." Fee of attorney for commonwealth

Deputies of collectors may be appointed.

103. Whenever the auditor of public accounts shall hereafter appoint a collector of taxes under the ordinance of the Virginia convention, number sixty-five, entitled an ordinance providing for the appointment of the commissioners of the revenue and collectors of taxes in certain cases, and providing for the absence of the auditor of public accounts, passed June twenty-sixth, eighteen hundred and sixty-one, it shall be lawful for such collector to appoint deputies in the same manner that deputy sheriffs are by law appointed, who shall possess all the powers which are now exercised or possessed by deputy sheriffs in the collection of taxes, militia fines, county levies and poor rates, and shall be subject to the same liabilities and restrictions which appertain to deputy sheriffs, and 'the principal shall be liable for his official acts as such, and such deputy collector shall be a resident of the county for which he is appointed. When and how collectors may appoint deputies

Confederate treasury notes receivable in payment of taxes.

109. The act entitled an act authorizing the receipt of Confederate States treasury notes in payment of taxes and other public dues, passed March twenty-second, eighteen hundred and sixty-two, shall be and the same is hereby amended and re-enacted so as to read as follows:

"Confederate States non-interest bearing notes of the denomination of, or over five dollars, dated and issued on and after the first day of April eighteen hundred and sixty-three, shall hereafter be receivable in payment of taxes and other public dues to the state." What confederate notes receivable for taxes

110. The auditor of public accounts shall cause the preceding section to be published in at least five newspapers in the city of Richmond, and in the papers of the cities of Lynchburg and Petersburg, and in the towns of Danville, Staunton and Wytheville, for at least four weeks. Preceding section to be published

When taxes may be distrained for.

111. The fourth section of chapter thirty-six of the Code (edition of eighteen hundred and sixty) shall be and the same is hereby amended and re-enacted so as to read as follows:

"§ 4. No distress shall be made for taxes or levies, where the sheriff or collector has had more than two years to collect the same, unless it be for taxes returned delinquent, and sent out by the auditor for collection, as provided by law. But a sheriff or collector of a former term may, notwithstanding the expiration of his term of office, by himself or by his deputies, have the same powers of dis- When taxes not to be distrained for
When taxes may be distrained for tress and sale as he possessed before said term expired; and which right of distress and sale shall continue for the term of two years from the time such right first accrued; but no deputy shall be permitted to qualify for such collections after the principal's office has expired. And it shall be lawful for a sheriff or collector to receipt for, and collect by distress, within said two years, any taxes or fees remaining unpaid to his predecessor. Such sheriff shall be liable to his predecessor, or his personal representative, for the taxes and fees collected, in the same manner he is liable for clerks' fees collected by him."

Liability of sheriff

Commissioners to ascertain the number, &c. of all slaves that escape to the enemy.

Lists of slaves escaping to enemy

112. Commissioners of the revenue for each district, in taking lists of the personal property in the several counties, cities and towns of this commonwealth, shall enquire into and ascertain, as far as practicable, the number of all slaves that have escaped to the enemy during this war, and have not been recovered, and make a return of such lists to the auditor of public accounts, with the names, sexes and ages of such slaves, and the names of the owners thereof; to be filed and preserved in the office of said auditor.

No license to issue to aliens. Exception

113. That no license under this act shall be issued to any alien, except as provided in the act passed March thirty-one, eighteen hundred and sixty-two, entitled an act defining the persons who may obtain license, and except as to such aliens as shall not, on account of being aliens, have claimed exemption from service in the army of the Confederate States: and no alien who has claimed exemption as such, from service in the army of the Confederate States, shall act as an agent for any citizen of this state licensed under this act.

Repealing clause.

Repealing clause

114. Chapter one, entitled an act imposing taxes for the support of government, passed March twenty-seventh, eighteen hundred and sixty-two, shall be and the same is hereby repealed, so far as the same is not herein before re-enacted.

Commencement

115. This act shall be in force from its passage.

CHAP. 2.—An ACT appropriating the Public Revenue for the fiscal year 1862-3.

Passed March 28, 1863.

Taxes appropriated

1. Be it enacted by the general assembly, that the public taxes and arrears of taxes due prior to the first day of October eighteen hundred and sixty-three, and not otherwise appropriated by law, which shall come into the treasury prior to the first day of October

eighteen hundred and sixty-three, shall constitute a general fund, and be appropriated for the fiscal year to close on the thirtieth day of September eighteen hundred and sixty-three, as follows, videlicet:

To pay the salary of the secretary to the commissioners of the sinking fund, three hundred dollars. *Salary of clerk of sinking fund*

To pay the per diem, mileage, and other expenses of the general assembly, incurred in the session of September eighteen hundred and sixty-two, forty-two thousand dollars. *General assembly*

To pay the per diem, mileage, and other expenses of the general assembly, incurred in the same session, in October eighteen hundred and sixty-two, and the session commencing in January eighteen hundred and sixty-three, sixty-five thousand dollars. *General assembly*

To pay expenses of comparing polls in sundry elections, one thousand dollars. *Elections*

To pay salaries and mileage of judges and other officers of the civil government, one hundred and eleven thousand dollars. *Judges*

To pay for arrest and support of prisoners, pay of jurors, witnesses, &c., as provided by law, sixty thousand dollars. *Prisoners, jurors, &c*

To pay for slaves condemned and executed, or sentenced to er reprieved for sale and transportation, twenty-five thousand dollars. *Slaves condemned*

To pay expenses for bringing condemned slaves to penitentiary, eight hundred dollars. *Expenses of, to penitentiary*

To pay Joseph W. Hancock, a judgment for the value of his female slave named Amanda, sentenced by the judgment of the county court of Chesterfield to sale and transportation, seven hundred and ninety dollars. *J. W. Hancock*

To pay for subsistence and other supplies for the support of convicts and transports in the penitentiary, fifty thousand dollars. *Convicts, &c*

To pay mileage to officers and guards, and expenses of convicts, in transporting convicts from the place of conviction to the penitentiary, five thousand dollars. *Mileage to officers and guards*

To pay the salary of the superintendent of the penitentiary, his assistant keepers, clerk, surgeon, and allowance to directors, eight thousand dollars. *Penitentiary*

To pay for printing records of the court of appeals and district courts, four thousand dollars. *Records court of appeals*

To pay contingent expenses of courts, sheriffs, clerks and other officers of the courts, fuel, stationery, &c., twenty thousand dollars. *Contingent expenses of courts*

To pay the expense of the militia establishment, to brigade inspectors, adjutants, clerks, musicians, &c., ten thousand dollars. *Militia*

To pay the salary of the adjutant general and his clerk, three thousand two hundred dollars. *Adjutant general*

To pay the annuity for the annual support of the Virginia military institute, thirteen thousand five hundred dollars. *Annuity to Virginia military institute*

To pay expenses chargeable to the military contingent fund, under an act to organize a military contingent fund, passed March fifteenth, eighteen hundred and sixty-two, fifty thousand dollars. *Military contingent fund*

To pay officers and privates, for rations, clothing and other allow- *Public guard*

FINANCIAL.—APPROPRIATIONS.

ances to the public guard, and ordnance sergeant at the military institute, including temporary quarters, sixty thousand dollars.

Interior guard at penitentiary — To pay allowances to the interior guard at the penitentiary, two thousand eight hundred dollars.

Transportation of arms — To pay for the transportation of arms collected and distributed, eight hundred dollars.

Commissioners of the revenue — To pay the commissions and other fees of commissioners of the revenue, and for lists of taxable property, and to clerks of courts, for examining commissioners' books, eighty thousand dollars.

Central lunatic asylum — To pay for support (in addition to the pay patient fund) and transportation of patients to the Central lunatic asylum, sixty-five thousand dollars.

Eastern lunatic asylum — To pay for support (in addition to the pay patient fund) and transportation of patients to the Eastern lunatic asylum, forty-eight thousand dollars; and also the sum of three hundred and twenty-four dollars and thirty-seven cents—of which sum one hundred and *Robert Saunders & al* twenty-six dollars shall be paid to Robert Saunders, and one hundred and twenty-six dollars to Edward H. Lively, for the hire of their servants for the year eighteen hundred and sixty-two—and to William H. Peirce, an officer, for services, the sum of seventy-two dollars and thirty-seven cents, balance due him for eighteen hundred and sixty-two.

William M. Hume — To pay to William M. Hume, sheriff of Fauquier county, or his legal representative, seventy-three dollars and sixty-cents, that being the amount to which he is entitled by law for conveying a lunatic from said county of Fauquier to the asylum at Williamsburg, which said amount is to be deducted from the appropriation to said institution for the fiscal year ending September thirtieth, eighteen hundred and sixty-two.

Lunatics in county jails — To pay expenses, &c. of lunatics confined in county jails, four thousand dollars.

Deaf, dumb and blind — To pay the support of the deaf, dumb and the blind, twenty-five thousand dollars.

Pensions — To pay pensions allowed by law, four hundred and thirty-two dollars.

To pay claims chargeable on the civil contingent fund, to be allowed and certified by the executive, one hundred thousand dollars.

Civil prosecutions — To pay expenses of civil prosecutions, eight thousand dollars.

Public warehouses — To pay for services of commissioners of public warehouses, one hundred and fifty dollars.

Governor's house — To pay for repairs to the governor's house, to be paid upon the certificate of the superintendent of public buildings, five hundred dollars.

Capitol — To pay for repairs of the capitol, to be paid upon the certificate of the superintendent of public buildings, five thousand dollars.

Grattan's Reports — To pay for the printing and binding of one thousand copies of the sixteenth volume of Grattan's Reports, two thousand two hundred dollars.

Leigh's Reports — To pay for reprinting and binding one volume of Leigh's Reports, as provided by law, one thousand six hundred dollars.

FINANCIAL.—APPROPRIATIONS.

To pay the annual allowance to the vaccine agent at Richmond, five hundred dollars. *Vaccine agent*

To pay for the services of a messenger in the office of the auditor of public accounts, eight hundred dollars. *Messenger in auditor's office*

To pay expenses of the registration of marriages, births and deaths, two thousand five hundred dollars. *Registration of marriages, &c*

To pay expense of printing for the general assembly and public officers, and for paper and books for public officers, forty-five thousand dollars. *Printing*

To pay for the services of temporary clerks in the office of the auditor of public accounts, four thousand five hundred dollars. *Temporary clerks in auditor's office*

To pay commissions to sheriffs, payable by warrants, two hundred dollars. *Commissions to sheriffs*

To pay sundry expenses out of the special appropriations to the New river navigation company, ten thousand dollars. *New river navigation company*

To pay the pages of the senate and house of delegates, the sum of three dollars per day for each day's services as such; to be paid upon the certificate of the clerk of the senate and of the clerk of the house of delegates respectively. *Pages*

To pay the clerk of the joint committee on salt, four dollars per day for the time of his services; to be paid on the order of the clerk of the house of delegates. *Clerk joint committee on salt*

To pay to the porter to the senate, for services as such, attention to the senate chamber and clerk's office of the senate, and for making fires for same, two dollars and fifty cents per day; to be paid upon the certificate of the clerk of the senate. *Porter of senate*

To pay the further expenses for making fires and superintending the furnaces in the capitol, the customary allowance of two dollars per day to each of the several persons entitled to the same, not exceeding two persons to be employed; to be paid upon the certificate of the superintendent of public buildings. *Fires, furnaces &c*

To pay the principal and interest on temporary loans, two million five hundred and nine thousand two hundred and eight dollars and ninety-five cents. *Temporary loans*

To pay the interest on loans under the act for the assumption of the Confederate States war tax, ninety-two thousand seven hundred and ninety-three dollars. *Interest on loans for war tax*

To pay the principal and interest of interest bearing treasury notes, three million three hundred and sixty-two thousand nine hundred and sixty-six dollars. *Interest bearing treasury notes*

To pay the salaries and allowances of naval officers on retired lists, five thousand three hundred dollars. *Naval officers*

To pay military expenses, other than the expenses of the state line and mountain rangers, to be paid upon the order of the auditing board, fifty thousand dollars; but the disbursements under this clause shall be limited to the payment of claims heretofore allowed by said auditing board; and all claims hereafter allowed by said board shall be reported to the general assembly for payment by appropriations by law, except claims embraced in the next following clause. *Military expenses*

FINANCIAL.—APPROPRIATIONS.

State line — To pay claims of officers and soldiers of the Virginia state line and mountain rangers, including the raising, clothing, subsistence, and otherwise supporting the same, to be paid upon the order of the auditing board, two million dollars.

Penitentiary — To supply the penitentiary with raw material for manufacturing purposes, twelve thousand dollars; to be paid to the order of the superintendent thereof.

Patrick Kean — To pay Patrick Kean, as reporter to the secret debates of the convention, upon the certificate of the secretary thereof, as ordered by the convention, three hundred dollars.

Hoyer & Ludwig — To pay Messrs. Hoyer & Ludwig for engraving and printing two hundred copies of the ordinance of secession, three hundred and ninety dollars.

J. D. Pendleton & al — To pay J. D. Pendleton and John Burwell, for clerical services rendered the senate during the indisposition of the clerk of the senate at the present session, sixty dollars each.

General fund — 2. Be it further enacted, that so much of the public revenue as may be received into the public treasury after the thirtieth day of September eighteen hundred and sixty-three, and the surplus of all other appropriations made prior to that date, unexpended within the fiscal year ending on the last day of September eighteen hundred and sixty-three, and all other moneys not otherwise appropriated by law, shall constitute a general fund, to defray such expenses authorized by law as are not herein particularly provided for, and to defray the usual allowances to lunatic asylums, and other current expenses of the commonwealth, in the fiscal year which shall commence on the first day of October eighteen hundred and sixty-three, and terminate on the thirtieth day of September eighteen hundred and

Disposal of general fund — sixty-four; and the auditor of public accounts is hereby authorized and required to issue his warrants in the same manner as if the same had been specifically mentioned, subject to such exceptions, limitations and conditions as the general assembly have prescribed, or may

Limitation — deem it proper to annex and prescribe by law: provided, that nothing in this act contained shall be so construed as to authorize the auditor of public accounts to issue his warrant or warrants in satisfaction of any judgment or decree of any court of law or equity against the commonwealth, for a sum exceeding three hundred dollars, without a special appropriation by law.

Payments, when made — 3. The payments to the military institute, for support, to the lunatic asylums, for support and transportation of patients; and to the institution for the education of the deaf and dumb and the blind, shall be made, one-fourth in advance, on the first day of October, one-half on the first day of January (if the visitors or directors so require), and the remaining one-fourth on the first day of April.

Commencement — 4. This act shall be in force from its passage.

CHAP. 3.—An ACT authorizing the payment of Interest on Bonds given for the Confederate States War Tax, after the day of payment.

Passed March 12, 1863.

1. Be it enacted by the general assembly, that any bond heretofore Bond, when to or hereafter given for the payment of money, in pursuance of the act of bear interest assembly entitled an act to provide for the assumption and payment of the Confederate States war tax, passed February twenty-first, eighteen hundred and sixty-two, shall continue to bear interest until presented for renewal. The holders of bonds heretofore paid after When holders the day of payment, to whom interest was refused after the said day rest entitled to interest of payment, shall be entitled to such interest; and the auditor of When auditor to public accounts shall issue his warrant on the treasury, payable out issue warrant of any money in the treasury not otherwise appropriated, in favor of the person whose bond may have been paid without such interest, for the amount of interest which would have accrued thereon, at the rate of six per centum per annum, from the day of payment until the Rate of interest same may have been paid.

2. This act shall be in force from its passage. Commencement

CHAP. 4.—An ACT to transfer the State Troops and Rangers to the Confederate Government.

Passed February 28, 1863.

1. Be it enacted by the general assembly, that the governor be Governor directed and he is hereby authorized and directed to cause, without delay, all rected to transfer state troops the state troops raised under an act of the general assembly, entitled Acts as to state an act to authorize a force of ten thousand men to be raised for the troops and rangers defence of the commonwealth, passed May fifteenth, eighteen hundred and sixty-two, and under any acts amendatory thereof, including all companies of rangers organized under the act of March twenty-seventh, eighteen hundred and sixty-two, entitled an act to authorize the organization of ten or more companies of rangers, or any other act of the general assembly, to be reorganized into companies, battalions and regiments, in accordance with the laws and regulations of the confederate service. In case there be four com- When officers panies of said rangers, including the company of Captain George may elect a major Dusky, at present acting with one of the regiments of said state troops, it shall be lawful for the officers of said companies (as intended by the said act of the twenty-seventh of March eighteen hundred and sixty-two) to elect a major therefor, who shall be commissioned by the governor as of the day preceding the date of the passage of this act: provided, that such election be made within ten days after the passage of this act; and such major, without waiting for his commission, shall be deemed one of the field officers who may be

MILITARY AFFAIRS.

Company officers, how elected — elected under the next succeeding section. Whenever two or more companies are consolidated into one to make up the complement of men required by said laws, the non-commissioned officers and privates may (under the superintendence of such officer as shall be designated by the governor for that purpose) elect, from among the officers of the same grade, a captain, a first lieutenant and two second lieutenants, who shall be assigned to the company thus formed, and the commissions of the other company officers shall thereafter be void.

Battalions and regiments, how formed
Field officers, how chosen

2. As soon as ten companies are thus formed, they shall be organized into two battalions and one regiment. From the field officers of the necessary grades now in commission in said state troops and rangers, the commissioned officers of the regiment may elect their field officers. In like manner, when another regiment is formed, the like proceeding shall be had until all the regiments that may be

Battalions — formed are completed. If there are any companies left after the formation of said regiments, they shall be formed into a battalion,

What field officers discharged — and officered in like manner. The field officers then remaining without commands shall be discharged, and their commissions shall be

How mustered into service of Confederate States — void. The regiments, and any detached battalion thus formed, shall be mustered into the service of the Confederate States by such mustering officer as shall be detailed by the secretary of war for that purpose; and when so mustered, complete returns thereof shall be immediately made by such mustering officer, to the adjutant general

How received — of this state at Richmond. The said troops are to be received in companies, battalions and regiments, with their respective officers.

Who may be discharged — They are to be mustered into the service for the war, but with the express reservation that those not subject to conscription, if they desire it, shall be discharged at the expiration of their present term

Inventory of arms, &c. how taken — of enlistment. The governor shall appoint an officer, to be present at the mustering of said troops into service, whose duty it shall be to take an inventory of all arms, accoutrements, ordnance, equipments, stores, munitions of war, horses and other property which may be in

How transferred to confederate government — the possession of said troops when so mustered into service; and the same shall be transferred to the confederate government, and shall be received and receipted for by the said mustering officer at the

Staff officers — time of receiving and mustering said troops as aforesaid. Such staff officers for said regiments and detached battalion, if any, as may be authorized by the laws of the Confederate States, shall be appointed by the colonels of the regiments when formed, according to the laws of the Confederate States; and when the said regiments are mustered into service, the said staff officers shall be received as a part of the force transferred, and be commissioned accordingly.

Arms, &c. how valued

3. All the arms, accoutrements, ordnance and equipments, stores, munitions of war and other property furnished and receipted for as aforesaid, shall be valued by the mustering officer aforesaid, and the officer appointed by the governor to make the inventory thereof, and

if they fail to agree, in such mode as may be agreed on by the governor and secretary of war; and the value thus ascertained shall, *Valuation, how* upon delivery thereof, be paid by the confederate government into *paid by confederate government* the treasury of the commonwealth, to the credit of the commonwealth.

4. All enlistments for the state troops and rangers shall cease from and after the passage of this act.

5. From and after the transfer of the said troops, as provided for *Payments not* in the second section of this act, no claim shall be allowed for the *allowed after transfer* payment of the officers and troops or otherwise, on account of said state troops and rangers, except in discharge of liabilities incurred prior thereto.

6. Such portion of said forces, including commissioned, non-com- *When pay, rations, &c, not to* missioned officers and privates, as shall not be reorganized and trans- *be received* ferred before the first day of April eighteen hundred and sixty-three, according to the provisions of this act, shall receive no pay, clothing, rations or other allowances for services thereafter.

7. This act shall be in force from its passage, and all acts and *Commencement* parts of acts inconsistent therewith are hereby repealed. *and repealing clause*

CHAP. 5.—An ACT to provide for the Discharge from active Military Service, of persons who have furnished Substitutes.

Passed February 5, 1863.

1. Be it enacted by the general assembly, that no person who has *When person* heretofore furnished, according to law, a substitute in the military *who has furnished substitute exempt* service of the Confederate States, for three years or the war, shall be *from military* liable to military service, under the proclamation of the governor of *service* the tenth day of January eighteen hundred and sixty-three, or any future proclamation calling for forces under now existing laws, to be turned over to the service of the Confederate States, except in cases in which such substitute may be himself liable, under the laws of the Confederate States, to perform his own tour of duty; but such per- *Entitled to discharge* son shall be entitled to his discharge.

2. In conformity to instructions of the governor, not inconsistent *Questions of ex-* with the provisions of this act, the board of exemptions provided for *emption, how determined* by act of October first, eighteen hundred and sixty-two, are empowered and directed to determine all questions of exemptions arising under said proclamation, or any future proclamations, claimed by any person by reason of his having furnished a substitute.

3. This act shall be in force from its passage. *Commencement*

CHAP. 6.—An ACT to amend and re-enact an act further to provide for the Public Defence, passed October 3, 1862.

Passed March 13, 1863.

Act amended and re-enacted

Be it enacted by the general assembly, that the act passed October third, eighteen hundred and sixty-two, entitled an act further to provide for the public defence, be amended and re-enacted so as to read as follows:

Slaves, how called into service of Confederate States

1. Be it enacted by the general assembly, that it shall be the duty of the governor of this commonwealth, and he is hereby authorized and required, whenever thereto requested by the president of the Confederate States, to call into the service of the Confederate States, for labor on fortifications and other works for the public defence within this state, from time to time, for a period not exceeding sixty days, a number of male slaves between the ages of eighteen and fifty-five years, not exceeding ten thousand at any one time, and not exceeding in any county, city or town, one-fifth of the number of male slaves therein between the ages specified, to be apportioned by the governor.

How apportioned

Such requisition shall be apportioned ratably among all the slaveholders in the several counties, cities and towns on which the requisition shall be made, so as to charge each slaveholder with the same proportion of his male slaves between the ages specified, capable of performing ordinary labor, to be judged of by the court,

When governor may exempt counties

which may be demanded from his county, city or town: provided, however, that the governor, in his discretion, may exempt wholly or partially, from the operation of this act, such counties as may have lost so large a portion of their slaves, in consequence of their escape to the public enemy, as will materially affect the agricultural products of such counties. And the governor may exempt such other counties as, from their geographical position or contiguity to the

Persons, how exempted

public enemy, he may deem expedient. And in any county, city or town partially exempted under this statute, any person who may satisfy its county or corporation court, or any person appointed by the governor for that purpose, that he or she has lost one-third part of his or her slaves liable to work on the public works, by said slaves going over to the enemy, shall be exempted from the operation of

Monthly allowance, &c. for slaves

this act. The sum of twenty dollars per month for each slave shall be paid by the Confederate States to the person entitled to his services, and soldiers' rations, medicines and medical attendance fur-

Value, when paid by confederate government

nished; and the value of all such slaves as may die during their term of service, or thereafter, from injuries received, or of diseases contracted in such service, or not be returned to their owners, shall be

Compensation for injuries

paid by the Confederate States to the owners of such slaves; and full compensation shall be made for all injuries to slaves arising from the act of the public enemy; and in like manner, full compensation shall be made for any injury to slaves arising from a want of due diligence on the part of the authorities of the Confederate States;

provided, that the Confederate States shall not be liable for any slave not returned by reason of fraud or collusion on the part of the owner or his agent; or if his death should be caused by the act of God, or by disease of such slave, existing when received by the confederate authorities; and in all cases the burden of proof shall be on the au- Burden of proof thorities of the Confederate States, to discharge the latter from liability to the former. Hired slaves shall be regarded as the slaves of Hired slaves, their temporary owners, in apportioning for the purposes of this act; garded how to be re but when hired slaves shall be held by persons owning other slaves, it shall not be lawful for the temporary owner to select one or more of the hired slaves to be sent to the public works; but in every such case, the slave or slaves to be sent shall be ascertained by lot, in which each of said slaves shall be drawn for by the court.

2. Be it further enacted, that so soon as the governor shall deter- Notice of call, mine to make a requisition for slaves under this act, he shall give how given notice thereof to the several counties, cities and towns on which the call may be made, by causing to be filed with the clerks of the several county and corporation courts, copies of the requisition made on their respective counties, cities and towns; and thereupon it shall Duty of clerks be the duty of the said clerks forthwith to issue a summons to all the of courts acting justices of their respective counties and corporations, requiring them to meet at the courthouses of their counties and corporations, on a day to be named in the summons, not later than six days from the filing of the requisition, to carry the same into effect; which summons shall be directed to and executed by the sheriff of the Duty of sheriffs county or sergeant of the corporation, as the case may be.

3. It shall be the duty of the several county and corporation courts, Number of after being duly convened as aforesaid, and not less than five justices requisition, how being present, to ascertain, by the assistance of the commissioners of ascertained the revenue of their respective counties and corporations, or otherwise, the entire number of male slaves therein between the ages specified, subject to requisition under this act; and after ascertaining Apportionment, the same, to apportion the requisition aforesaid, without delay, among how made all the holders of such slaves, so as to charge each slaveholder, as near as may be, with the same proportion of his male slaves between the ages of eighteen and fifty-five, capable of performing ordinary labor, as may be demanded from his county, city or town, throwing into classes, when necessary, the holders of but one or a few slaves, and of fractions of slaves, and ascertaining by lot, or agreement between the parties, or otherwise, the slave or slaves to be sent to the public works from such classes, and giving, as far as practicable, relief to those upon whom the lot or draft may have fallen under any preceding requisition: provided, that in no case of a soldier in ser- Proviso as to vice, or a widow having a son therein, or whose husband has died in slave of widow. such service, owning or hiring but one male slave, shall such slave &c be subject to requisition under this act. But no slaveholder shall be exempted by reason of having slaves in the employment of the state or confederate government.

How slaves delivered

4. So soon as the apportionment aforesaid shall be made, it shall be the duty of the courts of the several counties and corporations to require each slaveholder to deliver, on a day and at a place appointed by the court, his quota of slaves to the sheriff or sergeant, as the case may be, to be delivered by such sheriff or sergeant to an agent or officer of the Confederate States in the city of Richmond, at the expense of the Confederate States. All slaves delivered by the holders on the day and at the place designated as aforesaid, to be returned at the expiration of sixty days. Slaves not delivered in accordance with the order of the court, shall be seized by the sheriff or sergeant, as the case may be, and delivered, at the expense of the owner, to the agent or officer of the Confederate States authorized to receive them, and may be held, on the terms and conditions aforesaid, for a period not exceeding ninety days, unless sufficient cause for the failure shall be shown to the court of the county or corporation in which such failure may occur, and there entered on record; in which event, the expenses of said delivery shall be paid by the Confederate States, and a certified copy of such order shall be conclusive evidence of such sufficient cause; and moreover, the holder of such slaves shall be fined not less than three dollars nor more than ten dollars for every day each slave shall be withheld; and it shall be the duty of the sheriff or sergeant to report to the court, at its next succeeding monthly term, all persons failing or refusing to deliver their slaves as aforesaid; and unless good cause be shown for such failure or refusal, the court shall impose said fines, for which an execution shall be forthwith issued by the clerk of the court; which fines shall be repeated from time to time, until the order of court is complied with. Any sheriff failing to discharge the duties imposed by this act, shall be fined not less than fifty dollars nor more than two hundred dollars.

When returned

How seized, and when

Expenses, how paid

Fine

Sheriff to report delinquents

Fine and execution therefor

Detail of slaves, how made

5. It shall be lawful for the proper authorities of the Confederate States, whenever in their opinion the public interest may require it, to detail for labor in the business and at the place from which they have been taken, any slaves drafted under the provisions of the act hereby amended, or of this act; but in no case shall the deficiency in labor on the public works, caused by such detail, be supplied by a new draft on the other slaveholders of the county, city or town in which the detail may be made; and any slaves which shall be exempted from impressment or draft by any law of the Confederate States, shall be regarded as detailed under the provisions of this act.

Clerk and sheriff to attend court

6. The clerk and sheriff or sergeant shall attend the sessions of the court as in other cases, and the court may adjourn from time to time until the business shall be completed.

Duty of clerk

7. Should any county or corporation court fail or refuse to discharge the duties hereby imposed on them, wholly or in part, it shall be the duty of the clerk of such court immediately to notify the

governor thereof; and thereupon it shall be the duty of the latter, *Duty of governor* unless good and sufficient reasons be stated by the court for such failure or refusal, by officers and agents of his own selection, with the aid of the commissioners of the revenue of such county or corporation, who are hereby required to render such aid when required, to impress from said county or corporation such proportion of the slaves demanded by him therefrom as may not have been furnished under the provisions of this act. The slaves thus impressed, together with such as may have been furnished by such county or corporation under this act, shall not exceed one-fifth of the number of male slaves therein between the ages specified, capable of performing ordinary labor; shall be apportioned among the slaveholders, as herein above set forth, and shall be turned over to an authorized officer or agent of the Confederate States, to be held not longer than sixty days, for the uses and upon the terms and conditions set forth in the first section of this act. Separate receipts shall in all cases be executed to *Receipts, how given* the owners by the sheriff or other person seizing or taking possession of slaves under this act; and receipts shall in like manner be taken by the sheriff or other person holding them, when slaves may be turned over to the agent or officer of the Confederate States. Slaves coming into the possession of the sheriffs, sergeants or agents of the governor under this act, shall be regarded as in the possession and service of the Confederate States and at their expense, until redelivered to their owners. For every seizure of a slave by a sheriff or *Fee of sheriff* sergeant under this act, he shall be entitled to a fee of five dollars, to be paid by the person failing to deliver such slave.

8. In making the requisition authorized by this act, the governor *Requisition to be equalized* is required to equalize the burden, as near as may be, among the several counties, cities and towns of the commonwealth, and amongst the citizens thereof, having, when practicable, due regard to the number of slaves theretofore furnished by any counties or corporations, or the citizens thereof, under the provisions of the act of October third, eighteen hundred and sixty-two, and of this act, and under any call heretofore made by the president or secretary of war, or any officer of the confederate army; and for this purpose, it shall be the *Number and time of service to be forwarded* duty of the county and corporation courts, as soon as may be, to forward to the governor the number and time of service, of any slaves heretofore furnished under any call as aforesaid, so that the equalization intended by this section may be made to apply to any future call for labor by the confederate government.

9. Under any requisition made upon any county, city or town, it *Slaves to be in charge of overseer or agent* shall be lawful for any number of persons who may be required to furnish not less than thirty nor more than forty slaves, to place such slaves in charge of an agent or overseer selected by such owners, who shall deliver them to the confederate authorities, at the place where the labor is to be performed, at the expense of the Confederate States; and such agent or overseer, if a fit and proper person, shall

MILITARY AFFAIRS.

How discharged — be employed by the confederate government as the agent or overseer in charge of the slaves during their service of sixty days; and such overseer or agent shall not be discharged by any officer of the confederate government, except for good cause, to be approved by the secretary of war: provided, that if the requisition on any county, city or town shall amount to only twenty slaves and less than thirty, in such case an overseer or manager may be selected as aforesaid.

Subsistence — 10. The owners of slaves may furnish them subsistence and provisions, and in such event shall be allowed commutation in money in lieu of rations, equal to the commutation allowed soldiers in the service.

Slaves sent voluntarily — 11. All slaves sent voluntarily by their owners to the confederate authorities, and accepted by them, shall stand on the same footing as if sent under the proceedings required by this act.

Act to be communicated to president — 12. This act shall be forthwith communicated by the governor to the president of the Confederate States. Any request for slaves hereafter made by the president on the governor shall be regarded an assent to and acceptance of all the provisions of this act by the Confederate States.

Commencement — 13. This act shall be in force from its passage.

CHAP. 7.—An ACT to amend and re-enact the 12th section of an act passed March 13th, 1863, entitled an act to amend and re-enact an act further to provide for the Public Defence, passed October 3d, 1862, and to amend the title of said act.

Passed March 30, 1863.

Act of 1863 amended — 1. Be it enacted by the general assembly, that the twelfth section of the act passed March thirteenth, eighteen hundred and sixty-three, entitled an act to amend and re-enact an act further to provide for the public defence, passed October third, eighteen hundred and sixty-two, be amended and re-enacted so as to read as follows:

How amended As to impressments — "§ 12. This act shall be forthwith communicated by the governor to the president of the Confederate States, and shall be regarded an act regulating the mode in which and the terms upon which slaves in this state shall be impressed by the confederate authorities, under the act of congress entitled an act to regulate impressments, approved March twenty-sixth, eighteen hundred and sixty-three, to the extent provided for in the act to which this act is amendatory. Any call for slaves hereafter made by the president on the governor, shall be regarded an assent to and acceptance of all the provisions of this act by the Confederate States."

Title amended — 2. Be it further enacted, that the title of said act of March thirteenth, eighteen hundred and sixty-three, be amended and re-enacted so as to read as follows:

"An act to amend and re-enact an act further to provide for the public defence, passed October third, eighteen hundred and sixty-two, and to regulate the impressment of slaves by the Confederate government." Title

---

CHAP. 8.—An ACT to amend and re-enact section 3d of an act passed May 14th, 1862, entitled an act to organize a Home Guard.

Passed March 30, 1863.

1. Be it enacted by the general assembly, that the third section of an act passed May fourteenth, eighteen hundred and sixty-two, entitled an act to organize a home guard, be amended and re-enacted so as to read as follows: Act of 1862 amended

"§ 3. The said companies shall operate as a guard and police for their respective counties during the war, and shall arrest all deserters from the army found within the limits thereof; and the officer in command is hereby authorized to order such force to rendezvous at any point that he may determine upon, whenever in his opinion the interests of the county may require it. Whenever two or more companies shall be organized in a county, they may elect a major, who shall be commissioned by the governor to command the whole: provided, however, that the troops hereby authorized to be raised shall not be marched beyond the limits of their respective counties, against their consent, or kept in active service for more than thirty days at any one time." Guard, &c
Deserters, how arrested

When major may be elected
Proviso

2. This act shall be in force from its passage. Commencement.

CHAP. 9.—An ACT to refund Money received for Exemption from Military Duty.

Passed January 19, 1863.

Whereas the exemptions intended and provided by the act of assembly entitled an act providing for the exemption of certain parties upon religious grounds, passed March twenty-ninth, eighteen hundred and sixty-two, by subsequent legislation of the congress of the Confederate States, may have been rendered of none effect to parties who, upon the faith of said act of assembly, have paid money to the state according to the provisions thereof: Therefore, Preamble

1. Be it enacted by the general assembly of Virginia, that in all cases where such persons have served in the army of the Confederate When money to be refunded by auditor

States, in pursuance of the legislation of the Confederate States, or shall have paid the commutation for such service, as specified in the legislation aforesaid, the auditor of public accounts be authorized and required to issue his warrant upon the treasury of the commonwealth, in favor of any such person from whom commutation money may have been or may hereafter be received into the treasury under said act of assembly, or who may have served in the confederate army, and shall have continued in service or been discharged therefrom, for the amount actually so received, but not including any costs attending the collection.

When sheriff may refund

2. That any sheriff of a county or collector of taxes for a city or town, who may have in his hands commutation money received under the provisions of the said act of assembly, and not yet paid into the state treasury, be authorized and required to refund the same, deducting his commissions for collection, to such person or persons as aforesaid, from whom the same may have been collected; and the receipts of the parties to whom such repayments shall be made, shall be vouchers to such officers in their settlements with the auditor of public accounts, required by said act of assembly.

Commencement

3. This act shall be in force from its passage.

CHAP. 10.—An ACT to amend and re-enact the 1st section of an act entitled an act to refund Money received for Exemption from Military Duty, passed January 19, 1863.

Passed February 5, 1863.

Act of 1863 amended

1. Be it enacted by the general assembly, that the first section of the act entitled an act to refund money received for exemption from military duty, passed January nineteenth, eighteen hundred and sixty-three, be amended and re-enacted so as to read as follows:

When auditor to issue warrant

"§ 1. Be it enacted by the general assembly of Virginia, that the auditor of public accounts be authorized and required to issue his warrant on the treasury of the commonwealth, in favor of any person from whom commutation money may have been or may hereafter be received into the treasury, under said act of assembly, for the amount actually so received, but not including any costs attending the collection."

Costs

Commencement

2. This act shall be in force from its passage.

CHAP. 11.—An ACT to amend and re-enact the 1st section of an act entitled an act to refund Money received for Exemption from Military Duty, passed January 19, 1863, and for other purposes.

Passed March 19, 1863.

1. Be it enacted by the general assembly, that the first section of an act entitled an act to refund money received for exemption from military duty, passed January nineteenth, eighteen hundred and sixty-three, as amended and re-enacted by an act entitled an act to amend and re-enact the first section of an act to refund money received for exemption from military duty, passed February fifth, eighteen hundred and sixty three, be amended and re-enacted so as to read as follows: *Acts of 1862 amended*

"§ 1. Be it enacted by the general assembly of Virginia, that the auditor of public accounts be authorized and required to issue his warrant on the treasury of the commonwealth, in favor of any person, or his personal representative, from whom it may appear, by the returns of the sheriffs or other satisfactory evidence, commutation money may have been or may hereafter be received into the treasury, under said act of assembly, for the amount so actually received, but not including any costs attending the collection of the same." *When warrant to be issued*

2. This act shall be in force from its passage. *Commencement*

CHAP. 12.—An ACT to amend the 15th section of chapter 23 of the Code, so as to allow but one Major to each Regiment.

Passed February 7, 1863.

1. Be it enacted by the general assembly, that the fifteenth section of chapter twenty-three of the Code be amended and re-enacted so as to read as follows: *Code amended*

"§ 15. There shall be a major general for each division; a brigadier general for each brigade; a colonel, lieutenant colonel and a major for each regiment; a captain, first lieutenant and second lieutenant, four sergeants and four corporals for each company." *What officers there shall be for separate military organizations*

2. This act shall be in force from its passage. *Commencement*

CHAP. 13.—An ACT authorizing the Auditing Board to pay Junior Majors of Militia Regiments, for Service actually performed.

Passed March 19, 1863.

1. Be it enacted by the general assembly, that whenever any regiment of Virginia militia has been called into service by competent *Junior majors when paid*

authority, in which there shall have been two majors appointed and commissioned according to law, and the junior major shall have actually served therein, it shall be lawful for the auditing board, upon proof of such service, to allow compensation to the said junior major for the time he shall have actually served, at the rate of one hundred dollars per month; to be paid as other allowances made by them are paid.

Commencement 2. This act shall be in force from its passage.

CHAP. 14.—An ACT amending and re-enacting an ordinance of the Convention concerning the Aids to the Governor.

Passed March 25, 1863.

Ordinance amended 1. Be it enacted by the general assembly, that the ordinance passed June twenty-ninth, eighteen hundred and sixty-one, entitled an ordinance concerning the appointment of aids by the governor of the commonwealth, shall be and is hereby amended and re-enacted so as to read as follows:

Number of aids governor may appoint "§ 8. The governor of the commonwealth is authorized to appoint, during the war, three aids, with the rank of lieutenant colonel *Who to receive pay* of cavalry; but only one of said aids, to be designated by the governor, shall receive any pay, emoluments or perquisites for his services; and he shall be entitled to the pay of captain of cavalry."

Commencement 2. This act shall be in force from its passage.

CHAP. 15.—An ACT establishing an Agency in the City of Richmond, for receiving and forwarding Clothing, Shoes and other supplies to Virginia Soldiers.

Passed March 9, 1863.

Agent, how appointed, and duties of 1. Be it enacted by the general assembly, that the governor be and he is hereby authorized to appoint an agent, who shall reside in the city of Richmond, whose duty it shall be to receive and forward to the soldiers and officers in the confederate service from the state of Virginia, any contributions of clothing, shoes or other supplies which may be furnished by the families or friends of such soldiers or officers. The said agent shall also receive and take care of all hospital stores that may be contributed or purchased for the use of the sick or wounded soldiers of Virginia, and shall give out and dispense the same on requisitions from the attending physicians or surgeons of such sick or wounded soldiers.

Depot, how provided 2. The agent so appointed shall, under the direction of the gover-wor, provide a suitable place in the city of Richmond, for the deposit and safe keeping of such contributions until the same can be transported to the places of their destination. He shall make such arrangements as may be practicable with the quartermaster's department of the Confederate States, for the safe and speedy transportation of such contributions; and he may hire means of transportation, or with the approval of the governor, he may purchase wagons and teams for that purpose, and employ teamsters and other agents to aid and superintend the safe and speedy transmission of articles deposited with said agent. *Transportation*

3. It shall be the duty of said agent, as soon as he shall have received his appointment, and shall have secured a suitable place of deposit for the contributions which may be made, to advertise for three months, in all the newspapers published in the city of Richmond, the purposes and objects of his agency, and the place of his location. He shall receive a salary not exceeding fifteen hundred dollars, and shall, if necessary, employ clerks, not exceeding two in number, who shall receive a salary not exceeding seven hundred dollars each: provided, that nothing herein contained shall prevent the detailing of soldiers unfit for field duty, to act as the agent or clerks, in lieu of the officers aforesaid, whenever the consent of the Confederate States government can be obtained therefor: provided, that before the agent to be appointed by the governor shall proceed to discharge the duties of his agency, he shall enter into bond with approved security, before the clerk of the circuit court of the city of Richmond, in the penalty of twenty thousand dollars, with a condition for the faithful performance of all the duties required by this act. And any party who may be injured by the default or negligence of said agent, may recover judgment against him, by motion, upon ten days' notice, before the circuit court of the city of Richmond. *Duty of agent as to advertising. Salary. Clerks. Soldiers may be detailed. Bond, how given. Remedy against agent*

4. In order to carry out the purposes of this act, the sum of twenty-five thousand dollars is hereby appropriated. *Appropriation*

5. This act shall be in force from its passage. *Commencement*

CHAP. 16.—An ACT to authorize the use of the Jails of the State by the Confederate States.

Passed March 16, 1863.

1. Be it enacted by the general assembly, that any person who has been or may be hereafter arrested upon due authority, and charged with violating any military law of the Confederate States, shall, upon the warrant of commitment of the officer or person making the arrest, be received into jail by the jailor of any county *When persons arrested under confederate laws may be committed to jails*

or corporation of this commonwealth, and by him safely kept, according to the warrant of commitment, until discharged by the proper authorities, or by due process of law. But this section shall not be construed to exclude from such jail any prisoner who has been or may be committed thereto by any of the authorities of this commonwealth.

Proviso

2. The jailor shall, for the support of any such prisoner, be paid by the Confederate States the same amount allowed by law for keeping and feeding other prisoners. And the jailor, for a failure of duty as to any such prisoner, shall be liable to the Confederate States in like manner as he would to the state in case of a prisoner committed under its authority.

Fees of jailor
Duty of jailor

3. This act shall be in force from its passage, and continue in force during the present war.

Commencement

CHAP. 17.—An ACT to provide for the Production and Distribution of Salt.

Passed March 30, 1863.

1. Be it enacted by the general assembly, that there shall be and is hereby created the office of "superintendent of salt works," with an annual salary of five thousand dollars, payable quarter yearly. Such superintendent shall be elected by the general assembly, at its present session, and annually thereafter, while this act is in force, and shall be removable only by joint vote of the two houses, or in the recess of the assembly, by the board of supervisors herein after mentioned. He shall, within thirty days after his election, enter into bond, with sufficient sureties, before the secretary of the commonwealth, to be approved by him, in the penalty of two hundred thousand dollars, conditioned for the faithful discharge of his duties under this and any future act. In case said superintendent fail to execute said bond as required, or from any cause a vacancy may occur, another shall be appointed by said board, subject to the same terms and conditions. And that whenever the superintendent shall become interested directly or indirectly in the manufacture or sale of salt, his office shall be declared vacant, and his successor appointed by the board of supervisors: and provided, that the superintendent who shall be elected by the general assembly, shall in no event become interested in the property leased to or purchased by the state, as sub-lessee or sub-contractor, or otherwise.

Superintendent of salt works
Salary
How elected
How removable
Bond, how given
In case of vacancy

2. The superintendent shall, under the control and management of the board of supervisors, manage and dispose of the property, real and personal, leased, acquired and held of Stuart, Buchanan and Company, under a contract made by the commonwealth with said Stuart, Buchanan and Company, bearing date the twenty-fifth day of

Duties of superintendent

March, eighteen hundred and sixty-three, and such other property as may be acquired under the provisions of this act. He shall also, under the like control of said board, have power to lease any real property, and to purchase any personal property necessary to secure a supply of salt for the people of the commonwealth, and the distribution of the same; to contract for all needful supplies, and to hire all necessary labor for operating the said works; and if unable to agree upon the prices to be paid for said leases or personal property, supplies and labor, with the owners, he shall have power to impress the same, under the control of said board; and if the said Stuart, Buchanan and Company shall fail to comply with their said contract, or any part thereof, the said superintendent shall have the like power and authority to impress their property described in said contract. *Powers, under control of board*

3. The board of public works shall, ex-officio, constitute a board of supervisors. The members of said board, in addition to the salary and expenses now paid them by law, shall be paid their necessary traveling expenses under this act. *Board, how constituted*

4. It shall be the duty of the superintendent, under the control of the board, to confirm and continue the existing leases of the four furnaces now leased to Clarkson, Friend, Kelley and Gardner, except that in the event of the failure of any of these lessees to comply with the terms and provisions of their contracts of lease, he shall resume possession of the same, and either relet the furnace to other parties, or he shall operate it for the commonwealth, as shall appear expedient. And as to the six remaining furnaces acquired under the contract aforesaid, the said superintendent shall have power and authority in like manner to either lease the same, or any of them, or else to operate them for and on behalf of the commonwealth, as shall appear best. *Duty of superintendent to confirm and continue leases. Exception. Other furnaces*

5. The superintendent shall have power to appoint, and remove at his discretion, the following assistants, viz: one deputy manager, at a salary of two thousand dollars, and one clerk, at a salary of two thousand dollars. *Superintendent to appoint assistants. Their salaries*

6. The superintendent, under the control of the board of supervisors, shall have control of transportation on the several rail roads in the commonwealth, for the conveyance of supplies to the salt works, and for distribution of salt throughout the state, with power, if necessary, under like control, to impress the same. He shall make distribution among the several counties, cities and towns, from day to day, or from time to time, and in quantities proportioned to their whole populations repectively, as he may be directed by the said board of supervisors: provided the superintendent, under the direction of the board of supervisors, shall distribute salt with reference to cattle and other stock requiring salt, after distributing twenty pounds to each person. *Control of transportation. Salt, how distributed*

7. For the purpose of ascertaining the value of the property, real *Value of im-*

SALT.

impressed property, how ascertained

and personal, impressed under the second section of this act, it shall be lawful for the superintendent to appoint one assessor, and the owner or owners another assessor, and these two shall appoint a

Duty of assessors

third; and it shall be the duty of these three, or a majority of them, to assess the value of all property impressed under this act. They shall make duplicate statements of every such assessment, and which being endorsed by the superintendent, they shall return one copy thereof to the board of supervisors, and deliver the other to the owner of the property taken. Upon such certified statement, the owner may demand and receive payment from the treasury of the amount so assessed. If the owner in any case fail or refuse to ap-

How, in case owner refuse to appoint assessor

point an assessor, the assessment shall be made by the assessor appointed by the superintendent; and thereupon, like proceedings shall be had as in other cases.

Assessors of real property, how appointed

8. For an assessment for the use of real property, the board of supervisors shall appoint the assessor on behalf of the commonwealth, and said board shall select the arbitrator to be chosen by the state, under the contract with Stuart, Buchanan and Company, for ascertaining the price to be paid for the lease and property agreed to be sold by said contract.

Appeal, when allowed

9. Appeal shall lie from the decision of the assessors to the circuit court of the county or corporation in which the property is impressed; and the proceedings shall be, mutatis mutandis, according to the eleventh and twelfth sections of chapter fifty-six of the Code of Virginia, edition of eighteen hundred and sixty; except that the commonwealth shall not be required to pay the money into court, nor to the party entitled thereto, before the decision of the appeal; nor

No injunction to be granted

shall any court or judge grant injunction, for any cause, to restrain the commonwealth from taking possession of the property impressed.

Valuation, how paid

10. The superintendent's certificate, approved by the board of supervisors, shall entitle the holder, whose property may have been purchased or hired, to present the same to the auditor of public accounts, and receive payment thereof; and in like manner shall entitle Stuart, Buchanan and Company to receive the amount that may be ascertained to be due them under the contract aforesaid.

Salt, how sold and delivered

11. The salt so manufactured shall be sold at cost, for cash, and be distributed to the different counties, cities and towns, through duly accredited agents, to be appointed by the county and corporation courts respectively, or where said courts cannot meet because of the presence or proximity of the public enemy, by the board of supervisors, on the recommendation of any three or more justices of said county, or of the senator and delegate or delegates representing such

Price, how fixed

county in the general assembly; and in order to do so, it shall be the duty of the board of supervisors from time to time to ascertain, as near as may be, the actual cost of production and distribution, and fix the price accordingly, so as to cover such entire cost.

SALT.

12. Any surplus of salt, after supplying the wants of the people *Surplus, how disposed of* of this state, may be sold to the confederate government, or to any of the states, or to citizens thereof, under rules and regulations to be prescribed by the board of supervisors.

13. The superintendent shall make monthly reports of his trans- *Monthly reports by superintendent* actions to the board, and shall account to them for all funds received by him, and shall pay the same into the treasury, when ordered by the said board.

14. The board of supervisors shall make report of their proceed- *Monthly reports of board of supervisors* ings under this act, monthly to the governor, and shall also report to the general assembly, at each of its sessions during the continuance of this act.

15. The sum of one million of dollars is hereby appropriated to *Amount appropriated* carry into effect the provisions of this act, to be paid out of any money in the treasury not otherwise appropriated; and such additional sums are hereby appropriated as may be paid into the treasury from time to time from the proceeds of the sale of salt, or so much thereof as may be necessary for the purposes of this act.

16. All acts and parts of acts inconsistent with this act are hereby *Repealing clause* repealed.

17. This act shall be in force from its passage. *Commencement*

CHAP. 18.—An ACT to authorize the appointment of an Inspector of Salt.

Passed March 30, 1863.

1. Be it enacted by the general assembly, that the board of public *Inspector of salt, how appointed* works shall appoint an inspector of salt, to reside at Saltville; and for every five bushels thereof inspected, one-half of one cent shall be charged, and at that rate for any less quantity than five bushels; which fees shall be paid to the inspector by the producer of the salt; and no salt shall be transported, sold and delivered, or removed from *Salt to be inspected* the place where it is produced, unless inspected.

2. The board of public works may cause the salt produced by the *Salt of state to be inspected* state to be inspected in like manner, and for which like fees may be paid to the inspector. If any person shall transport or remove, or attempt to transport or remove, or sell, or offer to sell any salt, without the same having been inspected, he shall forfeit five dollars for each barrel, cask, box or bag so transported, removed or offered for sale.

3. The board of public works may prescribe further rules and re- *Rules and regulations, how prescribed* gulations for the inspection of salt; but no inspection shall be had of salt manufactured by the agents manufacturing for other states.

4. Any inspector, with the approbation of the board of public works, may appoint one or more deputies to assist him, for whose acts his principal shall be liable, and be entitled to the same fees as his own.

5. All acts and parts of acts inconsistent with the provisions of this act are hereby repealed.

Commencement

6. This act shall be in force from its passage.

CHAP. 19.—An ACT to amend and re-enact an act entitled an act to amend section 11 of chapter 29 of the Code, so as to exempt the property of persons in the military service of the State from distress for rent payable in money, passed February 19th, 1862.

Passed February 16, 1863.

Act of 1862 amending Code amended

1. Be it enacted by the general assembly, that the act entitled an act to amend the eleventh section of chapter twenty-nine of the Code, so as to exempt the property of persons in the military service of the state from distress for rent payable in money, passed February nineteenth, eighteen hundred and sixty-two, be amended and re-enacted so as to read as follows:

Legal proceedings against persons in military service

"§ 11. No proceeding shall be had at law or in equity against the person or property of any one ordered into actual service, whether of this state or the Confederate States, or against his surety, from the time such person shall be ordered to the place of rendezvous until thirty days after his term of service shall have expired; and if any such proceeding has been or shall be commenced, the court in which, or the justice before whom it may be had, at any stage of such proceedings, in the discretion of said court or justice, may dismiss, discontinue or stay the same, or make such other order in regard thereto as may be deemed proper to give effect to the provisions of this section: nor shall the property of any person be sold under any deed of trust while he is in such actual military service, nor for thirty days after his term of service shall have expired. The exemption provided by this section shall not apply to proceedings in criminal cases, nor to any suit or proceedings against any person for a tort, nor to any person who shall have incurred a liability as an officer of the commonwealth or of any court, or to any of his sureties as such officer, or to any person who shall have employed a substitute to perform his tour of duty; nor shall it prevent the granting or reinstating of any injunction: provided, however, that trials in actions for tort against such persons may be stayed by the court in its discretion in which such action is brought, so long as such person may be in such actual military service."

Commencement

2. This act shall be in force from its passage.

.CHANGES IN CODE. 57

CHAP. 20.—An ACT amending and re-enacting the 19th section of chapter 61 of the Code of Virginia (edition of 1860), so as to require Rail Road Companies to give receipts showing the Weights for Freights.

Passed March 11, 1863.

1. Be it enacted by the general assembly, that the nineteenth sec- *Code amended* tion of chapter sixty-one of the Code of Virginia (edition of eighteen hundred and sixty), be amended and re-enacted, so as to read as, follows:

"§ 19. On a rail road on which different rates are not prescribed by *Rates of transportation on* law, the following rates of toll may be charged for transportation, to *persons and produce* wit: Of a person and his baggage, within a hundred and fifty pounds, not exceeding six cents per mile: of produce and other articles, except gypsum, lime, guano, and other specific manures, not exceeding eight cents per ton per mile; and gypsum, lime, guano, and other specific manures, not exceeding four cents per ton of twenty-two hundred and forty pounds per mile; and for the transportation of any person, or of any produce or other articles for a distance less than ten miles, a charge may be made at the foregoing rates as for ten miles: and where articles weigh less than four pounds to the cubic foot, a *What rates when articles* toll may nevertheless be charged on each cubic foot as for four pounds *weigh less than four pounds* weight: and when the articles in any one consignment weigh less than one hundred pounds, a toll may be charged on the same as for one hundred pounds weight. If for the transportation of any person with his baggage, or for any consignment, the whole charge at the rates before mentioned would be less than twenty-five cents, the same may nevertheless be charged as a minimum. Receipts shall be *Receipts, how given* given for transportation of articles, in which shall be specified the weight of such articles, and the rates of toll thereon charged, according to such weight, except where such articles weigh less than four pounds to the cubic foot. For the weighing, storage and delivery *Charge* of articles at any depot or warehouse of the company, a charge may also be made, not exceeding the ordinary warehouse rates charged in the town in which or nearest to which the depot or warehouse is situated."

2. This act shall be in force from its passage. Commencement

CHAP. 21.—An ACT to amend the 43d, 44th and 45th sections of chapter 87 of the Code, so as to increase the Fees of Tobacco Inspectors.

Passed March 3, 1863.

1. Be it enacted by the general assembly, that the forty-third, forty- *Code amended* fourth and forty-fifth sections of chapter eighty-seven of the Code of Virginia (edition of eighteen hundred and sixty), be amended and re-enacted so as to read as follows:

Fees to inspectors

"§ 43. There shall be paid to said inspectors, for each hogshead or cask inspected by them, one dollar for opening, inspecting, coopering up, furnishing nails, marking and weighing it.

Fees

"§ 44. For every hogshead or cask of the weight aforesaid, of inspected tobacco, received on storage at any warehouse, there shall be paid to the inspector thereof one dollar for opening one head, breaking the tobacco in one place, coopering up the same, the necessary nails, and turning it into the house again.

"§ 45. There shall be paid to the inspectors, for each hogshead or cask delivered out of their warehouse, fifty cents; and for putting into good order each hogshead or cask noted by them to be in bad order, seventeen cents."

Commencement

2. This act shall be in force from its passage, and until the expiration of six months after the conclusion of the existing war.

CHAP. 22.—An ACT to amend and re-enact section 41, chapter 58 of the Code of Virginia (edition of 1860), so as to authorize Banks to increase their Contingent Funds.

Passed March 7, 1863.

Code amended

1. Be it enacted by the general assembly, that section forty-one, chapter fifty-eight of the Code of Virginia (edition of eighteen hundred and sixty), be amended and re-enacted so as to read as follows:

Rate of dividend
Surplus fund

"§ 41. There shall be no dividend of profits of a higher rate than six per centum per annum on the capital paid in, until the bank shall have a surplus or contingent fund arising from profits, of at least five per centum of its capital stock: nor shall any dividend of profits be made, by which such fund is reduced below the said five per centum. But the said fund is not at any time to be more than twenty per centum (on the capital paid in) over and above the bad and doubtful debts. So much of said fund as may have accrued at any branch, shall be left with such branch until it may be wanted to meet losses sustained by the bank."

Limitation of surplus fund

Commencement

2. This act shall be in force from its passage.

CHAP. 23.—An ACT to amend and re-enact section 22 of chapter 108 of the Code of Virginia (edition of 1860).

Passed January 24, 1863

Code amended

1. Be it enacted by the general assembly of Virginia, that the twenty-second section of chapter one hundred and eight of the Code

of Virginia (edition of eighteen hundred and sixty), be amended and re-enacted so as to read as follows:

"§ 22. The commissioner shall alphabetically arrange each of the books so to be kept by him, and shall make and subscribe an affidavit therein, to the effect that he has pursued the directions in this act, according to the best of his skill; and he shall return his said books to the clerk of the court of his county, on or before the first day of June. In addition to the compensation now allowed by law to commissioners of the revenue, the sum of three cents shall be paid to every such commissioner, for each birth and death listed and reported to the county or corporation clerk in said commissioner's district, under the provisions of this chapter, and that the same be paid out of the public treasury, upon the certificate of the county or corporation court, setting forth the number of births and deaths returned, and that the said returns have been accurately and fully made, according to the laws regulating the same, and within the time prescribed thereby. If the auditor of public accounts shall be of opinion that the failure to return a report of the births and deaths to the clerk within the time prescribed by law, was unavoidable, he may, notwithstanding such failure, pay such claim." *Duty of commissioner* *Compensation* *Duty of auditor in certain cases*

2. This act shall be in force from its passage. *Commencement*

CHAP. 24.—An ACT to amend the 12th section of chapter 10 of the Code of Virginia, so as to extend the time for filing Complaint in cases of Contested Elections.

Passed January 27, 1863.

1. Be it enacted by the general assembly, that the twelfth section of chapter ten of the Code of Virginia (edition of eighteen hundred and sixty), be amended and re-enacted so as to read as follows: *Code amended*

"§ 12. The returns of the elections of justices of the peace, of clerks of the county and circuit courts, of attorneys for the commonwealth, surveyors, sheriffs, commissioners of the revenue, constables and overseers of the poor, under this act, shall be subject to the enquiry, determination and judgment of the respective county and corporation courts, or of the county court, in case the election was for a county and city, upon complaint of fifteen or more of the qualified voters of the county or corporation, or of the proper district, when the officer is elected by a district, of an undue election or false return; two of whom shall take and subscribe an oath or affirmation that the facts set forth in such complaint are true, to the best of their knowledge and belief. And the said courts shall, in judging of said elections, proceed upon the merits thereof, and shall determine finally concerning the same, according to the constitution and laws of this commonwealth: and such complaint shall not be valid, *Returns, how enquired into* *Complaint, how made* *Duty of courts* *Time when com-*

plaint shall be filed	or regarded by the court, unless the same shall have been filed within twenty days after the election, in the clerk's office of the proper court: and when the complaint is of undue election or false return of a justice of the peace, the clerk of the said court shall immediately certify to the governor the decree of said court, when made, and in whose favor such contested election shall have terminated; and the governor shall then commission such person in whose favor
Duty of clerk	such contested election terminated. And in said last mentioned contested elections, in case such complaint be filed in due time, the clerk shall transmit by mail, immediately to the governor, a certified copy thereof: and in such case, no commission shall be issued until the court shall have determined and adjudged on such complaint as
Proviso	aforesaid: provided, however, that when the complaint is of the undue election and false return of a justice of the peace, all the justices composing the court shall be summoned for the trial of the complaint, and a majority of those not interested in the contest shall be present."
Commencement	2. This act shall be in force from its passage.

CHAP. 25.—An ACT amending and re-enacting the 2nd and 5th sections of chapter 34 of the Code of Virginia, entitled Virginia Military Institute.

Passed March 30, 1863.

Code amended	1. Be it enacted by the general assembly, that the second section of chapter thirty-four of the Code of Virginia be amended and re-enacted so as to read as follows:
Board of visitors, how appointed	"§ 2. There shall be a board of visitors for the institution, composed of the adjutant general and eight other persons, two of whom shall be appointed from each grand division of the state, and four new members shall be appointed every second year; the appointments to be made by the governor, by and with the advice of the
Board a corporation	senate. They shall be and are hereby declared to be a corporation, and as such, may sue and be sued for any cause or matter which has heretofore arisen, as well as for any cause or matter which may hereafter arise."
Code amended	2. That the fifth section of the thirty-fourth chapter of the Code of Virginia (edition of eighteen hundred and sixty), is hereby amended and re-enacted so as to read as follows:
	"§ 5. Such reasonable expenses as the visitors may incur in the discharge of their duties, shall be paid out of the funds of the institute."
Commencement	3. This act shall be in force from its passage.

CHAP. 26.—An ACT to amend and re-enact the 12th section of chapter 20 of the Code of Virginia, so as to compensate the Printer to the Senate for printing and binding the Journals of the Senate at Extra Sessions.

Passed March 4, 1863.

1. Be it enacted by the general assembly, that the twelfth section of chapter twenty of the Code of Virginia be amended and re-enacted so as to read as follows: *Code amended*

"§ 12. The senate may appoint annually a printer for that body, who shall, for his annual salary, print and have bound two hundred copies of the Journal of the Senate, with the index thereto of its regular sessions, and perform such other duties as the senate by its rules requires; and all other work which he may do by order of the senate, shall be deemed extra work, and paid for as is extra work done by the public printer." *Annual salary of printer to senate* *Extra work*

2. This act shall be in force from its passage. *Commencement*

CHAP. 27.—An ACT increasing the Compensation of the Interior Guard at the Penitentiary.

Passed March 26, 1863.

1. Be it enacted by the general assembly, that the fifty-first section of chapter two hundred and thirteen of the Code of Virginia (edition of eighteen hundred and sixty), be amended and re-enacted so as to read as follows: *Code amended*

"§ 51. The compensation of the said guard shall be allowed and certified by the board, at a rate not exceeding two dollars per diem for each person, and paid by the general agent." *Compensation of guard*

2. This act shall be in force from its passage. *Commencement*

CHAP. 28.—An ACT to amend and re-enact the 16th and 18th sections of the 14th chapter of the Code of Virginia, so as to increase the Salaries of certain Officers of the Penitentiary.

Passed March 28, 1863.

1. Be it enacted by the general assembly, that the sixteenth and eighteenth sections of the fourteenth chapter of the Code of Virginia be amended and re-enacted so as to read as follows: *Code amended*

"§ 16. The superintendent of the penitentiary shall receive the sum of two thousand dollars; the first assistant keeper one thousand dollars; the second, third, fourth, fifth, sixth and seventh assistant *Salary of superintendent* *Salary of assistants* keepers, each nine hundred dollars. Moreover, each of the said assistant keepers shall be allowed one hundred dollars worth of the manufactures of the penitentiary, at the prices fixed by the directors, every year the labor and the manufactures shall amount to the sum

Salary of surgeon of thirty-two thousand dollars. The surgeon of the penitentiary and public guard shall receive the sum of one thousand dollars."

Directors "§ 18. The directors of the penitentiary shall receive the sum of three dollars each for every day's attendance on the board: provided, that no director shall receive more than one hundred and fifty dollars

Salary of clerk per annum. The clerk of the penitentiary shall receive one thousand dollars."

Proviso 2. Provided, that the compensation for services herein before prescribed shall remain and be payable until the expiration of one year after the ratification of a treaty of peace between the Confederate States and the United States, and no longer.

Commencement 3. This act shall be in force from its passage.

CHAP. 29.—An ACT concerning Bonds of Sheriffs.

Passed January 16, 1863.

Code, &c. amended 1. Be it enacted by the general assembly, that chapter sixteen, entitled an act to amend the fifth section of chapter forty-nine of the Code of Virginia, as amended by an act passed June third, eighteen hundred and fifty-two, concerning bonds of sheriffs and other collectors of taxes, and bonds of constables, passed December twenty-third, eighteen hundred and fifty-seven, be amended and re-enacted so as to read as follows:

Bond of sheriffs and sergeants "From every person elected sheriff of any county or corporation, and from every sergeant of a corporation who is collector of the taxes assessed therein, the court of such county or corporation shall take bond with sufficient security, in such penalty as it may deem suffi-

Amount cient; which shall not be less than double the aggregate amount of all taxes, militia fines and other public dues and the county levy and poor rates assessed and collectable in such county or corporation for the year next preceding the official term of such sheriff or sergeant; but the penalty of such bond shall in no case be in a sum less than thirty thousand dollars. Such bond shall be for the term for which such sheriff or sergeant may have been elected or may continue in

When security deemed insufficient office. If the security in the bond of any sheriff or sergeant shall be deemed insufficient, or if such officer shall fail to pay the taxes,

Auditor may petition militia fines and other public dues; or if the same be in a penalty less than this act requires, the auditor of public accounts may petition the court of the county or corporation for a new bond; and it shall be the duty of the court to examine into the facts of such petition;

or it may, without such petition, require the execution of a new bond in a penalty according to this act, with good and sufficient security, and may at once suspend the official duties of such officer until such new bond be executed; and if the same be not executed within a reasonable time, shall remove such officer, and direct an election to fill the vacancy." New bond
When court to remove

2. This act shall be in force from its passage. Commencement

CHAP. 30.—An ACT to amend the 39th section of chapter 184 of the Code of Virginia, so as to increase the Compensation of Clerks of Courts for public services.

Passed March 11, 1863.

1. Be it enacted by the general assembly, that the thirty-ninth section of chapter one hundred and eighty-four of the Code of Virginia (edition of eighteen hundred and sixty), be amended and re-enacted so as to read as follows: Code amended

"§ 39. There shall be chargeable in every county or corporation such sum as the court thereof may, for services to the public of the county or town, allow its clerk and the sheriff or sergeant attending it, not exceeding for one year four hundred dollars to its clerk, and seventy-five dollars to its sheriff or sergeant; and the corporation court of Richmond may make such allowance as it may deem proper to its clerk and sergeant, for services for which no other compensation is made by law." Compensation for services to clerks
Corporation of Richmond

2. This act shall be in force from its passage. Commencement

CHAP. 31.—An ACT increasing the Compensation of Clerks of Courts during the existing war.

Passed March 24, 1863.

1. Be it enacted by the general assembly, that the tenth section of the one hundred and eighty-fourth chapter of the Code of Virginia, of eighteen hundred and sixty, be amended and re-enacted so as to read as follows, to wit: Code amended

§ 10. *A clerk of a county or corporation court.*

Where a writing is admitted to record under chapter one hundred and twenty-one, for every thing relating to it, except the recording in the deed book, to wit: For receiving proof or acknowledgment, entering orders, writing on it clerk's certificate, statement of deed in list returned to court, re- Fee for recordation of writing

	cording in minute book, and posting same, and embracing it in list for commissioner of the revenue,	$0 75
Recordation of plat	For recording a plat of not more than six courses, or for a copy thereof,	75
Course	For every course above six,	5
Deed book	For recording in the deed book such writing and all matter therewith, except plats, or for recording any thing not otherwise provided for, for every thirty words,	5
	In lieu of the said allowance of five cents for thirty words, the clerk may, for recording in the deed book, elect to	
Deed of trust or mortgage	charge the following specific fees, to wit: Where the writing is a deed of trust or mortgage, or is a conveyance of real and personal estate, or of real estate only,	1 20
	And where it is not such,	50
Swearing witnesses	For swearing the witnesses, and entering in the order or minute book all orders in relation to the proof of a will which is admitted to record without contest, and copying such orders on the will,	75
Recordation of will	For recording a will, and the matter recorded therewith, in the will book, at the option of the clerk, five cents for every thirty words, or a specific fee of	50
Order as to decedent's estate	If there be an order committing a decedent's estate to an officer, for entering and copying such order, and the orders of appraisement,	75
Swearing personal representative	If any personal representative qualify, for swearing him and his surety, making out bond, entering and copying on the will order granting probate or administration, making one copy of such order for the representative, entering and copying orders of appraisement, and including case in said list,	1 50
One fee where more than one	If several personal representatives qualify on the same estate, during the same term, only the same fee shall be charged as if one had qualified, to wit,	1 50
Licenses	For entering and copying an order granting a license and administering an oath where necessary,	1 20
Marriage license	On an application for a marriage license, for administering and writing certificate of oath, issuing and registering license, and recording and giving receipt for certificate of the marriage,	1 50
Search	For a search for any thing above a year's standing, except where the clerk, at the request of counsel, searches for papers in a pending cause,	15
Certificate	For recording a certificate and posting a copy thereof under the second section of chapter one hundred,	75
Injunction bond	For making out an injunction bond, administering all necessary oaths, writing proper affidavits, making out release of errors, copying same and endorsing on the summons that such bond and release are filed,	1 20

CHANGES IN CODE.

For making out any other bond, administering all necessary oaths, and writing proper affidavits, - -	$1 20	Any other bond
For issuing a writ in the nature of an ad quod damnum, -	1 30	Writ of ad quod damnum
On receiving the copy of a caveat, for entering such copy, -	40	Caveat
For issuing a summons to answer a bill, with an endorsement thereon of an injunction, or of an order of attachment, and recording return of same, - - -	50	Summons to answer bill
For issuing any other summons, or any writ not particularly provided for, and for recording the return where proper to do so, - - - - -	30	Any other summons
For each copy of any process which goes out of the office (with such process), to be used in serving it, one-half the fee for issuing such process.		Copy of process
For noting in the process book any decree, order or process (except a summons for a witness), and taking a receipt therefor, - - - - -	30	Noting
For postage paid by the clerk on a decree, order or process, and putting in or taking out of post office same, double the amount of such postage.		Postage
For entering in any suit, or in a motion for judgment for money, all the attorneys for each party, or the appearance in proper person of a party having no attorney who so appears, - - - - -	15	Appearance
For endorsing and filing each petition, declaration, bill, answer, or other written pleading, each bill of exceptions, demurrer to evidence, special verdict or case agreed, each written notice of the defence relied on in ejectment, or of a motion for judgment for money, and each report of a commissioner, and for entering each plea, replication or other pleading which is not written, - - -	30	Filing and endorsing petition
For endorsing and filing all the depositions and affidavits of witnesses, filed on the same side at any time, or all the written interrogatories at one time from one party to another, or all the answers filed at one time to such interrogatories, or the exceptions filed at one time by either party to a commissioner's report, - - -	30	Depositions
If papers be filed on the side of the plaintiffs, for which no particular fee is allowed, a fee (not for each, but for the whole) of - - - - -	30	Filing papers for plaintiffs
So, also, if papers be filed on the side of the defendants, for which no particular fee is allowed, a fee (not for each, but for the whole) of - - - - -	30	Filing for defendants
For issuing an attachment, with a copy of the rule or order for the same (if sent out therewith), and recording the return thereof, where proper to do so, - -	65	Issuing an attachment
For issuing a scire facias, and recording the return thereof, or for issuing a commission to examine witnesses, adminis-		Scire facias

5.

CHANGES IN CODE.

	tering oath when necessary as the foundation thereof, and writing affidavit, - - - -	$0 80
Rules	For all the rules entered in any case on the same side, at the rules for one month, where any thing is done on such side at said rules, besides entering or filing a pleading or continuing the case, - - - -	40
	Where no proceedings are had in a case during any rules, except to continue it, the fee shall be at the rate of thirty cents for every quarter of a year the case is so continued, and no more.	
Docketing	For docketing any suit, or any motion for judgment for money (to be charged only once), - - -	15
	Except that where an action or motion is on the court docket at a quarterly term, if no decision or continuance be entered on it, there shall be a fee for putting it on the docket at the next term, of - - - -	30
Jury	Where a jury is impanneled, for swearing the jury and witnesses, - - - -	1 00
Where no jury is impanneled	Where no jury is impanneled, if witnesses be examined by the court, for swearing such witnesses for either party, -	30
Swearing witness	Where a witness claims for his attendance, for administering an oath to him, and entering and certifying such attendance, - - - -	50
Administering oath	For administering any oath not before provided for, and writing a certificate thereof, where the case requires one, -	25
Judgments, decrees, &c	For all judgments, decrees, orders and proceedings (except entries of pleadings and matter otherwise provided for), which are entered on the same day, for the same persons, at the election of the clerk, five cents for every thirty words (actually written on the minute or order-book, or upon the rule book, when final judgments are entered therein), or a specific fee of - - -	30
Docketing	For docketing, under chapter one hundred and eighty-six, a judgment, decree, bond or recognizance, - -	40
Taxing costs	For taxing costs in any case, on one side, - -	30
	And if the case has been pending more than a year, then for every additional year, - - -	15
Execution returned by constable	When an execution is returned by a constable in a case wherein there is no appeal from the justice's judgment, for filing the papers, - - -	20
	And if the clerk issue an execution in the case, for such execution and all his other services in the case, until and including the record of the return of said execution (if it be returned before another issues); - - -	60
	For any other execution, the entry in the execution book, and the record of the return, - - -	60
Transcript of record	For making out a transcript of the record and proceedings in any case, in due form, so that the same may be used in	

CHANGES IN CODE.

an appellate court, for every thirty words, five cents; and for making out, in any other manner than copying, any paper to go out of the office, which is not otherwise provided for, the same, or in lieu thereof, if the clerk elect, a specific fee of - - - - - $0 40

For any copy to go out of the office, if it be not otherwise provided for, five cents for every thirty words, or in lieu thereof, if the clerk elect, a specific fee of - - 40   *Copy*

For annexing the seal of the court to any paper, writing the certificate of the clerk accompanying it, and writing certificate for the judge or presiding justice, if the clerk be requested so to do, - - - - 60   *Annexing seal*

2. That the eleventh section of said chapter be amended and re-enacted so as to read as follows: *Code amended*

§ 11. *A clerk of a circuit court.*

For a writ of supersedeas or other writ not used in a county court, - - - - - 75   *Writ of superse- deas*

For making out the bond upon issuing any such writ, administering necessary oath, and writing proper affidavits, 75   *Bond*

Upon any such writ, for endorsing and filing the petition therefor, or when the writ is returned, for filing it, with the return thereon, - - - - 25   *Endorsing writ*

For filing the record upon an appeal, or on such writ, - 25   *Filing record*

When the clerk of the court of appeals issues process on an appeal, writ of error or supersedeas, for making out the bond, administering the necessary oaths, writing proper affidavits, and endorsing on the process a certificate of the execution of the bond, and of the names of the sureties thereon, - - - - - 1 25   *Fees when clerk of court of appeals issues process*

For docketing any case, a fee of twenty-five cents, or if the clerk elect, in lieu thereof, five cents for every thirty words entered on the rule book when it is first docketed; this fee for docketing to be charged but once, except that when any case, either at law or in equity, is on the court docket, if at any time it be left undecided, without an order of continuance, there shall be a fee for putting it on the docket at the next term, of - - - 40   *Docketing*

For all judgments, decrees, orders and proceedings (except entries of pleadings and matters otherwise provided for), which are entered on the same day for the same persons, at the election of the clerk, five cents for every thirty words (actually written on the order book, or upon the rule book, when final judgments are entered therein), or a specific fee of - - - - - 60   *Judgments, &c*

After a decision by the circuit court or court of appeals, as an appellate court, for issuing an execution, making copy thereof in the execution book, and recording the return, 1 20   *Orders*

CHANGES IN CODE.

Unless the decision be by the court of appeals, in a case wherein the first judgment or decree was in a county or corporation court, in which case the fee shall be	$1 35
Damages — For taxing the damages to which a party may be entitled by reason of an injunction, appeal, writ of error or supersedeas,	60

For all other services, the same fees as a clerk of a county or corporation court for similar services; except that the clerk of a circuit may charge—

In chancery cases:

For issuing attachments — For issuing an attachment or summons, with an endorsement of an order of attachment or injunction,	75
Process — For process for which no higher fee is allowed,	35
Exhibits — If when a bill or answer is filed, there be filed at the same time an exhibit, on which the clerk endorses the name of the case and the day it is filed, for every such exhibit,	5
Exhibits with commissioner's report — When more than three exhibits are returned with a commissioner's report (but not annexed thereto), for endorsing and filing such exhibits, a fee, not for each, but for all filed with the same report, of	40
Filing — If papers be filed on the side of the plaintiffs, for which no fee is before provided, a fee, not for each, but for the whole of such papers, of	40
And if papers be filed on the side of the defendants, for which no fee is before provided, a fee, not for each, but for the whole of such papers, of	40
Rules — For entering in the rule book the return of all process returnable to the same rule day, a fee, not for each defendant named therein, nor for every such process, but for the whole of the defendants named in all such process, of	50
For all the rules entered in any case on the same side at the rules for one month, when any thing is done on such side at said rules, besides entering or filing a pleading or continuing the case,	75
Execution — For any execution, the entry of the case in the execution book, and the record of the return, unless a higher fee be allowed therefor,	75

Commencement and continuation — 3. This act shall be in force from its passage, and continue in force until the ratification of a treaty of peace between the Confederate States and the United States, whereupon the laws in force immediately before the passage of this act, regulating the fees of clerks of courts, shall be deemed to be in force.

CHAP. 32.—An ACT to authorize Town Councils and County Courts to condemn land for Hospital purposes.

Passed January 26, 1863.

1. Be it enacted by the general assembly of Virginia, that the first section of chapter eighty-six of the Code of Virginia (edition of eighteen hundred and sixty), be amended and re-enacted so as to read as follows:

Code amended

"§ 1. The council of any town or the court of any county may establish in such county, or in or near such town, hospitals, which shall be subject to regulations not contrary to law, made by such council or court; and if they cannot agree with the owners upon terms of purchase or rent of houses and land necessary for that purpose, they are hereby authorized to condemn and take possession of the same forthwith, and to hold and occupy for such time as may be deemed necessary. A just compensation to the owners thereof to be ascertained in the manner provided for in the fifty-sixth chapter of the Code of Virginia (edition of eighteen hundred and sixty), and allowance shall be made therefor in the next county or town levy: provided, that this act shall not be construed so as to authorize the condemnation or seizure of any of the buildings of the university, or of any college or academy, or any building used for a school: and provided further, that no dwelling house actually occupied as such by any white person, shall be condemned under the provisions of this act."

Powers of council or court

Lands and houses, how condemned

Limitation

Proviso

2. This act shall be in force from its passage.

Commencement

CHAP. 33.—An ACT to enlarge the Power of Special Terms of Circuit Courts in certain cases.

Passed January 19, 1863.

1. Be it enacted by the general assembly, that the thirty-second section of chapter one hundred and fifty-eight of the Code of Virginia (edition of eighteen hundred and sixty), be amended and re-enacted so as to read as follows:

Code amended

"§ 32. Whenever the situation of a prisoner confined in jail for trial in a circuit court makes it proper that his case should be disposed of before the next regular term thereof, the judge of such court may appoint a special term to be holden for the trial of the case, in the same manner as if the same had stood for trial at the next preceding term, and the court had adjourned without disposing thereof. At a special court thus held, any prisoner may be tried with his consent, and that of the attorney for the commonwealth, en-

Trial

Special term

Trial of prisoner at special term

tered of record, whether he be embraced or not in the warrant appointing such special term, and whether he shall have had his examination before or after the date of such warrant."

Commencement   2. This act shall be in force from its passage.

CHAP. 34.—An ACT to limit the production of Tobacco and increase the production of Grain.

Passed March 12, 1863.

Preamble   Whereas the comfortable support of our soldiers in the field, and the maintenance of their helpless families at home, is not only a duty of patriotism and humanity, but is absolutely essential to the successful prosecution of the struggle for independence in which we are engaged: and whereas the actual or threatened occupation of a large portion of the state by the public enemy, and the devastation of other portions of it, leaves but a small portion, comparatively, in which the pursuits of agriculture can be peacefully and safely followed, and from which both army and people are to be subsisted: and whereas it is of the last importance that the labor of this portion of the state shall not be diverted from the production of grain into other channels, so as to incur the hazard of a want of bread:

Production of tobacco limited

Number of plants to each hand

Proviso

1. Be it therefore enacted by the general assembly, that it shall not be lawful for any person, either for himself or another, to plant, within the limits of this state, in any one year, a larger quantity of tobacco than twenty-five hundred plants for each hand between the ages of sixteen and fifty-five years, actually and regularly employed in the cultivation thereof, as a field hand: provided, that it shall be lawful for any planter to plant a crop of ten thousand plants; and no planter shall plant a crop of more than eighty thousand plants.

List of field hands to be rendered on oath

List to be returned with property books

2. It shall be the duty of every person engaged or intending to engage in the cultivation of tobacco, either for himself or another, annually to render on oath to the commissioner of the revenue of the county and district in which such person may reside, an accurate list of all such field hands; which list the said commissioner is hereby required to take and return with the property books.

Penalty for violating first section

Amount of fine

Forfeiture of the value of tobacco

How forfeiture disposed of

3. Any person violating the provisions of the first section of this act shall be deemed guilty of a misdemeanor, and shall be fined in a sum not less than five hundred dollars nor more than five thousand dollars; and shall moreover forfeit the full value of all the tobacco produced by him beyond the amount specified in said first section; to be paid to the county court of the county in which the offence may have been committed, and applied in defraying the expenses incurred by such county in providing for soldiers in service, and supporting their families.

4. For a violation of the second section of this act, either by a planter or commissioner of the revenue, the offender shall be deemed guilty of a misdemeanor, punishable by a fine of not less than ten dollars for each offence. *Penalty for violating second section*

5. It shall be the duty of the judges of the circuit courts, and of the attorneys for the commonwealth in the county courts, to give this act specially in charge to the grand juries of the several counties; and it shall be the duty of the commissioners of the revenue to inform the attorneys for the commonwealth in their respective counties, of all violations thereof which may come to their knowledge; and the said attorneys shall cause the offenders to be prosecuted. *Duties of the judges of circuit courts and attorneys for the commonwealth. Duty of commissioners of the revenue*

6. This act shall be in force from its passage, and shall continue in force during the existing war with the United States, and no longer. *Commencement*

CHAP. 35.—An ACT to secure Representation in the General Assembly for Senatorial Districts, Counties, Cities and Election Districts within the power of the Public Enemy.

Passed March 9, 1863.

1. Be it enacted by the general assembly, that whenever, in consequence of the presence of the public enemy, vacancies exist in the representation of any senatorial district, city, county or election district, it shall be lawful for the senator or delegate, as the case may be, who last represented such district, county or city in the general assembly, provided he be a loyal citizen of this commonwealth, to continue to discharge the duties of the office until successors, respectively, may be duly elected and qualified. *When senator or delegate may be admitted*

2. So soon as the presence or power of the public enemy is withdrawn from any such district, county or city, writs shall be issued, in the manner prescribed by law, for an election to fill the office for the residue of the term. The compensation of the office shall be payable to the persons discharging the duties thereof, for the times only of their respective service. *When writ to be issued*

3. This act shall be in force from its passage, and continue in force during the existing war. *Commencement*

CHAP. 36.—An ACT to provide for voting by persons in the Military Service, and persons absent from their respective Counties and Corporations on account of the presence of the Public Enemy, in Elections for Members of Congress, and for Governor, Lieutenant Governor and Attorney General, and for Members of the General Assembly, and to amend and re-enact the 3d section of chapter 8 of the Code of Virginia (edition of 1860).

Passed March 26, 1863.

1. Be it enacted by the general assembly, that during the present *When persons in*

Military service may vote

war the qualified voters of this commonwealth, who may be in the military service of the state or of the Confederate States, on the day of any general or special election for members of the house of representatives of the Confederate States, or of any election for governor, lieutenant governor and attorney general of this state, may vote in such election, at such place or places within their regiment as the commandant of such regiment shall designate, whether such regiment be within the limits of this state or not.

Commissioners, how appointed

2. For each place of voting the commandant of the regiment shall detail a superintendent, three commissioners, and as many clerks as shall be necessary, who, after being first duly sworn by him, shall perform the duties required of and be liable to the penalties imposed upon such officers by the election laws of the state. The qualified voters in any company or battalion unattached, or on detached service, may vote in like manner, the officer in command detailing similar officers to perform similar duties, who shall be liable to like penalties.

Polls for members of congress

The said commissioners shall open polls on the day of any such election for members of congress, for each district entitled to representation in said congress, for which there shall be voters in said regiment, battalion or company desiring to vote; and on the day of any election for governor, lieutenant governor and attorney general, they shall also open polls for such last named officers. The qualified voters who present themselves to vote, shall be asked by said commissioners from what district they come, and each voter shall vote for a person to represent the district from which he comes; and his name shall be recorded on the poll book opened for that district, and also on the poll book for governor, lieutenant governor and attorney general, when an election for such last named officers shall be held: and when the polls taken as aforesaid shall be closed, the commissioners holding the said election shall make and certify a statement of the said polls to the senior officer commanding the troops at the point where such regiment may be, if there be any such officer, and if not, then to the commandant of the regiment, unattached or detached battalion or company, who shall appoint some person whose duty it shall be to take all the polls and statements which may have been so taken and certified to the secretary of the commonwealth, within fifteen days after the commencement of such election.

Name, how recorded for governor

Duty of commissioners

Polls to be taken to secretary of commonwealth

When qualified persons may vote

3. The qualified voters of any county or corporation, absent therefrom because of the presence of the public enemy, on the day appointed for any such election as is mentioned in the first section, may, during the existing war, vote in any such election in which they would be entitled to vote if in the county or corporation of their domicil, at the courthouse of any county or corporation in the state where they may happen to be on the day of said election. If any other election is held at the same time, the officers holding said election shall open the poll and receive the votes herein authorized to be polled, as prescribed by law in cases of other elections; but if no

other election be then held than such at which the persons mentioned in this section are authorized to vote, then a poll shall be opened by the clerk of the county court. Any such person desiring to vote in such election, shall make oath before the clerk, or other officer conducting the election, that he believes he would be entitled to vote therein if in the county or corporation of his domicil; and thereupon his vote shall be recorded on the proper poll. When such polls shall be closed, the officer conducting the election shall certify the result and the correctness of the polls at the foot thereof, and shall transmit such poll book, so certified, by mail, prepaying the postage thereon, to the secretary of the commonwealth, within fifteen days after the commencement of the election. *When oath to be taken*

4. Be it further enacted, that the third section of chapter eight of the Code of Virginia (edition of eighteen hundred and sixty), be amended and re-enacted so as to read as follows: *Code amended*

"§ 3. In cases of elections for election districts, or senatorial or congressional districts, the commissioners superintending the election at the courthouses of the several counties or corporations forming such districts, shall, within three days after such election is concluded, deliver a certified statement of the result of the election in said county, to be ascertained by comparing the polls of the different voting places in said county, and striking therefrom such votes as are required by law to be stricken therefrom, to the officer conducting the election at the courthouse of said county, or to such other officer as may legally act for him; which said statement shall be written in words and not in figures, and shall conform as near as may be to the form of the return required to be made in case of the election of governor. The officers conducting the election at the courthouses of the several counties, shall meet at the courthouse of the county or corporation first named in the law prescribing such districts, which may not be in the possession or power of the public enemy, on a certain day after that appointed by law for the commencement of such election; which certain day, in the case of an election from a district of a delegate, shall be the eighth; of a senator, shall be the twelfth, and of a representative in congress, shall be the fifteenth after such commencement. They shall compare the returns from their respective counties, and shall declare elected the person having the greatest number of votes in the whole district. If the greatest number of votes be equal for two or more persons, the officers attending shall decide to which of them they will give the certificate of election; and if the votes of said officers be equal also, they shall decide forthwith by lot to whom such certificate shall be given. A notice of said election shall forthwith be given at the door of the courthouse where the meeting is held. In case of special elections to supply vacancies, the time for the meeting of the returning officers shall be earlier, if required in the writ of election: provided, that during the existing war, in all elections for members of the house of representatives of *Duty of commissioners of election* *Certificate, how written* *When officers to meet* *Returns, how compared* *Notice given* *Special elections* *Certified statement to secretary*

74   ELECTION LAWS.

tary of commonwealth the Confederate States, the officer conducting the election at the courthouses of the several counties shall transmit the certified statement of the result of the election in his county, herein above required, by mail, prepaying the postage thereon, to the secretary of the commonwealth, within twenty days after the commencement of such election."

Duty of secretary of commonwealth 5. It shall be the duty of the secretary of the commonwealth, within thirty days from the commencement of any such election as is mentioned in the preceding sections, to examine the polls returned to him as aforesaid, and certify the state of the same to the governor, who shall declare and make proclamation of the result; and in case two or more candidates have an equal number of votes for the same office, the governor shall decide by lot to whom the return shall be given, and declare the result accordingly.

Duties of secretary of commonwealth 6. Be it further enacted, that upon the receipt of any polls under the provisions of the ordinance (No. 99) passed December the sixth, eighteen hundred and sixty-one, the secretary of the commonwealth shall perform the duties required by law to be performed by the commissioners and officers to conduct the elections at the courthouse, or by either of them, in the same manner he is required by law in case such polls had been received by him from the county or district for which the election was held: and all other proceedings shall be the same as in such cases.

Proclamation of governor, when to be issued 7. Be it further enacted, that it shall be the duty of the governor of the commonwealth to issue his proclamation, giving notice to the qualified voters of the state in the military service of the state or of the Confederate States, or who may be absent from the county or corporation of their residence, because of the presence of the public enemy, of their right to vote for members of the general assembly, by virtue of the provisions of the first, second and fourth sections of the ordinance passed by the convention of Virginia (No. 99) on the sixth day of December eighteen hundred and sixty-one, and also to all whom it may concern, of the passage of this act, and of the rights and duties set forth in its provisions; and it shall further be his duty to request the president of the Confederate States to issue an order to all commandants of camps, posts and detachments in command of Virginia troops, requiring them to give their aid in the due execution of the ordinance aforesaid and of this act.

Result of vote, how forwarded 8. The result of the votes in camps and the result of the votes of persons absent from their counties, cities or towns, by reason of the presence of the enemy, shall be forwarded by mail, when practicable, directed to the secretary of the commonwealth, when required to be returned to said secretary, and directed to the clerk of the county, city or town, when required to be returned to the county, city or town. The officer conducting such elections shall so forward the result, and

ELECTION LAWS.   75

preserve a duplicate of the result so to be forwarded, verified by certificates of the officer, and by not less than two other disinterested persons.

9. This act shall be in force from its passage.   *Commencement*

CHAP. 37.—An ACT to prescribe the mode of ascertaining and certifying Elections of Delegates and Senators during the existing war.

Passed March 24, 1863.

1. Be it enacted by the general assembly, that in all elections, *Elections of senator or delegate* during the existing war, for delegates for any county, corporation or election district, or for senators for any senatorial district, no part of which is in the possession of the public enemy, in which elections votes are authorized, by law or ordinance of convention, to be polled in military encampments, as well as in the county, corporation or election district, the commissioners of election, who are required by law to meet and compare the polls and ascertain the election, shall meet in each case at the place prescribed by law, on the thirtieth *When commissioners to meet* day from the commencement of the election; examine and compare the several polls taken in the county or corporation, and those taken in the several encampments for delegate or senator, as the case may be, for such county, corporation, election or senatorial district; strike therefrom any votes which are by law directed to be stricken from the same, and attach to the poll a list of the votes stricken therefrom, and the reason therefor. The result of the election shall then be ascertained, delivered and certified as prescribed by law, in each case respectively.

2. So much of the first, second and third sections of chapter eight *Code suspended* of the Code of Virginia (edition of eighteen hundred and sixty), as is in conflict with this act, shall be and the same is hereby suspended so long as this act shall continue in force, which shall be during the continuance of the present war and no longer, and thereafter the part of said sections hereby suspended shall be in full force.

3. This act shall be in force from its passage.   *Commencement*

CHAP. 38.—An ACT to provide Representation for the Counties where the Courthouses are in the possession or power of the Public Enemy.

Passed March 24, 1863.

1. Be it enacted by the general assembly, that in cases of election *When districts partially in power of enemy* districts or senatorial districts partially in the possession or power of the public enemy, the officers conducting the elections at the court-

houses of the several counties, or the persons substituted therefor by the provisions of this act, shall meet at the courthouse of the county or corporation first named in the law describing such district, which may not be in the possession or power of the public enemy, and perform the duties required of them by the third section of chapter eight of the Code of Virginia (edition of eighteen hundred and sixty).

<small>When election cannot be held at courthouse</small>

2. That whenever, by reason of the presence or power of the public enemy, no election can be held at the courthouse of any county, it shall be lawful for the commissioners or freeholders present, and agreeing to act as commissioners, at any regular place of voting in said county, to appoint a conductor at such place, if none be present, who shall be vested with the same powers and take the same oath, be subject to the same penalties and perform the same duties as now provided by law, except as they may be herein after otherwise directed. The officer conducting the election at such places of voting shall deliver or cause to be delivered the polls, within fifteen days after the commencement of such election, to the secretary of the commonwealth, who, after receipt of the polls, shall perform all the duties now required by law to be performed by the commissioners at the courthouse, and, except when herein after directed to perform the duties in person, shall appoint some one to perform the duties of the officer conducting the election at the courthouse.

<small>Duty of officer conducting election</small>

<small>Duty of secretary of commonwealth</small>

3. If the courthouse of any county entitled to one or more representatives in the general assembly, or all the courthouses of any election or senatorial district, are in the possession or power of the public enemy, the secretary of the commonwealth, after the receipt of the polls, shall perform all the duties of the commissioners and officers to conduct the elections at the courthouse or courthouses.

<small>Time within which duty to be performed</small>

4. When the secretary of the commonwealth, or any one appointed by him to perform the duties of the officer to conduct the election at the courthouse, are required to perform any act, either separately or conjointly with others, the time in which such act is to be performed shall be thirty days after the time now fixed by law.

<small>Commencement</small>

5. This act shall be in force from its passage.

CHAP. 39.—An ACT to provide for the Election of County Officers in certain cases.

Passed March 11, 1863.

<small>When county prohibited from holding an election</small>

1. Be it enacted by the general assembly, that in all cases where, on account of the occupation of any county, city or town by the public enemy, or from any cause connected therewith, the people of such county, city or town have heretofore been or hereafter may be prevented from holding elections for county or corporation officers, at

the times and in the manner prescribed in section three, chapter seven of the Code of Virginia (edition of eighteen hundred and sixty), the county or corporation courts, as the case may be, shall, us soon as such causes are removed, order writs of election, in the manner prescribed in chapter seven, section twenty-two of said Code, for filling vacancies, said elections shall be held and all proceedings relative thereto conducted in the manner and according to the provisions provided for filling vacancies in such offices. *Court may order writ of election*

2. Such elections shall be for the unexpired terms of the offices thus filled. *Unexpired terms*

3. This act shall be in force from its passage. *Commencement*

CHAP. 40.—An ACT changing the times of holding the Circuit Courts of the 14th Judicial Circuit.

Passed February 13, 1863.

1. Be it enacted by the general assembly, that an act passed March third, eighteen hundred and fifty-four, be amended and re-enacted so as to read as follows: *Act of March 1854 amended*

"The circuit courts for the fourteenth circuit shall hereafter be holden on the following days, viz: For the county of Craig, on the fifteenth day of March and August; for the county of Roanoke, on the twenty-second day of March and August; for the county of Botetourt, on the first day of April and September; for the county of Alleghany, on the thirteenth day of April and September; for the county of Pocahontas, on the twenty-third day of April and September; for the county of Greenbrier, on the first day of May and October; for the county of Monroe, on the twelfth day of May and October." *Terms of courts in 14th circuit*

2. This act shall be in force from and after the first day of July next. *Commencement*

CHAP. 41.—An ACT to enlarge the Powers of the Circuit Courts of the several Counties and Corporations in cases of Attachments against Non-residents.

Passed February 16, 1863.

1. Be it enacted by the general assembly, that during the continuance of the present war, the circuit courts of the several counties and corporations of this state, or the judge of any such court in vacation, in all cases of proceedings by way of attachment against non-residents, wherein slaves may be levied upon, shall have power *Attachments against non-residents* *Sale of slaves, how ordered*

to order the sale thereof, when, by reason of the destruction of the jail of said county or corporation, or from other cause, said slaves cannot be safely kept, or when, by reason of the great expense attending the support and maintenance of said slaves, during the pendency of said attachment, it may, in the opinion of said court, be proper to order such sale.

How made
2. Any sale directed to be made under the foregoing section, shall be ordered and made in accordance with the provisions of section sixteen of chapter one hundred and fifty-one of the Code of Virginia (edition of eighteen hundred and sixty), except that such sale may be ordered to be made elsewhere than in the county in which said attachment may be pending.

Commencement
3. This act shall be in force from its passage.

CHAP. 42.—An ACT to extend the time within which to institute Proceedings for Misdemeanors in Counties, Cities and Towns in possession of or threatened by the Enemy.

Passed March 23, 1863.

Limitation
1. Be it enacted by the general assembly, that in such of the counties, cities and towns of this commonwealth as are or may hereafter be so occupied or threatened by the public enemy, as that the courts cannot sit regularly for the trial of causes, the period between the passage of this act and six months after the ratification of a treaty of peace between the Confederate States of America and the United States of America, shall be excluded from the computation of the time within which, by the terms or operation of any statute or rule of law, it may be necessary to institute or commence proceedings or prosecutions against parties who may commit any misdemeanor.

Commencement
2. This act shall be in force from its passage.

CHAP. 43.—An ACT to amend the act passed March 10th, 1862, entitled an act to amend and re-enact an ordinance extending the Jurisdiction of the County Courts in certain cases, passed by the Convention on the 26th day of June 1861.

Passed March 23, 1863.

Act of 1862 amended
Be it enacted by the general assembly, that the act passed March tenth, eighteen hundred and sixty-two, entitled an act to amend and re-enact an ordinance extending the jurisdiction of the county courts in certain cases, passed by the convention on the twenty-sixth day of June eighteen hundred and sixty-one, be and the same is hereby amended and re-enacted so as to read as follows:

"1. Be it enacted by the general assembly, that an ordinance passed by the convention on the twenty-sixth day of June eighteen hundred and sixty-one, be amended and re-enacted so as to read as follows: *Ordinance amended*

'When the court of any county shall fail to meet for the transaction of business, or the people thereof, or any of them, shall be prevented from attending thereupon by reason of the public enemy, the court of the county next thereto, where such obstruction does not exist, and the clerk thereof, or the circuit court of the city of Richmond, and the clerk thereof, shall have jurisdiction of all matters, and authority to do and perform all acts which, as the law now is, are referable to the court or to the clerk of the county so obstructed: provided, however, that the authority to admit to record the writings mentioned in the fifth and sixth sections of chapter one hundred and eighteen of the Code of Virginia, shall by this act be extended only to the circuit court of the city of Richmond, and the clerk thereof: and further, that such admission to record shall be invalid unless such writing shall be duly admitted to record, according to the laws of this commonwealth in force prior to the twenty-sixth June eighteen hundred and sixty-one, within twelve months after the ratification of a treaty of peace between the United States and the Confederate States of America.' *Jurisdiction of courts*

"2. No tax shall be charged on the admission to record of any such writing in the circuit court of Richmond. *Where no tax to be charged*

"3. It shall be the duty of the clerk of the circuit court of the city of Richmond, whenever the said clerk has notice, on the face of any such writing or otherwise, in what county or corporation said writing ought to be recorded, within twelve months after a treaty of peace between the United States and the Confederate States, to transmit for recordation a copy of such writing to the clerk of the court of the county or corporation in which such writing should be recorded, according to the laws of this commonwealth in force, prior to the twenty-sixth day of June eighteen hundred and sixty-one; and in case of the failure of the clerk of the said circuit court to perform the duty herein required of him, he may, upon motion of any party injured by such failure, after ten days' previous notice, be fined by said circuit court not less than ten dollars nor more than one hundred dollars for every such failure; to be paid to the party injured. It shall be lawful for the clerk of said circuit court to charge a fee for such copy of said writing so transmitted, and the postages allowed by section ten of chapter one hundred and eighty-four of the Code of Virginia (edition of eighteen hundred and sixty); which fees and postages shall be collected as other clerks' fees. *Duty of clerk* *Penalty for failure* *Fees and postage*

"4. This act shall be in force from its passage." *Commencement*

CHAP. 44.—An ACT authorizing the Court of Appeals to hold its Sessions at other places than Lewisburg.

Passed March 12, 1863.

Place for holding sessions may be changed

1. Be it enacted by the general assembly, that the annual sessions of the supreme court of appeals, provided by law to be held at Lewisburg in the county of Greenbrier, may, during the continuance of the present war with the United States, be held at such other place on the western side of the Blue Ridge of mountains as the said court, or a majority of the judges thereof in vacation, may from time to time direct and appoint; of which removal due notice shall be given, by publication thereof in one or more of the newspapers printed in the city of Richmond; and all laws now in force applicable to the said court when its sessions are held at Lewisburg, shall apply in like manner to said court and its sessions when held at any other place, under the provisions of this act.

Notice to be given of removal

Removal of library and records

2. The said court, or a majority of the judges thereof in vacation, may order the removal of the library and the records of said court at Lewisburg to such place as the said court may, under the provisions of this act, appoint for its sessions; and a sum not exceeding one thousand dollars is hereby appropriated for the purposes of such removal; to be paid upon the order of such court, out of any moneys in the treasury not otherwise appropriated.

Commencement

3. This act shall be in force from its passage.

CHAP. 45.—An ACT to amend and re-enact the 1st section of an act entitled an act to increase Jailors' Fees for keeping and supporting Prisoners, passed September 24, 1862.

Passed March 17, 1863.

Act of 1862 amended

1. Be it enacted by the general assembly, that the first section of the act entitled an act to increase jailors' fees for keeping and supporting prisoners, passed September twenty-fourth, eighteen hundred and sixty-two, be amended and re-enacted so as to read as follows:

Jailors' fees

"§1. Jailors shall hereafter be allowed one dollar per day for keeping and supporting persons confined in the jails of this commonwealth, and a fair proportion of said sum for any time less than twenty-four hours; and in all cases the allowance shall be made on an account stating the time for which the person or persons remained in jail: provided, that the county and corporation courts of the commonwealth may establish, in their discretion, a different rate, not less than thirty-five cents nor more than one dollar and twenty-five cents per diem."

Power of courts

Commencement

2. This act shall be in force from its passage.

FIDUCIARIES.

[...] authorizing Fiduciaries to invest Funds in their hands [in] certain cases, and for other purposes.

Passed March 5, 1863.

[... enacte]d by the general assembly, that whenever any guar- *When fiduciary may invest* [...]mittee, executor, administrator or other fiduciary *funds.* [...] [ha]ve in his hands moneys received in the due exer[cise ...] [be]longing to the estate or trust fund held by him as [suc]h, which moneys any such fiduciary or trustee may, [... o]f his trust, or for any cause whatever, be unable to [... the per]sons que tr[u]e or parties entitled thereto, it shall [be lawful for such] fiduciary or trustee to apply, by motion or petition, [to the] circuit court in vacation, for leave to invest the [amount] of such moneys in interest bearing bonds or certi- *In what funds* [ficates of the Con]federate States or of the state of Virginia, or any *may be invested* [... bo]nds or securities of or within the said state; and [the judge ma]y, in his discretion, grant such leave. The bonds, [etc., so taken] shall be taken in the name of such fiduciary or [in his fid]uciary character: and whenever such investment [is made, suc]h fiduciary or trustee shall be released from respon[sibility for mo]neys thus invested; but it shall be his duty to pre[serve the bon]ds taken, and to exercise due diligence in collect[ing interest ac]cruing thereon, and in making a proper application [... provided] that nothing herein contained shall authorize said [fiducia]ries to change the character of an existing invest[ment or inv]estment made under the provisions of this law, [except b]y the decree of a circuit court of competent juris[diction; prov]ided further, that the provisions of the foregoing [shall not b]e so construed as to interfere with the powers now [of court]s of chancery over the subject.

[... Be it furthe]r enacted, that whenever any fiduciary or fiducia- *As to joint fidu-* [ry or tru]stees, residing in this state, have been or may be *ciaries* [called to exer]cise any power or to do any act jointly with one or [more t]rustee or trustees, residing within the limits of the [... it s]hall be lawful for the fiduciary or fiduciaries, trus[tees, re]siding in this state, to exercise any such power or [... act] without the concurrence of the non-resident fidu[ciarie]s, trustee or trustees; and the act of the resident [fiduc]iaries, trustee or trustees, shall have the same force [and in]tents and purposes, as if it had been the joint act [of all the fiducia]ries or trustees.

[... This act sha]ll be in force from its passage, and continue in *Commencement* [force until the ex]piration of six months after the ratification of a *and continuation* [treaty of peace b]etween the Confederate States and the United [States.]

FIDUCIARIES.—BANKS.

CHAP. 47.—An ACT to provide against the Forfeiture of Compensation to Fiduciaries in certain cases.

Passed March 11, 1863.

What allowed when fiduciary in military service.

1. Be it enacted by the general assembly, that when a compliance on the part of any fiduciary, with the seventh section of chapter one hundred and thirty-two of the Code of Virginia, has been or shall be, during the present war, prevented by the occupation or invasion of a county by the public enemy; the absence of the commissioner authorized to settle the accounts of such fiduciary; the employment of such fiduciary in the military service of the state or of the Confederate States, or by any other cause growing out of the present war, rendering such compliance impracticable, such fiduciary shall not, for such failure, forfeit a compensation for his services: provided such fiduciary shall, within six months after the removal of such cause of failure, exhibit before the proper commissioner the statement and vouchers mentioned in said section.

Commencement.

2. This act shall be in force from its passage.

CHAP. 48.—An ACT authorizing the Banks of the Commonwealth, during the existing war, to convert Confederate Treasury Notes in their possession into other obligations of the Confederate States.

Passed March 24, 1863.

Code amended.

1. Be it enacted by the general assembly, that the thirty-third section of the fifty-eighth chapter of the Code of Virginia (edition of eighteen hundred and sixty) be amended and re-enacted so as to read as follows:

When bank may loan money.

"§ 33. Any bank authorized to carry on business as a bank of circulation, deposit and discount, may loan money for a period not exceeding six months, and discount any bill of exchange, promissory note or other negotiable paper for the payment of money, which will be payable within six months from the time of discounting the same.

What interest bank may take.

A bank may take interest on its loans and discounts at the rate of one-half of one per centum for thirty days, and the interest may be received in advance. Each bank shall so regulate its loans and discounts that they shall not exceed twice the amount of the capital actually paid in: provided, however, that during the existing war, and until six months after the ratification of a treaty of peace between the Confederate States and the United States, any bank may convert the treasury notes and other evidences of debt of the Confederate States into the notes or obligations of said Confederate States, to an amount not exceeding the amount of its capital stock, in addition to its other loans and discounts in this section authorized, and to treat the same as part of its loans and discounts: and pro-

Loans, how regulated.

Provision as to treasury notes.

BANKS.

vided further, that said banks shall be authorized to convert only the treasury notes of the Confederate States, issued and dated prior to the first of April eighteen hundred and sixty-three."

2. This act shall be in force from its passage.   *Commencement*

CHAP. 49.—An ACT to amend and re-enact section 1, chapter 57, of an act passed March 1, 1861, entitled an act for the Relief of the Banks of this Commonwealth.

Passed March 18, 1863.

1. Be it enacted by the general assembly, that the first section of the act, entitled an act to amend and re-enact section first, chapter fifty-seven of the Acts of eighteen hundred and sixty-one, be amended and re-enacted so as to read as follows: *Act of 1861 amended*

"§ 1. Be it enacted by the general assembly, that so much of all or any acts as now may subject any bank or banking corporation incorporated by the laws of this commonwealth, now in operation, or which may be put in operation whilst this act is in force, to the forfeiture of its charter, or to any other penalty, for failing or refusing to pay or redeem its notes or debts in specie, shall be and the same are hereby suspended until the first day of March eighteen hundred and sixty-three, and until otherwise provided by the general assembly of Virginia: and if any such bank or banking corporation, shall have forfeited its charter by failing or refusing to pay in specie any notes or other debts due from such bank, the forfeiture thereby incurred shall be remitted, and the charter of such bank, with all the rights and powers thereby conferred, except such portions thereof as are herein before suspended, shall be and the same is hereby declared to be in full force and effect, to all intents and purposes: provided, that nothing herein contained shall be so construed as to prevent the recovery of the amount of any note or debt due from any such bank, with legal interest thereon, in the mode prescribed by law."   *Forfeiture of charter was pended*   *Charter in force*   *Proviso*

2. This act shall be in force from its passage.   *Commencement*

CHAP. 50.—An ACT authorizing the Branch of the Exchange Bank of Virginia at Richmond to declare a Dividend.

Passed February 28, 1863.

1. Be it enacted by the general assembly, that so long as the Exchange Bank of Virginia at Norfolk shall remain within the lines of the public enemy, it shall be lawful and the duty of the branch of said bank at Richmond to declare dividends of profit at the same   *Bank at Richmond to declare dividend*

times and to the same extent, and in the same manner the parent bank might do, if situated within our own lines. When such dividend shall be declared, it shall be lawful and the duty of said branch bank to demand contribution from the other branches of said bank, in the same manner the parent bank might do, to make payment thereof; and upon satisfactory evidence being furnished of the names of persons holding shares, and the amount so held, to pay the dividend, the tax thereon, and the bonus on the capital stock of said bank, within the time and in the manner the parent bank would be required to do, if a dividend had been declared by said parent bank. The said branch bank may at any time declare a dividend for the six months ending on the first day of December last, in pursuance of this act.

Contribution from other banks, how demanded

2. This act shall be in force from its passage.

Commencement

CHAP. 51.—An ACT amending and re-enacting the 5th and 6th sections of the act passed March 13, 1862, entitled an act to convert the Northwestern Bank of Virginia at Jeffersonville into a separate and independent Bank.

Passed March 11, 1863.

1. Be it enacted by the general assembly, that the fifth and sixth sections of the act passed March thirteenth, eighteen hundred and sixty-two, entitled an act to convert the branch of the Northwestern Bank of Virginia at Jeffersonville into a separate and independent bank, be amended and re-enacted so as to read as follows:

Act of 1862 amended

"§ 5. At any time within three months from the passage of this act, any loyal holder of stock in the Northwestern Bank of Virginia, whose stock in said bank was purchased through said branch, or whose dividends have usually heretofore been credited to him at said branch, may return and assign to the said Graziers Bank of Virginia such stock, and demand and receive in lieu thereof a certificate for a like number of shares of stock in said Graziers Bank of Virginia: provided, however, that if before the first day of July eighteen hundred and sixty-three, satisfactory reasons shall be shown to the board of directors of the Graziers Bank for the failure of any such stockholder to avail himself of the benefits of the foregoing provision, the said board shall certify such reasons, with their opinion on the same, to the governor.

When loyal stockholder may demand transfer

"§ 6. As soon as may be after the expiration of the said three months from the passage of this act, the governor of the state shall cause certificates of the stock held by the state in the said Northwestern Bank of Virginia, for an amount equal to the balance of the capital stock of said branch, not exchanged under the previous sec-

Certificates of stock, how returned and assigned

tion, to be in like manner returned and assigned to said Graziers. Bank of Virginia, for a like number of shares of the stock thereof: provided, however, that on the certificate authorized in the preceding section being received by the governor, it shall be his duty to transfer to the stockholder to whom the same shall be given, out of the stock herein directed to be transferred to the state, a quantity thereof equal to the amount held by such stockholder in the Northwestern Bank, together with any dividends thereon which may have accrued to the state under the sixth section of said act."

2. This act shall be in force from its passage. *Commencement*

CHAP. 52.—An ACT authorizing the Sale of the Roanoke Valley Rail Road.

Passed February 13, 1863.

1. Be it enacted by the general assembly, that the Roanoke valley rail road company shall have power to sell at public auction, to the highest bidder, their road, together with all their property of every sort and description: provided, that a notice of sixty days of said sale shall be published in one or more of the Richmond papers: provided further, that said sale shall be subject to the approval of the board of public works, to a majority of the stockholders, and that the proceeds of said sale shall be sufficient to pay all the debts of said company; and the purchasers under this act shall have and enjoy all the rights, privileges and immunities which the said Roanoke valley rail road company had under its charter, and the acts amendatory thereof: provided, however, that the purchasers under this act shall give guarantees, satisfactory to the board of public works, that the use of said road shall be continued as heretofore: provided further, that the sale hereby authorized shall not be valid, if, on or before the day of sale, a majority of the mortgage creditors of said company, whose claims are not due, shall object to such sale—such objection, if made, to be signified in writing to the president of the company: and provided also, that a majority of the holders of the mortgaged bonds of said corporation shall give their assent in writing to the making of such sale. *Power to sell* *Notice of sale* *Sale subject to approval of the board of public works* *Proviso*

2. Be it further enacted, that out of the proceeds of such sale the debt of said company shall first be paid, and then shall be paid to the state of Virginia the preferred stock held by said state in said company; and what remains of the proceeds of said sale shall be divided ratably among the stockholders of said Roanoke valley rail road company. *Proceeds of sale*

3. This act shall be in force from its passage. *Commencement*

CHAP. 53.—An ACT to convert into Stock, to be held by the State, the Interest in arrear, due by the South Side Rail Road Company to the State.

Passed March 25, 1863.

Amount of interest to be converted into stock.

1. Be it enacted by the general assembly, that under the superintendence of the board of public works, the whole amount of the interest in arrear from the South side rail road company to the commonwealth of Virginia, to wit, the sum of one hundred and ninety-six thousand dollars, be converted into stock, to be held by the state as owner of so much stock in the said rail road, in conformity with the resolution of the stockholders in said rail road, adopted by them on December third, eighteen hundred and sixty-two, in general meeting assembled on that day in the city of Petersburg: provided, that the said one hundred and ninety-six thousand dollars shall be a preferred stock, and six per centum thereon shall be paid into the treasury of the commonwealth, whenever any dividend shall be declared by the company: and provided further, that the amount of interest hereby authorized to be converted into preferred stock shall be appropriated exclusively to the construction of the new line of road near Farmville, as provided by the act passed the twenty-sixth day of January, eighteen hundred and sixty-two, for that purpose: and provided further, that this act shall not continue to be in effect, unless the construction of the new line referred to is commenced within one year and completed in three years from the passage of this act; and upon a failure to complete the same as aforesaid, the sum hereby appropriated, with interest, shall be paid into the treasury by said company.

Proviso

Commencement

2. This act shall be in force from its passage.

CHAP. 54.—An ACT to amend and re-enact an act entitled an act to amend and re-enact an act entitled an act to prevent the unnecessary Consumption of Grain by Distillers and other Manufacturers of Spirituous and Malt Liquors, passed October 2, 1862.

Passed March 11, 1863.

Act of 1862 amended.

1. Be it enacted by the general assembly, that the first section of an act passed on the second day of October eighteen hundred and sixty-two, entitled an act to amend and re-enact an act entitled an act to prevent the unnecessary consumption of grain by distillers and other manufacturers of spirituous and malt liquors, be amended and re-enacted so as to read as follows:

Distillation prohibited

"§ 1. It shall not be lawful for any person hereafter to make or cause to be made any whiskey, or other spirituous or malt liquors, out of any corn, wheat, rye or other grain, or out of potatoes, sugar, molasses, sugar cane, molasses cane or sorghum; and any person so

offending shall be deemed guilty of a misdemeanor; and upon con- Penalties
viction thereof, shall be fined for every offence not less than one
hundred dollars nor more than five thousand dollars, and be subject
to imprisonment in the county jail not exceeding twelve months, at
the discretion of the court: provided, that this act shall not be so Proviso
construed as to impair the obligation of any existing contract legally
entered into under the existing laws, or any rights growing out of any
such contract: but this proviso shall not be construed to refer to any
other contracts than those made directly with the confederate authorities, under the provisions of the law of October eighteen hundred
and sixty-two."

2. This act shall be in force from its passage. Commencement

CHAP. 55.—An ACT to repeal the act passed October 1st, 1862, entitled an
act legalizing the Manufacture of Alcohol.

Passed March 11, 1863.

1. Be it enacted by the general assembly, that the act passed Act of 1862
October first, eighteen hundred and sixty-two, entitled an act le- repealed
galizing the manufacture of alcohol, be and the same is hereby
repealed.

2. This act shall be in force from its passage. Commencement

CHAP. 56.—An ACT for the Relief of certain persons engaged in the
Distillation of Fruit.

Passed March 28, 1863.

1. Be it enacted by the general assembly, that any person who When person
has heretofore paid the tax and the penalty imposed by the thirty- may appear
third section of an act passed the twenty-seventh of March eighteen
hundred and sixty-two, or by an act passed the second of October
eighteen hundred and sixty-two, amending and re-enacting said section, may appear before the court of his county or corporation, and
make oath that he failed to obtain license for the distillation of fruit,
only through ignorance or misapprehension of the law. Said person
shall thereupon be examined on oath by the attorney for the commonwealth; and if the court be satisfied that the failure to obtain When court sa-
license was for the cause alleged, and not with intent to defraud the tisfied as to fail-
commonwealth, the court shall order the clerk to give to said person ure
a certificate to that effect; and whenever such certificate shall be Auditor to issue
presented to the auditor of public accounts, with satisfactory proof warrant
of the payment of the tax and penalty into the treasury, the auditor
shall issue his warrant on the treasury, payable out of any money

therein not otherwise appropriated, in favor of said person for a sum equal to the penalty, minus the commissions of the sheriff: and upon a like certificate and proof that any person has in like manner satisfied the court of his county or corporation that he has heretofore paid the tax imposed by either of said acts, and that he has distilled spirits from fruit only for his own use, and has not distilled more than thirty-three gallons, the auditor shall issue his warrant, payable in like manner, in favor of said person, for a sum equal to the tax paid by him, less the expenses of collection.

Duty of sheriff   2. That upon a like certificate, it shall be the duty of the sheriff of any county or corporation to release from payment of the penalty imposed by either of said acts, any person heretofore engaged in distilling ardent spirits from fruit without license therefor; but such person shall pay the tax imposed by said acts prior to his release from said penalty; and the said certificate shall serve as a voucher for the sheriff in his settlement with the auditor.

Attorney to be present   3. That in every case the said certificate of the court shall state that the attorney for the commonwealth defended the case, and shall be authenticated by the seal of the county or corporation.

Commencement   4. This act shall be in force from its passage.

CHAP. 57.—An ACT concerning Officers of the State who have taken an Oath to support an Usurped Government within the limits of this State.

Passed March 26, 1863.

What, when oath taken by officer   1. Be it enacted by the general assembly, that any officer who has been regularly elected or appointed according to the laws of this state, who has, since the seventeenth day of April eighteen hundred and sixty-one, or who shall hereafter, voluntarily take an oath or affirmation to support any usurped government established or attempted to be established within the limits of this state, and who acts in such office, claiming to act under such usurped government, shall be held to be an officer under such usurped government, and to *Acts void* have vacated his office under this state, and all his acts thereafter *To whom act also to apply* shall be absolutely null and void. This section shall also be held to apply to judges of the circuit courts, and to county and corporation courts composed, in whole or in part, of justices who may have been justices on the seventeenth day of April eighteen hundred and sixty-one, and who may have held courts under the authority of such usurped government, or otherwise may have recognized or acted under the authority of such usurped government, and shall have taken an oath or affirmation to support the same.

Oath or affirmation   2. An oath or affirmation taken before any person to support any such usurped government, whether the person administering it be

CHARTERED COMPANIES.—LUNATIC ASYLUM. 89

authorized to administer an oath or not, shall be held to be an oath, within the meaning and intention of this act, and within the meaning and intention of any other act in which such oath may be brought in question.

3. No record evidence of the election, appointment or qualification of any officer under such usurped government shall be required, but the person's acting in the capacity of an officer, claiming to act under such government, shall be sufficient to establish his official character.   *Record evidence not required*

4. This act shall be in force from its passage.   *Commencement*

CHAP. 58.—An ACT to authorize the transfer and issue of new Certificates of Stock in Chartered Companies in certain cases.

Passed March 20, 1863.

1. Be it enacted by the general assembly, that whenever any shares of stock in a chartered company shall be sequestered and sold under an order or decree of a district court of the Confederate States, as the property of an alien enemy, the proper officers of such company shall, upon application of the receiver making the sale, assign or transfer the same to the purchaser on the books of the company, without requiring the production of the certificate for such shares, and shall issue new certificates of stock to such purchaser.   *When property sold and sequestered*

2. Be it further enacted, that whenever a certificate of stock in any chartered company belonging to a loyal citizen of the Confederate States, shall be beyond his control by reason of the public enemy, upon the production of proper evidence to the board of directors of the company, of the ownership of such stock, a new certificate therefor shall issue to the owner, and the old certificate annulled by an order of the said board entered on the records of the company.   *New certificate, how granted. Old certificate destroyed*

3. This act shall be in force from its passage.   *Commencement*

CHAP. 59.—An ACT making an Appropriation for the Central Lunatic Asylum.

Passed March 6, 1863.

1. Be it enacted by the general assembly, that the auditor of public accounts be and he is hereby authorized and directed to issue his warrant on the treasury, payable out of any money therein not otherwise appropriated, for the sum of sixty-five thousand dollars, for the support of the Central lunatic asylum at Staunton, for the fiscal year ending the thirtieth September eighteen hundred and sixty-   *Amount appropriated*

three. Said amount, or any part thereof, to be paid upon the order of the board of directors of said institution, and to be in addition to the amount received from the pay patient fund.

Commencement 2. This act shall be in force from its passage.

CHAP. 60.—An ACT amending and re enacting the 1st and 2d sections of an act entitled an act to repeal the Fence Law of Virginia as to certain Counties, and to authorize the County Courts to dispense with Enclosures in other Counties, passed October 3d, 1862, and to legalize the Action of County Courts held under said Law.

Passed February 13, 1863.

Act of 1862 amended 1. Be it enacted by the general assembly, that the first and second sections of an act entitled an act to repeal the fence law of Virginia as to certain counties, and to authorize the county courts to dispense with enclosures in other counties, passed October third, eighteen hundred and sixty-two, be amended and re-enacted so as to read as follows:

First section amended "§ 1. Be it therefore enacted by the general assembly of Virginia, that the first section of the ninety-ninth chapter of the Code of Virginia, so far as it applies to the counties of Hanover, Henrico, York, Warwick, Elizabeth City, Alexandria, Fauquier, Stafford and King George, be and the same is hereby repealed.

Second section amended
Power of courts "§ 2. Be it further enacted, that the county courts of the counties of Augusta, Frederick, Clarke, Warren, Culpeper, Rappahannock, Norfolk, Princess Anne, Mercer, Shenandoah, Page, Prince William, Spotsylvania, Hampshire, Berkeley, Caroline, Rockingham, Richmond, Westmoreland, Loudoun, Jefferson, Orange, Essex, King & Queen, Goochland, Giles, Bland, Fairfax, Greenbrier, New Kent, Charles City, James City, Prince George and Nansemond shall have power, all the justices having been summoned, and a majority thereof being present, to dispense with the existing laws in regard to enclosures, so far as their respective counties may be concerned, or such parts thereof, to be described by metes and bounds, as in their discretion they may deem it expedient to exempt from the operation of such law."

Action of county courts legalized 2. Be it further enacted, that in case the county courts of any of the counties specified in the foregoing section shall have taken action in pursuance of the provisions of the act passed the third day of October eighteen hundred and sixty-two, entitled an act to repeal the fence law of Virginia as to certain counties, and to authorize the county courts to dispense with enclosures in other counties, since the passage thereof, such action is hereby legalized and made valid to the same extent as it would be, had such counties been specifically included in the second section of said act.

Commencement 3. This act shall be in force from its passage.

WAREHOUSE.—FLOUR.

CHAP. 61.—An ACT to establish an Inspection of Tobacco at Keen's Warehouse in the Town of Danville.

Passed March 10, 1863.

1. Be it enacted by the general assembly, that an inspection of tobacco be and the same is hereby established at a warehouse to be located on Loyal and Lynn streets in the town of Danville, and called "Keen's Warehouse," agreeably to the provisions of chapter eighty-seven of the Code of Virginia (edition of eighteen hundred and sixty). *Warehouse established*

2. This act shall be in force from its passage. *Commencement*

CHAP. 62.—An ACT to provide for an Inspection of Flour in the Town of Danville.

Passed March 11, 1863.

1. Be it enacted by the general assembly, that an inspection of flour be and the same is hereby authorized to be established in and for the town of Danville, under such regulations as shall be prescribed by the ordinances of said town, and subject to the provisions of chapter eighty-eight of the Code of Virginia (edition of eighteen hundred and sixty). *To authorize inspection of flour*

2. This act shall be in force from its passage. *Commencement*

PRIVATE OR LOCAL ACTS.

CHAP. 63.—An ACT to incorporate the Farmville Insurance Company.

Passed March 3, 1863.

1. Be it enacted by the general assembly of Virginia, that James W. Dunnington, Howell E. Warren, Frank. N. Watkins, Clement C. Read, James L. Hubard, Norval Cobb, Stephen O. Southall, Richard McIlwaine, Christopher C. Lockett, Archibald Vaughan, and others who may associate under this act, not less than twenty, are hereby created and declared to be a body politic and corporate, by the name and style of The Farmville Insurance Company; and by that name may sue and be sued, plead and be impleaded in all the courts of law and equity in this state and elsewhere; and to make and have a common seal, and the same to break, alter or renew at their pleasure; to ordain and establish such by-laws, ordinances and regulations, and generally to do every act and thing necessary to carry into effect this act, or to promote the object and design of this corporation: provided, that such by-laws, ordinances, regulations or acts be not inconsistent with the laws of this state or of the Confederate States. *Company incorporated*

2. To make insurance upon dwellings, houses, stores, and all other kind of buildings, either in town or country, and upon household furniture, merchandise and other property, against loss or damage by fire; to make insurance upon lives; to cause themselves to be reinsured, when deemed expedient, against any risk or risks upon which they have made or may make insurance; to grant annuities; to receive endowments; to contract for reversionary payments; to guarantee the payment of promissory notes, bills of exchange or other evidences of debt; to make insurance upon vessels, freights, goods, wares, merchandise, specie, bullion, profits, commissions, bank notes, bottomry and respondentia interests, and to make all and every insurance connected with marine risks and risks of transportation and navigation. *Insurance, how and upon what made*

3. To receive money on deposit and grant certificates therefor, in accordance with the conditions set forth in sections four and five, chapter fifty-nine of the Code of Virginia; but in no case are such deposits or the certificates therefor to be held liable to make good any policy of insurance issued by this company. *Money received on deposit*

4. The funds of this company, however derived, may be invested in or loaned on any stock or real or personal security. *Investments, how made*

INSURANCE COMPANIES.

Capital stock, how payable

5. The capital stock of said company shall be not less than twenty thousand dollars nor more than four hundred thousand dollars, to be divided into shares of fifty dollars each. The said capital stock shall be payable by each subscriber at such time or times as it may be called for by the president and directors, and in such proportions as they may deem necessary; and if any subscriber shall fail to pay the same so called for, upon each and every share so held, within twenty days after the same has been so called for and demanded, then the amount so called for may be recovered by motion, upon twenty days' notice in writing, in any court of record in the county or place of residence of the holder of stock.

Affairs of company, how managed

6. The affairs of said company shall be managed by a president and board of directors, nine in number, five of whom shall constitute a quorum. Said directors shall be elected by ballot from among the stockholders of said company, in general meeting assembled, by a majority of the votes of said stockholders present in person or by proxy, according to a scale of voting to be hereafter prescribed; and the directors thus chosen at their first meeting, shall choose from amongst themselves or the stockholders at large, a president, and allow him a reasonable compensation for his services: the said president and directors to continue in office one year, or until their successors are appointed. In case of a vacancy in the office of president or directors from any cause, the remaining directors may elect others to supply their places for the remainder of the term for which they were chosen.

Officers, how appointed

7. The president and directors of said company shall appoint a secretary and such other clerks and officers as they may find necessary for the proper conducting of the business of the company, and shall allow them suitable compensation for their services: all of which officers shall hold their places during the pleasure of the board of directors; and the said officers so appointed shall not, by reason of their being stockholders in said company, be incapacitated from giving evidence in any suit to which said company may be a party, unless said officers have other personal interest in said suit, or unless they shall own stock to the amount of fifty shares.

Agents

8. The president and directors shall have power to appoint agents in any part of this state or elsewhere; and it shall be the duty of said president and directors to appoint such agents in any city or county in this state, when requested so to do by not less than ten stockholders, residents of such city or county, holding not less than one hundred shares of stock; such agents being removable at the pleasure of the president and directors.

Scale of voting

9. The scale of voting at all meetings of said company shall be, one vote for each share of stock not exceeding twenty: one vote for every two shares exceeding twenty and not exceeding two hundred; one vote for every four shares exceeding two hundred; and every

stockholder not in debt to the company may, at pleasure, by power of attorney or in person, assign and transfer his stock in the company, on the books of the same, or any part thereof, not being less than a whole share; but no stockholder indebted to the company shall be permitted to make a transfer or receive a dividend until such debt is paid or secured to the satisfaction of the board of directors.

10. The president and directors shall have power to declare such dividends of the profits of the company as they may deem proper: provided, that no dividend shall be declared, when, in the opinion of a majority of the board, the capital stock would be impaired thereby. They shall also make and publish at the end of every year, except that in which the company goes into operation, a report showing the condition of the company in regard to its business for the current year. Dividends, how declared.

11. The members of the company shall not be liable for any loss, damage or responsibility other than the property they have in the capital of the company, to the amount of the shares respectively held by them, and any profits arising thereupon and not divided.

12. The persons named in the first section shall be commissioners, whose duty it shall be, within six months after the passage of this act, at some suitable place in the town of Farmville, and elsewhere in Virginia, to open books to receive subscriptions to the capital stock of said corporation; and five days' notice shall be given by said commissioners of the time and place of opening said books, in the newspapers published in the city of Richmond; which books shall not be closed in less than twenty days from the time of opening. The said commissioners shall give a like notice for a meeting of the stockholders to choose directors; and they shall supervise the first election of said officers, and shall deliver over to them, when so elected, any property belonging to the corporation that may have come into their hands. Stockholders how responsible

13. Nothing in this act shall be so construed as to authorize said company to issue and put into circulation any note in the nature of a bank note. Restriction

14. This act shall be in force from its passage, and subject to modification, amendment or repeal, at the pleasure of the general assembly. Commencement

---

CHAP. 64.—An ACT incorporating the Insurance and Savings Society of Petersburg.

Passed March 10, 1863.

1. Be it enacted by the general assembly of Virginia, that Reuben Ragland, Nathaniel F. Rives, David B. Dugger, Charles H. Cuth- Company incorporated

96   INSURANCE COMPANIES.

bert, Robert W. Brodnax, Thomas A. Proctor,
James Chieves, Edmund H. Osborne, Philip H.
Claiborne, Robert Y. Jones, Thomas R. Moore
Harrison, and their associates and successors, who
come subscribers or stockholders, be and they are
and made a body politic and corporate, under the

Privileges of the The City Insurance and Savings Society of Peter
company name, shall have perpetual succession, and be a
sued, plead and be impleaded in all courts in this st
and to have a common seal, and the same to alter
pleasure; and to make and ordain such ordinanc
and generally to do all such acts and things as m
carry into effect this act, and promote the object
corporation.

Capital stock 2. The capital stock of said corporation shall n
How divided hundred thousand dollars, to be divided into sha
dollars each, with power to increase the same to a
one million of dollars, whenever a majority of t
interest shall in general meeting, from time to t
to do.

How capital 3. The capital stock shall be paid as follows:
stock to be paid share before or at the general meeting for the
company, to the four associates herein first name
appointed commissioners (any three of whom may
due thereafter as may be required by the presiden

When meeting 4. Whenever it shall appear to the commissio
to be called two hundred thousand dollars of the capital has be
forty thousand dollars thereof has been paid to the
commissioners shall, by service of personal notic
a general meeting of the subscribers or stockho

President and time and place in said city, to organize said cor
directors, how meeting the subscribers or stockholders shall pro
elected spection of the commissioners, to elect a preside
tors. The commissioners shall forthwith, after
over, as the president and directors may order, a
by them from the subscribers to the capital stock of
deliver up all books and papers in their hands co

Management 5. The affairs of the corporation shall be man
dent and three directors, being stockholders (a
shall constitute a quorum), who shall be chosen l
in general meeting, and continue in office for o
Vacancies, how others are elected in their stead; and in case of
filled tion or disqualification of the president or any of
remaining members of the directory shall elect of
cancies for the residue of the term for which they

Who to consti- 6. In all general meetings of the stockholder
tute a quorum

The stockholders in interest being present in person or by proxy, shall constitute a quorum for the transaction of business. Each stockholder shall be entitled to as many votes as he may hold shares in said company. The stockholders in general meeting shall have power to fix the time and place of the annual meetings, and to prescribe the mode in which general meetings of the stockholders may be called by the directory, and the manner in which the stockholders shall be notified of all meetings of their body. The stockholders shall determine and fix the compensation of the president. *Compensation of president*

7. The president and directors may appoint and dismiss at their pleasure, a secretary and such other officers as may be necessary for the transaction of the business of the company, and allow such compensation for their services as they may deem reasonable; and may require such secretary and other officers to enter into bonds with security for the faithful discharge of their duties. *Secretary and other officers, how appointed. Bond and security to be given*

8. Every stockholder, not in debt to the company, may, subject to such regulations and upon such terms as the stockholders may prescribe, in person or by attorney, assign his stock, or any number of his shares, on the books of the company; but no stockholder indebted to the company shall assign or make a transfer of his stock or receive a dividend, until such debt is paid, or secured to the satisfaction of the board of directors. *Assignment of stock*

9. The president and directors are authorized to make insurance upon vessels, freights, merchandise, specie, bullion, jewels, profits, commissions, bank notes, bills of exchange, and other evidences of debt, bottomry and respondentia interests, and make all and every insurance connected with marine risks, and risks of transportation and navigation. *Authority to make insurance upon vessels, &c*

10. To make insurance on dwellings, houses, stores and other kinds of buildings, and upon household furniture and other property, and merchandise against loss or damage by fire. *Insurance upon dwellings*

11. To make insurance on lives; to grant annuities; to guarantee the payment of notes, bonds and bills of exchange; and to make all kinds of contracts for the insurance of every description of property; to receive money on deposit, and to pay interest thereon, as may be advantageous to the stockholders; to provide for the investment of funds of the company in any way which may be deemed most beneficial; and to invest the same in any stock of any kind, or loans or otherwise, as may be judged best for the interest of the company: provided always, that nothing in this act shall be construed to authorize said company to issue or put into circulation any note of the nature of a bank note, or to own more land than is necessary for an office building. *Insurance upon lives, &c. To receive money upon deposit. Proviso*

12. All policies of insurance and other contracts made by the said company, signed by the president and countersigned by the secretary, *Effect of the policies*

INSURANCE COMPANIES.

shall be obligatory on said company, and have the same effect as if the said policies and contracts had been attested by a corporate seal.

Dividends to be declared

13. The president and directors may declare semi-annual or other dividends of the profits of the company, as they may deem proper; but no dividend shall be declared when in the opinion of a majority of the board the capital stock would be impaired thereby.

General meeting to be called

14. The president and directors may, at any time when deemed necessary by them, call a general meeting of the stockholders; and any number of stockholders owning not less than one-fourth of the whole number of shares, may require the president and directors to call such meeting, and on their refusal to do so, may themselves call such meeting, giving fifteen days' notice thereof in one or more of the newspapers published in the city of Petersburg.

Agent to be appointed

15. The president and directors may appoint an agent in any of the cities, towns or counties of this state or elsewhere, to receive offerings for insurance, and for the transaction of such business of the company as may be confided to him.

16. The corporation hereby created shall be subject to the provisions of the Code of Virginia, so far as the same are applicable to it, and not inconsistent with the provisions of this act; and this act shall be subject to alteration, amendment or repeal, at the pleasure of the general assembly.

Commencement

17. This act shall be in force from its passage.

———————

CHAP. 65.—An ACT to incorporate the Confederate Insurance Company.*

Passed February 4, 1862.

Company incorporated

1. Be it enacted by the general assembly of Virginia, that James L. Cabell, H. Howard, N. H. Massie, B. C. Flannagan, W. P. Farish, J. T. Randolph, James Fife, A. P. Abell, E. J. Timberlake, William A. Bibb, and others who may associate under this act, not less than twenty, are hereby created and declared to be a body politic and corporate, by the name and style of The Confederate Insurance Company; and by that name, may sue and be sued, plead and be impleaded in all the courts of law and equity in this state and elsewhere; and to make and have a common seal, and the same to

By-laws, &c

break, alter or renew at their pleasure; to ordain and establish such by-laws, ordinances and regulations; and generally to do every act and thing necessary to carry into effect this act, or to promote the

Proviso

object and design of this corporation: provided, that such by-laws, ordinances, regulations or acts be not inconsistent with the laws of this state or of the Confederate States.

* Tax paid since publication of Acts of 1862.

INSURANCE COMPANIES.

2. To make insurance upon dwellings, houses, stores and all other kind of building, either in town or country, and upon household furniture, merchandise and other property, against loss or damage by fire; to make insurance on lives; to cause themselves to be reinsured, when deemed expedient, against any risk or risks upon which they have made or may make insurance; to grant annuities; to receive endowments; to contract for reversionary payments; to guarantee the payment of promissory notes, bills of exchange or other evidence of debt; to make insurance upon vessels, freights, goods, wares, merchandise, specie, bullion, profits, commissions, bank notes, bottomry and respondentia interests; and to make all and every insurance connected with marine risks of transportation and navigation. *To insure dwellings, lives &c.* *To insure vessels, &c.*

3. To receive money on deposit, and grant certificates therefor, in accordance with the conditions set forth in sections four and five, chapter fifty-nine of the Code of Virginia; but in no case are such deposits, or the certificates therefor, to be held liable to make good any policy on insurance issued by this company. *To receive money on deposit.*

4. The funds of this company, however derived, may be invested in or loaned on any stock or real security, or be used in purchasing bonds of this state or of the Confederate States. The said company shall have power to purchase or otherwise acquire, to have and to hold, and likewise to convey and to sell, any real or personal estate, for the purpose of securing any debt or debts that may be due to them, and to lend money upon personal or real estate. *Funds to be invested or loaned.* *Power to purchase and hold lands.*

5. The capital of said company shall be not less than twenty thousand dollars nor more than five hundred thousand dollars, to be divided into shares of fifty dollars each. The said capital stock shall be payable by each subscriber at such time or times as it may be called for by the president and directors, and in such proportions as they may deem necessary; and if any subscriber shall fail to pay the sums so called for upon each and every share so held, within twenty days after the same has been so called for and demanded, then the amount so called for may be recovered by motion, upon twenty days' notice in writing, in any court of record in the county or place of residence of the holder of stock. *Capital* *How capital stock payable*

6. The affairs of said company shall be managed by a president and board of directors, seven in number, four of whom shall constitute a quorum. Said directors shall be elected by ballot from among the stockholders of said company, in general meeting assembled, by a majority of the votes of the stockholders present in person or by proxy, according to a scale of voting to be hereafter prescribed; and the directors thus chosen, at their first meeting shall choose from among themselves, or the stockholders at large, a president. The said president and directors to continue in office one year, or until their successors are appointed. In case of a vacancy in the office of *Management of the company* *Directors, how elected* *President, how chosen* *Term of office* *Vacancy, how filled*

president or directors, from any cause, the remaining directors may elect others to supply their places for the remainder of the term for which they were chosen.

Secretary, how appointed

Compensation

7. The president and directors of said company shall appoint a secretary and such other clerks and officers as they may find necessary for the proper conducting of the business of the company, and shall allow them suitable compensation for their services: all of which officers shall hold their places during the pleasure of the board of directors; and the said officers so appointed shall not, by reason of their being stockholders in said company, be incapacitated from giving evidence in any suit to which said company may be a party, unless said officers have other personal interest in said suit, or unless they shall own stock to the amount of one hundred shares.

Power to appoint agents

8. The president and directors shall have power to appoint agents in any part of this state or elsewhere; and it shall be the duty of said president and directors to appoint such agents in any city or county in this state, when requested so to do by not less than ten stockholders, residents of such city or county, holding not less than one hundred shares of stock; such agents being removable at the pleasure of the president and directors.

Scale of voting

Power to transfer stock

9. The scale of voting at all the meetings of said company shall be one vote for each share of stock not exceeding twenty; one vote for every two shares exceeding twenty and not exceeding two hundred; one vote for every four shares exceeding two hundred; and every stockholder not in debt to the company may at pleasure, in person or by power of attorney, assign and transfer his stock in the company, on the books of the same, or any part thereof, not being less than a whole share; but no stockholder indebted to the company as principal or endorser on paper due or to mature, shall be permitted to make a transfer or receive a dividend until such debt is paid, or secured to the satisfaction of the board of directors.

Dividends

To make and publish report

10. The president and directors shall have power to declare such dividends of the profits of the company as they may deem proper: provided, that no dividend shall be declared when, in the opinion of a majority of the board, the capital stock would be impaired thereby. They shall also make and publish at the end of every year, except that in which the company goes into operation, a report showing the condition of the company in regard to its business for the current year.

Liability of members

11. The members shall not be liable for any loss, damage or responsibility other than the property they have in the capital of the company, to the amount of the shares respectively held by them, and any profits arising thereupon, not divided.

Books of subscription to be opened

12. The persons named in the first section shall be commissioners, whose duty it shall be, within six months after the passage of this

act, at some suitable place in the town of Charlottesville, and at such other places as they may deem proper, to open books to receive subscriptions to the capital stock of said corporation; and five days' notice shall be given by said commissioners of the time and place of opening said books, in the newspapers published in the town of Charlottesville: which books shall not be closed in less than twenty days from the time of opening. The said commissioners shall give a like notice for a meeting of the stockholders to choose directors. They shall supervise the first election of said officers, and shall deliver over to them, when so elected, any property belonging to the corporation, that may have come into their hands.

margin: Commissioners to give notice

13. This act shall be in force from its passage; and the legislature of Virginia reserves to itself the power of altering, amending or repealing any of the provisions thereof.

margin: Commencement

CHAP. 66.—An ACT to amend the 4th section of an act to incorporate the Confederate Insurance Company, passed 4th February 1862.*

Passed March 4, 1862.

1. Be it enacted, that the fourth section of the act to incorporate The Confederate Insurance Company, passed fourth February eighteen hundred and sixty-two, be and is hereby amended and re-enacted so as to read as follows:

margin: Act amended

"§ 4. The company shall have power and authority to invest its capital stock and other funds in bank, state or other stocks; in the purchase of bonds issued by this or any other state, or of the Confederate States, and of bonds of any incorporated company; to lend money upon personal or real security; and to purchase or otherwise acquire, to have and to hold, and likewise to convey and sell any real or personal estate, for the purpose of securing any debt or debts that may be due to them, and for their own use and convenience."

margin: Funds, how invested

margin: Real or personal estate

2. This act shall be in force from its passage.

margin: Commencement

CHAP. 67.—An ACT to amend and re-enact section 12 of an act passed March 29, 1861, incorporating the Rockbridge Insurance Company.

Passed February 9, 1862.

1. Be it enacted by the general assembly, that the twelfth section of an act passed March twenty-ninth, eighteen hundred and sixty-one, entitled an act incorporating the Rockbridge insurance company, be amended and re-enacted so as to read as follows:

margin: Act of 1861 amended

* Tax paid since publication of Acts of 1862.

Commissioners	"§ 12. The persons named in the first section of said act shall be commissioners, whose duty it shall be, within six months after the passage of this act, at some suitable place in the town of Lexington,
Books	and at such other place as they may deem proper, to open books to receive subscriptions to the capital stock of said corporation; and five days' notice shall be given by said commissioners of the time and place of opening said books, in the newspapers published in the town of Lexington; which books shall not be closed in less than twenty days from the time of opening. The said commissioners shall give a like notice for a meeting of the stockholders to choose directors.
Property, how delivered	They shall supervise the first election of said officers, and shall deliver over to them, when so elected, any property belonging to the corporation that may have come into their hands."
Commencement	2. This act shall be in force from its passage.

Chap. 68.—An ACT to incorporate the Richmond Importing and Exporting Company.

Passed February 21, 1862.

Company incorporated	1. Be it enacted by the general assembly of Virginia, that Thomas W. McCance, John D. Harvey, Emanuel Miller, T. Edward Hambleton, Jr., Andrew L. Ellett, Alfred Moses, William Barrett, James L. Apperson, Robert H. Maury, William Boulware, William Allen, William G. Paine and Samuel J. Harrison, together with such other persons and firms as are now connected with them, under the name and style of the Richmond importing and exporting company, be and the same are, together with their successors and assigns,
Corporate name	hereby made and constituted a body corporate, under the said name
Powers	and style of The Richmond Importing and Exporting Company, for the purpose of owning, navigating and freighting ships and other vessels engaged in foreign and domestic commerce, trading from the
Capital	ports of the Confederate States of America. The capital of the said company shall not be less than five hundred thousand dollars nor more than two millions of dollars, and shall be held in shares of five
Affairs of company, how managed	hundred dollars each. The affairs of the company shall be managed by a president and board of directors, whose term of office and their number shall be determined and elected by the stockholders; and the said board of directors shall possess all the corporate powers of
Proviso	the company: provided, however, that nothing in this act shall change or affect the rights, obligations, exemptions and immunities of the said company, under the provisions of the laws of the Confederate States applicable to owners of vessels: and provided, that the said company shall be subject to such general laws as may affect corporations of this character.
Commencement	2. This act shall be in force from its passage, and shall be subject to repeal, modification or amendment, at the pleasure of the general assembly.

CHAP. 69.—An ACT to amend and re-enact an act entitled an act to incorporate the Richmond Importing and Exporting Company, passed February 21, 1863.

Passed March 12, 1863.

1. Be it enacted by the general assembly, that the act passed February twenty-first, eighteen hundred and sixty-three, entitled an act to incorporate the Richmond importing and exporting company, be amended and re-enacted so as to read as follows: *Company incorporated*

"Be it enacted by the general assembly of Virginia, that Thomas W. McCance, John D. Harvey, Emanuel Miller, T. Edward Hambleton, Jr., Andrew L. Ellett, Alfred Moses, William Barrett, James L. Apperson, Robert H. Maury, William Boulware, William Allen, William G. Paine and Samuel J. Harrison, together with such other persons and firms as are now connected with them, under the name and style of the Richmond importing and exporting company, be and the same are, together with their successors and assigns, hereby made and constituted a body corporate, under the said name and style of *Corporate name* The Richmond Importing and Exporting Company, for the purpose *Powers* of owning, navigating and freighting ships and other vessels engaged in foreign and domestic commerce, trading from the ports of the Confederate States of America, and with power to purchase and sell and otherwise to deal in the products and commodities so freighted or intended to be freighted."

2. The capital of the said company shall not be less than five *Capital* hundred thousand dollars nor more than two millions of dollars, and shall be held in shares of five hundred dollars each. The affairs of *Affairs, how managed* the company shall be managed by a president and board of directors, whose term of office and their number shall be determined and elected by the stockholders; and the said board of directors shall possess all the corporate powers of the company: provided, however, that nothing in this act shall change or affect the rights, obligations, exemptions and immunities of the said company, under the provisions of the laws of the Confederate States applicable to owners of vessels: and provided, that the said company shall be subject to such general laws as may affect corporations of this character.

3. This act shall be in force from its passage, and shall be subject *Commencement* to repeal, modification or amendment, at the pleasure of the general assembly.

CHAP. 70.—An ACT to incorporate the Prospect Tan-yard Company in the County of Prince Edward.

Passed February 2, 1863.

Company incorporated

1. Be it enacted by the general assembly of Virginia, that Joel Elam, James Venable, William Jones, S. F. Hunt, R. V. Davis, H. B. Brightwell, Isaac Glenn, T. Osborne, A. R. Venable, F. B. Watkins and J. J. Brightwell, and such other persons as may be associated with them, and their successors, shall be and are hereby incorporated and made a body politic, under the name and style of The Prospect Tan-yard Company; and by that name and style, may have a common seal, and be invested with all the rights and privileges, and made subject to all the limitations and restrictions contained in the Code of Virginia, so far as the same may be applicable, and not inconsistent with the provisions of this act.

Name of company *Rights and privileges*

Power to purchase real estate

2. The said company may purchase and hold real estate in the county of Prince Edward, not exceeding twenty acres, and such other property as they may deem necessary for the manufacture of leather, shoes and harness.

Capital

3. The capital stock of said company shall not exceed ten thousand dollars, and shall be divided into shares of fifty dollars each; and the shares shall be transferable agreeably to the by-laws of said company.

Commencement

4. This act shall be in force from its passage.

CHAP. 71.—An ACT to authorize the Bank of Rockingham to increase its Contingent Fund.

Passed January 29, 1863.

Contingent fund

1. Be it enacted by the general assembly of Virginia, that the Bank of Rockingham is authorized to increase its contingent fund to a sum not exceeding twenty per centum upon its capital stock paid in.

Commencement

2. This act shall be in force from its passage.

CHAP. 72.—An ACT to amend the Charter of the Bank of Rockingham.

Passed March 11, 1863.

1. Be it enacted by the general assembly, that the sixth, seventh, eighth, ninth, tenth and eleventh sections of the act passed on the twelfth day of January eighteen hundred and fifty-three, entitled an act to incorporate the Citizens Bank of Virginia, now known by the

name and style of the Bank of Rockingham, be and the same are hereby repealed.

2. That the twelfth section of the same act be and the same is hereby amended and re-enacted so as to read as follows: {*Charter amended*}

"§ 12. The charter of the said bank shall continue and be in force until the first day of April eighteen hundred and seventy-three." {*When charter expires*}

3. The treasurer of the state may retransfer to the said bank the certificates of the debt of the state and the bonds of internal improvement companies guaranteed by the state, now held by him in trust for the purposes of said bank, or any part thereof, upon receiving and canceling an equal amount of the notes of said bank countersigned by him; and if the notes of the said bank, so countersigned by him, have been so far returned and canceled as that the amount outstanding shall not exceed the sum of five thousand dollars, the said treasurer may retransfer the residue of said certificates or guaranteed bonds to said bank, upon receiving from at least five of the stockholders thereof, with at least five good and sufficient securities, to be approved by him, a joint and several bond, payable to the commonwealth of Virginia, in a penalty equal to at least three times the amount of such outstanding notes, and conditioned to pay the same on demand, at the place of business of said bank, or of either of the obligors therein: which bond shall be recorded in the manner prescribed in the fourth section of chapter one hundred and eighty-six of the Code of Virginia, and shall have the force of a judgment; and for every breach of the conditions thereof, execution may be issued, upon ten days' notice of the application therefor, in the name of the commonwealth, for the benefit of the holder of any such outstanding unredeemed notes, for the amount thereof and costs. {*Treasurer to retransfer certificates of debt held by him*} {*Bond and security to be given*} {*Bond to be recorded*} {*For breach of conditions, execution to issue*}

4. The bank shall not issue and pay out any notes for circulation, except of the denomination of five dollars, ten dollars, or some multiple of ten. {*Denomination of notes*}

5. Every quarterly statement of this bank shall, in addition to the information which the Code of Virginia requires to be made, also exhibit the aggregate debt due by the bank, the outstanding debts due to the bank, its discount of inland and foreign bills of exchange, its loans to directors, its specie, circulation and deposits on the first day of each month of the quarter it embraces. {*What to be exhibited in quarterly statements*}

6. The board of directors shall consist of not more than nine nor less than seven, as the stockholders may direct. {*Board of directors*}

7. Provided, that nothing in this act contained shall debar the Bank of Rockingham of the privileges contained in an act passed March twenty-ninth, eighteen hundred and sixty-two, entitled an act to provide a currency of notes of less denomination than five dollars. {*Proviso*}

8. This act shall commence and be in force from and after the {*Commencement*}

time when the provisions have been approved by the stockholders in said bank, convened in general meeting at any time before the first day of April eighteen hundred and sixty-four, and such approval shall have been made and certified by the president and cashier of said bank to the governor of the commonwealth.

CHAP. 73.—An ACT to legalize the Records, Proceedings and Acts of the County Court of Spotsylvania County, at the Terms of said Court held during the year 1862, at Places in the said County other than the Courthouse thereof.

Passed February 18, 1863.

Preamble

Whereas it has been represented to the general assembly of Virginia, that for the period of several months during the year eighteen hundred and sixty-two, the public enemy held military occupation of a large portion of Spotsylvania county, including the courthouse thereof; and that by reason of the interruption of the mail between said county and the city of Richmond, as well as the inexpediency of publishing any notice of the place where the sessions of the county court of said county might be held during such military occupation, it was deemed proper by the justices of said county not to apply to the governor of Virginia to designate some place other than the said courthouse, where the sessions of said court should be held, and that said justices accordingly proceeded to hold several terms of said court at places in said county other than said courthouse:

Records, proceedings and acts of court made at places other than court house legalized

1. Be it therefore enacted by the general assembly, that all the records, proceedings, acts and things made, ordered and done by the said county court, at the terms thereof held during the said year eighteen hundred and sixty-two, at places other than the said courthouse, which might have been legally made, ordered and done at said courthouse, are hereby declared and made legal and valid to the same extent as if ordered and done at the said courthouse.

Commencement

2. This act shall be in force from its passage.

CHAP. 74.—An ACT to enlarge the Powers of the Council of the City of Richmond.

Passed February 13, 1863.

Powers of council enlarged

1. Be it enacted by the general assembly of Virginia, that the council of the city of Richmond be and the same is hereby authorized to suppress riots and unlawful assemblies in the said city; to suppress gaming and gambling houses, tippling and tippling houses, and to prevent or regulate the sale of spirituous and fermented

liquors within the said city, and around the same to the boundaries to which the jurisdiction of its corporation courts or officers of police extends in criminal cases. And for the purposes of executing the powers and authority hereby vested in said council, the said council may enact ordinances and impose penalties for the violation thereof, not exceeding five hundred dollars, and imprisonment not exceeding three months; may authorize and empower the proper officers and police of the city to seize such liquors sold or kept for sale, for the use of the city, and to shut up the houses in which such liquors are so sold or kept for sale, and arrest the persons who shall sell or keep for sale or purchase the said liquors in violation of said ordinances, and hold them in custody until they shall give security for their good behavior in such penalty, not exceeding one thousand dollars, as the justice before whom they are taken shall prescribe. And the said officers and police shall have the same powers and authority in discharging their duties under said ordinances, as state officers have in cases of breaches of the peace. *Council may enact ordinances and impose fines, &c* *Persons to be arrested for violating ordinances* *Powers of officers, &c*

2. The said council may organize and establish an armed police, and appoint such officers thereof as to the council may seem expedient; and the said officers shall be accountable to, and under the supervision and control of the council, or such other body or officer as the council may prescribe. *Armed police organized*

3. This act shall be in force from its passage. *Commencement*

CHAP. 75.—An ACT to enlarge the powers of the Council of the city of Lynchburg.

Passed March 9, 1863.

1. Be it enacted by the general assembly, that the council of the city of Lynchburg be and the same is hereby authorized to suppress riots and unlawful assemblies in the said city; to suppress gaming and gambling houses, tippling and tippling houses, and to prevent or regulate the sale of spirituous and fermented liquors within the said city, and around the same to the boundaries to which the jurisdiction of its corporation courts or officers of police extends in criminal cases. And for the purposes of extending the powers and authority hereby vested in said council, the said council may enact ordinances and impose penalties for the violation thereof not exceeding five hundred dollars, and imprisonment not exceeding three months; may authorize and empower the proper officers and police of the city to seize such liquors sold or kept for sale, for the use of the city, and to shut up the houses in which such liquors are so sold or kept for sale, and arrest the persons who shall sell or keep for sale or purchase the said liquors in violation of said ordinances, and hold them in custody until they shall give security for their good behavior in such penalty, *Powers of council enlarged* *Council may enact ordinances and impose fines, &c* *Persons to be arrested for violating ordinances*

not exceeding one thousand dollars, as the justice before whom they are taken shall prescribe. And the said officers and police shall have the same powers and authority in discharging their duties under said ordinances, as state officers have in cases of breaches of the peace.

Powers of officers, &c

2. The said council may organize and establish an armed police, and appoint such officers thereof as to the council may seem expedient; and the said officers shall be accountable to, and under the supervision and control of the council, or such other body or officer as the council may prescribe.

Armed police organized

3. This act shall be in force from its passage.

Commencement

CHAP. 76.—An ACT to incorporate the Southern Female College of the City of Petersburg.

Passed January 27, 1863.

1. Be it enacted by the general assembly, that Dr. J. H. Claiborne, Col. R. M. Harrison, W. T. Joynes, T. L. H. Young, Wesley Gregg, J. H. Cooper, George B. Jones, P. H. Booth, George V. Scott, W. S. Harrison, Rev. B. R. Duval, Warner Eubank, Edwin Brown, R. H. Lyell and W. T. Davis, and their successors, be and they are hereby constituted a body politic and corporate, under the name and style of The Trustees of the Southern Female College of Petersburg, Virginia; and by that name shall have perpetual succession and a common seal, and may sue and be sued, plead and be impleaded in any court of law or equity. The said trustees of the Southern female college shall be capable in law to receive, hold and dispose of real and personal property, in order to carry out the purposes of their incorporation.

Institution incorporated

Trustees to hold real and personal property

2. The said Southern female college shall be under the control and management of the said trustees and their successors, who shall appoint a treasurer and all necessary officers and professors, and make such rules and regulations for the government of the institution as to them may seem fit, not inconsistent with the laws of Petersburg or of this state or of the Confederate States. Five of the trustees shall constitute a quorum for the transaction of business; and any vacancy in the said board of trustees, occasioned by death, resignation or otherwise, shall be supplied by appointment by the surviving trustees; and they may remove any member of their body, two-thirds of the whole number being present and concurring.

How managed

Quorum

How vacancy filled

3. The treasurer shall receive all moneys accruing to the college and property delivered to his care, and shall pay or deliver the same to the order of the board of trustees. Before entering upon the discharge of his duties, he shall give bond with such security and in such penalty as the board may direct, made payable to the trustees

Treasurer to receive moneys

To give bond

for the time being, and their successors, and conditioned for the faithful performance of the duties of his office, under such rules and regulations as the board may adopt; and it shall be lawful for the said trustees to obtain a judgment for the amount thereof, or for any special delinquency incurred by said treasurer, on motion in any court of record in this commonwealth against the treasurer and his or their executors or administrators, upon giving ten days' previous notice of the motion.

4. The said trustees are hereby authorized to raise by joint stock subscription, a sum not less than twenty thousand dollars nor more than one hundred thousand dollars, to be divided into shares of twenty-five dollars each; and from time to time shall declare such dividends on the same as the net profits of the college shall justify, and shall have power to collect the subscription to said stock in the manner now provided by law for collecting subscriptions to joint stock companies. *Amount of joint stock subscription. Dividends. Power to collect subscription.*

5. The board of trustees, in connection with the president and professors of the college, shall have power to confer such diplomas, medals, literary titles and honors as they may think best calculated to promote the cause of female education. *Power to confer diplomas.*

6. This act shall be in force from its passage, and shall be subject to amendment, modification or repeal, at the pleasure of the general assembly. *Commencement.*

CHAP. 77.—An ACT amending and re-enacting the 4th section of an act passed 22d January 1862, entitled an act to authorize the establishment of a Military School as a part of the Instruction of Randolph Macon College.

Passed March 11, 1863.

1. Be it enacted by the general assembly, that the fourth section of an act passed the twenty-second of January eighteen hundred and sixty-two, entitled an act to authorize the establishment of a military school as part of the instruction of Randolph Macon College, be amended and re-enacted so as to read as follows: *Act amended.*

"§ 4. They shall appoint such professors to give instructions in military science as they may deem proper, and may remove them for good cause, as already provided for in their charter." *Amendment.*

2. This act shall be in force from its passage. *Commencement.*

CHAP. 78.—An ACT authorizing the Sale, by the County Court, of the District School Houses, and the Lots of Land thereto attached, in the County of Henry.

Passed March 11, 1863.

Sale of district school houses authorized

1. Be it enacted by the general assembly, that the county court of Henry county, the justices of said county having been first duly summoned for that purpose, and a majority of the acting justices being present, is hereby authorized and empowered to order the sale of the district school houses in said county, and the lots of land thereto attached, which said houses were built under the act of assembly passed the twenty-fifth of February eighteen hundred and forty-six, authorizing the establishment of free schools in said county.

Power of court

Proceeds of sale, how disposed of

2. The said court shall have power to order the sale of all or a part of said school houses, as may be deemed most expedient;, and may prescribe the terms of the sale; but the proceeds thereof shall be used for the education of the indigent children of said county.

Court to appoint commissioners Bond and security to be given

3. For the purpose of carrying out the provisions of this act, the said court may appoint one or more commissioners, and take from them a bond with approved security, payable to the county, in such penalties as the said court may prescribe, with conditions for the faithful performance of their duties.

Commencement

4. This act shall be in force from its passage.

CHAP. 79.—An ACT authorizing the County Court of Henrico to establish a Public Pound.

Passed March 4, 1863.

Court to establish public pound

1. Be it enacted by the general assembly, that the county court of Henrico shall be and is hereby authorized to establish one or more public pounds within the limits of said county, at least one of which shall be within one mile of the city of Richmond, for confining such stock, horses, mules, cattle, hogs and sheep as may stray from their owners and be found trespassing upon the land of others.

What animals to be confined

Keepers to be appointed

2. Be it further enacted, that it shall be the duty of the county court (if they shall establish such pound) to appoint keepers or overseers of the same, and make such rules and regulations for the management thereof as they may deem proper.

How expenses are defrayed

Fines imposed

Proviso

3. Be it further enacted, that in order to defray the expenses of establishing and keeping the said pound (mentioned in the first section of this act), it shall be lawful for the county court aforesaid to impose such fine upon the owners of such stock as shall be confined in the same, as they may deem necessary for that purpose: provided,

that such fines shall not exceed the sum of two dollars per head for horses and mules, and fifty cents per head for all other stock.

4. When, after due notice, not less than five days, to be prescribed by the county court, any of the stock confined in said pounds shall not be reclaimed by their owners, the keepers or overseers of said pounds shall sell the same at public auction, at one of the market houses of the city of Richmond, after two days' notice stuck up at the said market house, and after defraying all the actual and necessary expenses incurred in connection with such stock (under rules prescribed by the county court), said bill of expenses to be assessed on the oath of the keeper or overseer, reserving to the owner the right of appeal from the decision of said keeper or overseer to the county court, shall pay over the balance to the owners of the same, or if the owners do not appear within sixty days, into the county treasury: provided, that said balance shall be paid to the owner, who may appear at any time within one year after such sale, and demand the same. *Stock nor claimed to be sold* *Where to be sold* *How bills of expenses assessed* *What amount to be paid to owners* *Proviso*

5. This act shall be in force from its passage. *Commencement*

CHAP. 80.—An ACT allowing the Lynchburg, Franklin, Citizens and Washington Building Fund Associations to purchase their Stock.

Passed March 11, 1863.

1. Be it enacted by the general assembly, that the president and directors of the Lynchburg building fund association of Lynchburg, the Franklin building fund association of Lynchburg, the Citizens building fund association of Lynchburg, and the Washington building fund association of Lynchburg, are hereby authorized to purchase (at their discretion) any portion of the stock of the said associations, when deemed by them to be to the interest of the said institutions to do so. *Power to purchase stock*

2. This act shall be in force from its passage. *Commencement*

CHAP. 81.—An ACT to incorporate the Richmond Harmonic Association.

Passed March 26, 1863.

1. Be it enacted by the general assembly of Virginia, that Charles Seibert, president, H. Wentzel, vice president, J. C. Fisher, secretary, C. Haase, cashier, J. T. Kohler, treasurer, and M. Tresh, librarian, and their associates, shall be and the same are hereby constituted a body politic and corporate, under the name and style of The Richmond Harmonic Association; and by that name and style, shall *Incorporated* *Name*

112 HARMONIC ASSOCIATION.—PRIVILEGES.

Rights, powers, &c be subject to all the rules, regulations and restrictions imposed, and invested with all the rights, powers and privileges conferred by chapters fifty-six and fifty-seven of the Code of Virginia (edition of eighteen hundred and sixty), and all other laws of this commonwealth applicable to such corporations.

Property to be held 2. That the said corporation may hold property, real and personal, to the value of forty thousand dollars.

Commencement 3. This act shall be in force from its passage, and shall be subject to amendment, modification or repeal, at the pleasure of the general assembly.

CHAP. 82.—An ACT allowing Sarah T. Thornton to remove certain Slaves from this State to the State of North Carolina.

Passed January 27, 1863.

Preamble Whereas it has been represented to the general assembly, that Sarah T. Thornton, relict of Dr. Richard Thornton of the county of Halifax, is possessed of a life estate in certain slaves received by her as dower from the estate of her said husband, and that said Sarah T. Thornton wishes to remove said slaves to the county of Granville, North Carolina:

County court to authorize removal of slaves 1. Be it enacted by the general assembly, that the county or circuit court of the county of Halifax shall have power, upon the petition of the said Sarah T. Thornton, to authorize her to remove said slaves to the said county of Granville, in such manner and upon such

Proviso terms as to the said court may seem proper: provided, that before such removal, a list of all the slaves to be removed, containing a description thereof, shall be filed in the clerk's office of the court autho-

Bond and security to be given rizing such removal: and provided further, that the said Sarah T. Thornton shall give bond and surety residing in Virginia, for the delivery of said slaves and their increase, at her death, to the persons

To report to court annually entitled to the same, and also for making annually a report of the increase of said slaves to the court granting said permission.

Court may require new bond to be given 2. Upon the application of any party interested, alleging the insolvency or insufficiency of the security in the said original or any subsequent bond, the court may, from time to time, after personal notice, or by publication, require a new bond, with ample security,

Penalty for failure to give new bond with condition similar to that herein before prescribed; and upon failure to give such bond and security, the forfeiture hereby intended to be saved shall be restored to those entitled to said property.

Commencement 3. This act shall be in force from its passage.

PRIVILEGES. 113

CHAP. 83.—An ACT for the relief of James M. Laidley and Thomas S. A. Matthews.

Passed March 21, 1863.

1. Be it enacted by the general assembly, that the auditor of public accounts be and he is hereby authorized to settle the judgment rendered against James M. Laidley and Thomas S. A. Matthews, commissioners of forfeited and delinquent lands for the county of Kanawha, by the circuit court of Richmond city, by allowing said Laidley to pay the principal due from them, after allowing proper credits, with interest at the rate of six per centum per annum, from the time the same was due and payable, after allowing reasonable time for money in transitu from the county of Kanawha to the city of Richmond, and the costs of said judgment; and upon such payment by said Laidley, the damages and the excess of interest over the six per centum embraced in said judgment, shall be deemed to be released. *Auditor autho- rized to make settlement*

Certain damages released

2. Be it further enacted, that in the event said Laidley shall pay the amount with which said commissioners are chargeable on the books of the auditor of public accounts, and he shall, at any time within twelve months from the date of a treaty of peace between the United States and the Confederate States of America, produce to the auditor of public accounts evidence of further credits and allowances to which said commissioners are, or may be entitled, then and in that event, said auditor shall refund to said Laidley such sum as he may have paid over and above the sum justly due from said commissioners. *In what event the auditor is to refund*

3. This act shall be in force from its passage. Commencement

CHAP. 84.—An ACT authorizing the Personal Representative of John M. Alderson, deceased, to deliver certain Militia Fines to the Sheriff of Greenbrier County.

Passed March 9, 1863.

1. Be it enacted by the general assembly, that it shall be lawful for the personal representative of John M. Alderson deceased, late sheriff of Greenbrier county, to deliver to the sheriff of said county any militia fines uncollected by said Alderson. *Militia fines to be delivered to the collector*

2. The sheriff shall give a receipt therefor, to account to the commonwealth for the same, within the time fixed by law from the time of delivery to him, and to have the same effect as if the said fines had been delivered on that day by the clerk of the regiment. Upon receipt of the sheriff being delivered to the auditor of public accounts, he shall charge the sheriff with the amount appearing due thereby, and give credit for a like amount to the account of the said Alderson. *Sheriff to give receipt*

Auditor to charge sheriff with the amount

3. This act shall be in force from its passage. Commencement

8

CHAP. 85.—An ACT for the relief of the Securities of William Paris, late Sheriff of Appomattox County.

Passed January 31, 1863.

Appropriation

1. Be it enacted by the general assembly, that the auditor of public accounts be and he is hereby authorized and required to issue his warrant on the treasury, payable out of any money not otherwise appropriated, in favor of John Johns, D. O. Bass, Silas P. Vawter, E. Legrand, W. W. Hamner, George S. Penn, Samuel J. Walker, Thomas R. Peers and N. Pamplin, securities of William Paris, late sheriff of Appomattox county, or their legal representatives, for the damages (less the costs of collection) on judgments in favor of the commonwealth against them as such securities, rendered by the circuit court of the city of Richmond on the thirteenth day of November eighteen hundred and fifty-eight: provided, that this act shall not be construed as releasing the said William Paris, late sheriff of Appomattox county, from the payment of any damages adjudged against him.

Amount

Proviso

Commencement

2. This act shall be in force from its passage.

CHAP. 86.—An ACT amending an act entitled an act for the relief of the Securities of William Paris, late Sheriff of Appomattox County, passed January 31st, 1863.

Passed February 20, 1863.

Relief to sureties

1. Be it enacted by the general assembly, that an act entitled an act for the relief of the securities of William Paris, late sheriff of Appomattox county, passed thirty-first of January eighteen hundred and sixty-three, be amended and re-enacted so as to read as follows:

Damages refunded

"That the auditor of public accounts be and he is hereby authorized and required to issue his warrant on the treasury, payable out of any money therein not otherwise appropriated, in favor of the securities of said William Paris, late sheriff of Appomattox, or their legal representatives, for the damages (less the costs of collection) on judgments in favor of the commonwealth against them as such securities, rendered by the circuit court of the city of Richmond, and the payment in pursuance thereof. But this act shall not be construed as releasing the said William Paris from the effect of said judgment and its payment, and any damages which may have been rendered against him by the judgments aforesaid: nor shall the money so paid by said securities and refunded by this act, be treated or held to be a payment on said judgment as to the said William Paris."

How this act shall be construed

How money refunded to be treated

Commencement

2. This act shall be in force from its passage.

PRIVILEGES. 115

CHAP. 87.—An ACT authorizing the Governor to deliver to B. B. and J. W. Cooley an Infant Child of a Slave named Harriet.

Passed March 10, 1863.

1. Be it enacted by the general assembly, that the governor of this commonwealth be and he is hereby authorized and directed to deliver to B. B. and J. W. Cooley, or their legal representatives, an infant child of the slave Harriet, who was condemned to be hung by the county court of the county of Frederick, and who died in the jail at Richmond before the sentence was carried into execution. *Governor to deliver to B. B. and J. W. Cooley infant child of Harriet*

2. This act shall be in force from its passage. *Commencement*

CHAP. 88.—An ACT authorizing the payment of a sum of money to B. B. and J. W. Cooley for a Slave condemned to be hung.

Passed February 17, 1863.

1. Be it enacted by the general assembly, that the auditor of public accounts be and he is hereby authorized and required to issue his warrant on the treasury, payable out of any money therein not otherwise appropriated, in favor of B. B. and J. W. Cooley, or their legal representatives, for the sum of four hundred dollars, that being the appraised value of a slave belonging to them, named Harriet, who was convicted of murder in the first degree, at the May term in the year eighteen hundred and sixty-one, of the Frederick county court, and who died in jail before the sentence was carried into execution. *Amount appropriated*

2. This act shall be in force from its passage. *Commencement*

CHAP. 89.—An ACT refunding a sum of money to Gordon and Brother, paid by them as a Merchant's License in the County of Fluvanna.

Passed March 19, 1863.

1. Be it enacted by the general assembly, that the auditor of public accounts be directed to issue his warrant on the treasury, payable out of any money therein not otherwise appropriated, in favor of Gordon and Brother, or to their personal representatives, for the sum of eighty-six dollars and forty cents, being the amount paid for a license as merchants in the county of Fluvanna. *Amount appropriated*

2. This act shall be in force from its passage. *Commencement*

PRIVILEGES.

CHAP. 90.—An ACT for the relief of Thomas Littleton, Jailor of Loudoun County.

Passed February 12, 1863.

Preamble

Whereas no court can be held for the county of Loudoun, by reason of the frequent inroads of the public enemy, and the usual certificate of such court cannot be obtained by Thomas Littleton, jailor of said county, to authorize payment of his account against this commonwealth for the keeping of prisoners, and for other matters: Therefore,

Auditor to pay account

1. Be it enacted by the general assembly of Virginia, that the auditor of public accounts be and he is hereby authorized to pay the account of said Thomas Littleton, jailor as aforesaid, upon such proof of the same as may be satisfactory to him.

Commencement

2. This act shall be in force from its passage.

CHAP. 91.—An ACT for the relief of George W. Chambers.

Passed March 16, 1863.

Preamble

Whereas the United States government was indebted to George W. Chambers in the sum of eight hundred and forty-nine dollars and forty cents, for twenty-two thousand six hundred and fifty pounds of castings made by him for said government, at the Harpers Ferry armory in Virginia, which said castings were taken possession of by the state of Virginia: and whereas the auditing board has recommended the payment of said claims by the legislature, on the ground that the state had seized the products of the labor of said George W. Chambers, for which he has received no compensation: Wherefore,

Amount appropriated

1. Be it enacted by the general assembly, that the auditor of public accounts be and he is hereby directed to issue his warrant on the treasury in favor of George W. Chambers, for the sum of eight hundred and forty-nine dollars and forty cents, in payment of the account of said Chambers, for twenty-two thousand six hundred and fifty pounds of castings, as recommended by the auditing board.

Commencement

2. This act shall be in force from its passage.

CHAP. 92.—An ACT for the relief of the Clerk of the Hustings Court of the City of Richmond.

Passed January 28, 1863.

Allowance to clerk in felony cases

1. Be it enacted by the general assembly, that the judge of the hustings court of the city of Richmond may make such allowance as

he may deem proper to the clerk of the said court for his services rendered in felony cases, not to exceed ten dollars for each felony case which may be disposed of in said court; to be paid by the council of the said city. *How paid*

2. This act shall be in force from its passage. *Commencement*

CHAP. 93.—An ACT for the relief of the Sergeant of the City of Richmond and the Sergeant of the City of Petersburg.

Passed January 29, 1863.

1. Be it enacted by the general assembly, that there be allowed and paid to Thomas U. Dudley, sergeant of the city of Richmond, and John H. Patterson, sergeant of the city of Petersburg, out of any moneys in the treasury not otherwise appropriated by law, the sum of twenty-five cents per day, in addition to the allowance heretofore authorized by law, for each person confined in the jails of the said cities, from the nineteenth day of May eighteen hundred and sixty-two, to the twenty-third day of September eighteen hundred and sixty-two, other than prisoners charged with or convicted of violation of any ordinance of the said cities: provided, however, that the number of such prisoners, and the date and the length of their confinement in said jails, shall be certified, sworn to and passed by the auditor of public accounts, in the manner prescribed by law for the allowance and payment of the accounts of sheriffs and sergeants for the maintenance, care and support of prisoners confined in the jails of this commonwealth. *Relief granted* *Amount appropriated* *Proviso*

2. This act shall be in force from its passage. *Commencement*

CHAP. 94.—An ACT to amend the 2d section of an act concerning the Estate of John Haskins, senior, a Lunatic, passed January 24, 1839.

Passed February 13, 1863.

1. Be it enacted by the general assembly, that section second of an act concerning the estate of John Haskins, senior, a lunatic, passed January twenty-fourth, eighteen hundred and thirty-nine, be amended and re-enacted so as to read as follows: *Act of 1839 amended*

"§ 2. That if the county court of the county of Brunswick should think it advisable, or to the interest of the parties interested, they shall have power and authority, upon the application of the said committee, or his successor, in the event of his death, or his powers being revoked, to authorize the said committee, or his successor, to sell the whole, or any part of said stock or stocks, acquired by the *Committee or successors to sell stock*

118 PRIVILEGES.

<small>To make investments</small>
proceeds of the sale of the estate of the said lunatic, under the provisions of the before recited act, and any stocks acquired under the provisions of this act, and to invest in like manner the proceeds arising therefrom, together with the annual surplus which may have accrued, or which shall hereafter accrue from the said estate, either from interest or otherwise, over and above the comfortable support and maintenance of the said lunatic, in stock of this commonwealth, or in any other stock authorized by the laws of this state, or in bonds or certificates of debt of the Confederate States, or in bonds of incorporated cities and towns; and the said county court, as well as the said committee, or his successor, as the case may be, shall be guided and governed by the provisions of the before recited acts, in all their proceedings except so far as the same may be herein altered or repealed."

<small>Commencement</small> 2. This act shall be in force from its passage.

CHAP. 95.—An ACT refunding to William M. Hume, Sheriff of Fauquier County, Damages paid by him as such.

Passed March 9, 1863.

<small>Appropriation</small> 1. Be it enacted by the general assembly, that the auditor of public accounts is hereby authorized and directed to issue his warrant on the treasury of the commonwealth, to be paid out of any money in the treasury not otherwise appropriated, in favor of William M. <small>Amount</small> Hume, for the sum of five hundred and thirty-two dollars and sixty-four cents (less the costs of collecting the same), being the amount of damages, at fifteen per centum, for default of the payment of license taxes for the county of Fauquier, due the thirtieth day of May eighteen hundred and sixty-one, recovered against the said Hume, by judgment rendered in the clerk's office of the circuit court of the city of Richmond, on the thirtieth day of July eighteen hundred and sixty-one; which damages, together with the amount of said licenses, with lawful interest thereon and costs, the said Hume has heretofore fully paid to the commonwealth; it appearing to the general assembly, that prior to the twenty-fifth day of May preceding the day when said license taxes became payable as aforesaid, the said Hume had deposited in the Farmers Bank of Virginia at Alexandria, money sufficient to pay the said license taxes, which, by reason of the public enemy taking possession of said town on the morning of the twenty-fifth of May aforesaid, he has been unable to the present time to realize.

<small>Commencement</small> 2. This act shall be in force from its passage.

PRIVILEGES. 119

CHAP. 96.—An ACT refunding to Samuel E. Lybrook, Sheriff of the County of Giles, a certain sum of money.

Passed March 19, 1863.

1. Be it enacted by the general assembly, that the auditor of public accounts be and he is hereby authorized and required to issue his warrant on the treasury, payable out of any money therein not otherwise appropriated, in favor of Samuel E. Lybrook, sheriff of Giles county, or his legal representative, for the sum of one hundred and ten dollars, that being the amount for taxes on ordinary licenses granted respectively to Warren A. Guy and to Stewart Rowan, for the year ending May eighteen hundred and sixty, each of said licenses amounting to fifty-five dollars; which said licenses were returned twice for the said year, and which erroneous assessment was ordered to be corrected by the county court of the county of Giles on April fourteenth, eighteen hundred and sixty-two. *Appropriation*

Amount

2. This act shall be in force from its passage. *Commencement*

CHAP. 97.—An ACT to pay E. W. Canfield and C. D. Bragg for services as Instructors of Artillery.

Passed March 17, 1863.

1. Be it enacted by the general assembly, that the auditing board be and they are hereby directed to allow and cause to be paid to E. W. Canfield, for three months and nine days' service as instructor and commander of artillery, under Brigadier General Carson, according to the pay per month of a first lieutenant of artillery in the confederate service; and to C. D. Bragg, for one month and seven days' service, at the same rate. *Payment to be made*

2. This act shall be in force from its passage. *Commencement*

CHAP. 98.—An ACT establishing an Election Precinct at Mill Swamp Meeting House, in the County of Isle of Wight.

Passed March 9, 1863.

1. Be it enacted by the general assembly, that at any general or special election for members of the general assembly, governor, lieutenant governor, attorney general, judges, commissioners of public works, for representatives in congress, and for electors of president and vice president of the Confederate States, polls shall be opened at Mill Swamp meeting house, in addition to the other places for voting now prescribed by law in the county of Isle of Wight. *Elections for governor, &c*

Where to be held

2. This act shall be in force from its passage. *Commencement*

RESOLUTIONS.

No. 1.—Resolution authorizing and directing the Governor to transfer the Prisoners, captured by the State Line, to the Confederate Government, except those held as Hostages for Colonel Zarvona and others.

Adopted March 28, 1863.

Resolved by the general assembly, that the governor be authorized and directed to transfer to the confederate government all the prisoners held by the state, mentioned in his communication of the ____ day of ____ (to be exchanged for Confederate States prisoners held by the United States government), except the prisoners who are detained as hostages for the release of Colonel Zarvona, Captain Duskey and Lieutenant Varner; and that he be authorized and requested to deliver up the said hostages for a similar purpose, as soon as he shall obtain the assurance of the confederate authorities that said hostages will be retained in their present confinement until arrangements are agreed on for the exchange of the prisoners for whose safety they are so held.

Transfer of prisoners

No. 2.—Resolutions expressing the high appreciation of the General Assembly of the patriotic fortitude and devotion displayed by the Women of Virginia, from the commencement of the present war.

Adopted March 26, 1863.

1. Resolved by the senate and house of delegates, that the grateful acknowledgments of the general assembly are due and are hereby cordially tendered to the women of Virginia, for their disinterested, generous and heroic devotion to the cause of their country during the pending war.

Patriotism appreciated

2. Resolved, that the civilized world cannot fail to regard with the highest admiration the sublime spectacle exhibited by the women of a whole community, elevated, refined, softened, purified by a high christian civilization, devoting all their energies to the public service, and beautifully blending a holy zeal for their country with humble piety to God.

Regarded with highest admiration

3. Resolved, that this inadequate tribute to their virtues be entered on the journals of both houses, as a lasting memorial of their exalted worth, that history may present to posterity so shining an example, and that our children's children, to the latest generation, may be incited thereby to deeds of heroism and public virtue.

Resolutions to be entered on journals

RESOLUTIONS.

No. 3.—Preamble and Resolutions in relation to the Disorderly Practices at the Virginia Military Institute in connection with the Case of Cadet William A. Daniel.

Adopted March 18, 1863.

Preamble

Whereas it appears, upon satisfactory evidence adduced before the general assembly, that Cadet William A. Daniel, then a junior cadet of the Virginia military institute, was on the eleventh day of November eighteen hundred and sixty-two, subjected to an unprovoked and cruel infliction of personal violence by cadets of the institute, and that no adequate protection was afforded him by the officers of the institution against a repetition of such violence; by which means said Cadet Daniel has been driven from the institute, and practically denied the benefits of its instruction: and whereas it appears also that the practice of such wanton violations of good order and humanity has been of long continuance and without proper restraint, at said institute: Therefore,

Unqualified condemnation

1. Resolved, that this general assembly hereby expresses its unqualified condemnation of such practice, as violative of good discipline, unjust to the peaceable and orderly cadets, injurious to the efficient administration of the institute, and unworthy the chivalrous character of our southern youth.

Instruction to officers

2. That the officers of said institution be and are hereby instructed to adopt such regulations and discipline in reference to said practice of wanton punishment of junior cadets, as will effectually discontinue

Disapprobation

and repress it; and that it is the opinion of the general assembly, upon the facts before them, that the efforts of the officers of said institute to suppress the vicious practice complained of, have not been such as meet with the approbation of this general assembly.

Requirement

3. That the officers of said institution be and they are hereby required, if Cadet William A. Daniel shall so desire, to reinstate him as a cadet of said institute, without prejudice to his position therein

Duty of officers

on account of his withdrawal therefrom in November last. And if the facts stated by him, in his letter to Mr. Robert Dabney, be substantially established, it is the further duty of said officers to drop from the rolls the name of every cadet who participated in the outrage.

No. 4.—Resolution to authorize the Governor to suspend the law of the 3rd October 1862, to further provide for the Public Defence, so far as it applies to those Counties whose loss of Slaves has been so great as to interfere with the Agricultural Products of said Counties.

Adopted January 27, 1863.

Action of law of October 1862 suspended

Resolved by the general assembly, that the governor be and he is hereby authorized to suspend the action of the law passed October third, eighteen hundred and sixty-two, to provide for the public defence, so far as it applies to those counties whose loss of slaves by the presence of the public enemy has been so great as to interfere with the agricultural products of such counties.

No. 5.—Resolution requesting the Governor to make application to the Secretary of War of the Confederate States for Passports for Members of the General Assembly, &c.

Adopted January 12, 1863.

1. Resolved by the general assembly, that the governor be and he is hereby authorized and requested to apply to the secretary of war of the Confederate States for passports to be issued to the members of the general assembly of this state, giving them the privilege of passing at will on any of the rail roads in the state, to and from the capital, or other place of holding their sessions, during the term for which they were elected, so that they may be saved the trouble of renewing their passports from time to time, under any general scheme of passports which may be put into operation applicable to other persons; and that the governor make a like application for similar passports for all the state officers who have occasion to pass to or from the capital. *Passports for members of the general assembly*

Passports for state officers

2. Resolved, that the foregoing resolution be certified, forthwith, after it is adopted, to Governor Letcher. *To be certified to governor*

No. 6.—Resolution in relation to Duration of the present Session of the General Assembly.

Adopted February 20, 1863.

Resolved, that the present session of the general assembly commenced on the fifteenth day of September last, under the proclamation of the governor bearing date on the nineteenth day of August eighteen hundred and sixty-two, and is not a continuation of the session which was commenced on the first day of April last, under the proclamation of the governor of that date, and continued in May following. *Commencement of session*

No. 7.—Preamble and Resolutions of Instruction to the Senators from Virginia, in relation to the subject of Impressment.

Adopted March 14, 1863.

Whereas it is of the utmost importance that a general impressment law should be passed, so that the burdens of this war should be *Preamble* to some extent equalized between the citizens of the states of the Confederate States: and whereas every day's delay in passing an impressment law is acting most injuriously and unjustly upon many citizens of this state, from the fact that their property is being seized, and the price paid for the same is far below the market value: and whereas the house of representatives of the congress of the Confederate States did, on the   day of   eighteen hundred and sixty-three, pass a bill entitled an act to authorize and regulate impressment of private property for the use of the army and other military purposes, which has been communicated to the senate of the Confederate States, but has not yet been finally acted upon by that body: and whereas the general assembly approve the principles and leading provisions of the said bill as it passed the house: Therefore,

Instruction to senators

1. Resolved by the general assembly, that our senators are hereby instructed to urge the passage of the said bill, or such bill as shall as effectually as possible, secure to the owner of property a just compensation, to be determined by an impartial board of assessors to be selected equally by both parties, so that it may become a law with as little delay as possible.

To be furnished to senators

2. Resolved, that a copy of the foregoing preamble and resolution be furnished to each of our senators.

No. 8.—Resolutions giving authority to Justices of the Peace, in a certain contingency, to appoint Commissioners of Elections.

Adopted March 30, 1863.

Justice of peace may appoint commissioners of elections

Resolved by the general assembly, that in such of the counties of this commonwealth as are in the occupation of the public enemy, so that the sessions of the county courts cannot be held therein, and commissioners of elections cannot be appointed, it shall be lawful, should such counties be temporarily or otherwise restored to our control, on the day of the next ensuing elections, and the county court shall not have time to act, for any justice of the peace to appoint commissioners of elections, and cause such elections to be held in pursuance of the laws now in force.

No. 9.—Joint Resolutions authorizing the Governor to demand of the President of the Confederate States to deliver C. J. A. Collins, who is confined, in prison, in North Carolina, to a Justice of the Peace in Prince George County, Virginia, to be tried.

Adopted March 5, 1863.

Preamble

Whereas, it is represented and believed, that C. J. A. Collins, a citizen of Prince George county, in the state of Virginia, and being a civilian in no way attached to the military service, was arrested by military orders, and was delivered to the provost marshal in the city of Petersburg, on the eighth of July eighteen hundred and sixty-two, who committed him to jail in said city, where he was confined until the eighteenth of November eighteen hundred and sixty-two, when and whence he was sent, under an armed escort, to Salisbury, in the state of North Carolina : and whereas, according to a memorandum in writing, furnished by the said provost marshal, as far as the records of his office show, the said Collins is still restrained of his liberty in that foreign jurisdiction : and whereas it is represented that other citizens of Virginia are in the same category :

1. Resolved, therefore, by the general assembly, that the governor be requested and is authorized to make application to the president of the Confederate States for the return to the jurisdiction of the commonwealth of the said C. J. A. Collins and any other citizens of Virginia that may now be imprisoned beyond the limits of the state. *Application for return of citizens imprisoned out of state*

2. Resolved, that the governor communicate any correspondence he may have with the president and other confederate officials on this subject. *Correspondence to be communicated*

No. 10.—Preamble and Resolutions tendering the Thanks of the General Assembly of Virginia to Major General John B. Floyd, and the Officers and Men under his command.

Adopted February 28, 1863.

The general assembly of Virginia, satisfied that the exigencies of the times require that the whole military strength of the Confederacy shall be united under one organization, and having under this conviction of public duty, transferred by law the state line under the command of Major General John B. Floyd, to the authorities of the Confederate States, and desirous of expressing to that eminent patriot and gallant soldier their high appreciation of his ability as a soldier, and of his unselfish course as a patriot, do resolve : *Preamble*

1. That the thanks of the general assembly of Virginia are due and are hereby tendered to Major General John B. Floyd, for the zeal, gallantry, ability and untiring devotion which he has exhibited in the command of the forces of this state. *Thanks to Gen. Floyd*

2. That the thanks of the general assembly are also tendered to the officers and soldiers under the command of Major General Floyd, for the efficiency and gallantry displayed by them while in the service of the state. *Thanks to officers*

No. 11.—Joint Resolutions directing the Auditor of Public Accounts to accompany his Biennial Report with the outline of a Tax Bill.

Adopted March 31, 1863.

Outline of tax bill to be reported by auditor.

Resolved by the general assembly, that the auditor henceforth accompany his biennial report with the outline of a tax bill, showing— 1. The aggregate amount of revenue proposed to be raised thereby. 2. The estimated amount of revenue expected to be yielded by every separate subject of taxation, and each different class of tax payers, with the principle and reasons on which the same is proposed to be levied. 3. Any recommendation of new subjects of taxation, or any suggestions on the general subject, which he may deem appropriate.

No. 12.—Resolution concerning the Transportation of Salt on Rail Roads and Canals.

Adopted March 31, 1863.

Control of board of public works over rail roads, &c explained.

Resolved by the general assembly, that in giving the board of public works the control over the rail roads and canals for the transportation of salt to be furnished pursuant to the act passed thirtieth March eighteen hundred and sixty-three, it is likewise the design of the general assembly that they should exercise like control over said roads and canals for the transportation of salt due or becoming due under the contracts with the counties.

No. 13.—Joint Resolution explanatory of a section of the act imposing Taxes for the Support of Government.

Adopted March 31, 1863.

Provision in favor of telegraph companies.

Resolved by the general assembly, that section eighty-three of the act imposing taxes for the support of government, which reads as follows: "No license shall be construed to grant any privilege beyond the county or corporation wherein it is granted unless it be expressly authorized," does not refer to telegraph companies whose lines run through more than one county or corporation.

No. 14.—Resolution ratifying the Contract with Stuart, Buchanan & Co.

Adopted March 30, 1863.

Ratification of contract with

Resolved by the general assembly, that the contract entered into on the twenty-fifth of March eighteen hundred and sixty-three, between Robert A. Coghill, chairman of the committee of the senate of Virginia, and H. B. Tomlin, chairman of the committee of the house of delegates of Virginia, the two committees constituting a joint committee of the general assembly, on the subject of a supply of salt, and Stuart, Buchanan and Company, in the following words and figures: Stuart, Buchanan & Co

Articles of agreement, made this twenty-fifth day of March eighteen hundred and sixty-three, between Robert A. Coghill, chairman of the committee appointed by the senate of Virginia, and Harrison B. Tomlin, chairman of the committee appointed by the house of delegates of Virginia, the two committees constituting a joint committee of the general assembly of Virginia, on the subject of a supply of salt, and acting as such, for and on behalf of the commonwealth, of the first part, and Stuart, Buchanan and Company, of the second part: Contract

Witnesseth, that the said Stuart, Buchanan and Company do propose, without the right to retract or withdraw the same, the following terms for the lease and sale of certain real and personal property necessary for the production of salt for the people of this commonwealth, and the parties of the first part do accept the same on behalf of the said joint committee—but their action shall not be binding on the said commonwealth, unless this agreement shall be ratified and confirmed by the general assembly of Virginia, at its present session:

The said Stuart, Buchanan and Company agree to lease to the commonwealth, for the term of one year, fully to be completed, commencing on the first day of April eighteen hundred and sixty-three, and ending one year thereafter, or after the day on which possession is actually given, the following property, viz:

1. A portion, from one hundred to two hundred acres, convenient to the "river works," of a certain tract of land, known as the "Preston estate," for agricultural purposes; which is to be laid off by the arbitrators herein after provided for. Description of property

2. The ten furnaces, counting the double furnace as two, four of which are now leased and operated by Friend, Clarkson, Kelley and Gardner, and four known as the "river works," including the conduits, fixtures, tools used in connection with said furnaces, the dwelling houses and stables at the "river works," and all stables and out houses at the upper works, under the control of Stuart, Buchanan and Company. And the said commonwealth shall have the privilege of cutting, quarrying and carrying away from any of the lands owned by Palmer and Stuart, outside of the Preston and King estates, or either of them, stone, wood and timber, and an equal right with the said Stuart, Buchanan and Company under their lease, to cut, quarry and remove stone, wood and timber from the King estate and the Preston estate; but the lease of the four furnaces now held by Friend, Clarkson, Kelley and Gardner is subject to the contract of

lease between them and Stuart, Buchanan and Company: and the state assumes the position of said lessors as to said lease.

Said Stuart, Buchanan and Company also bind themselves to pump to the surface and furnish to the commonwealth, salt water sufficient to supply and to keep in continued operation the said ten furnaces, to their full boiling capacity; and this stipulation means and intends that said supply of brine to the said ten furnaces is to be prior to any other supply to be furnished to any other contracting party, and prior to any right of user of brine by said Stuart, Buchanan and Company: but it is expressly agreed by the said Stuart, Buchanan and Company, that the commonwealth may lease or transfer to any other person the property and privileges hereby intended to be leased or conveyed, and that the sub-lessees or transferrees shall be entitled to all the rights and privileges hereby conveyed to the commonwealth.

Said Stuart, Buchanan and Company agree to sell and deliver to the commonwealth one-half of all the wagons, harness, horses, mules, sacks, provisions, forage and other personal property owned by them, and needful for the manufacture and distribution of salt; also one-half of all the wood now cut and in their possession, or contracted for and cut, and intended to be used by them for the manufacture of salt; also to deliver to the commonwealth all the slaves of Col. J. N. Clarkson hired by them, and one-half of all other slaves hired by them, at the same rate of hire for the residue of the year, at which they the said Stuart, Buchanan and Company have hired them; and the commonwealth agrees to assume all their liabilities as to said slaves.

It is further agreed that said Stuart, Buchanan and Company shall allow to said commonwealth good and convenient ways to and from said furnaces, together with wood yards and appurtenances, affording ample space for conveniently operating said ten furnaces.

Submission to arbitration, &c   And the said parties of the first and of the second parts, being unable to agree upon the price to be paid by the commonwealth for the foregoing lease and purchase and other privileges, do hereby mutually agree that the same shall be submitted to the arbitrament and award of three disinterested citizens of the commonwealth, or a majority of them, one of whom shall be chosen by the commonwealth or her authorized agent, and one by the said Stuart, Buchanan and Company; and the two so chosen to select a third; and if any of the said arbitrators should die, fail or decline to act, his place shall be supplied in the manner in which he was originally selected.

And the parties of the first part agree that the sum thus ascertained by the said board, each one of whom shall be sworn before proceeding to act, shall be paid in confederate currency to the said Stuart, Buchanan and Company whenever the value is so ascertained and possession delivered: and they the said Stuart, Buchanan and Company do agree to receive the same in full discharge of this contract to the said Stuart, Buchanan and Company by the commonwealth: but the commonwealth reserves the right to impress the whole of the property hereby intended to be conveyed, if the said Stuart, Buchanan and Company shall not in good faith execute this contract in all its parts.

Witness the following signatures:

R. A. COGHILL,
Ch'n of Senate Committee.

H. B. TOMLIN,
Ch'n of House Committee.

STUART, BUCHANAN & CO.

--be and the same is hereby ratified and confirmed.

No. 15.—Preamble and Resolution advising the people of the Commonwealth in relation to the increase and preservation of certain Agricultural Productions and Supplies.

Adopted March 31, 1863.

The general assembly of Virginia, moved by a deep sense of the importance, at this time, of raising, above all things, an abundance of provisions and of forage for the uses of our armies and of the people at large; confident in our ample resources of production, as well as in the public spirit and patriotic zeal of our citizens; and fearing no deficiency or serious inconvenience, beyond what at all times may occur from unfavorable seasons, except such as might result from over confidence in those resources, or from not sufficiently adverting to the large space of our territory temporarily disabled from furnishing its usual contribution to the public wants, and to other considerable portions of the Confederacy cut off for the present from their usual sources of supply; but still deeming it their highest duty to guard as far as possible, against even the chance of so great a calamity as a scarcity of provisions, do therefore resolve:

That they earnestly recommend to every citizen of the state that he shall aim to increase, greatly beyond his usual amount, all his agricultural products of every kind whatsoever; his grain and his grass crops; his live stock; his fruits and his garden vegetables; every thing, indeed, that goes to the sustenance of man and beast, before he shall apply his labor to any other object or employment whatever; that he constantly practice frugality in using his resources of food, and bear in mind always to consume first what is most perishable, in order that he may husband his whole stock to the best advantage; and they enjoin it upon and make it the special charge of every justice of the peace throughout all the state, not occupied by the enemy, to visit his neighbors and urge it upon them to act promptly and effectually on this recommendation, as a work of true patriotism, a sacred duty to the cause of the independence and safety

Increase of agricultural products, &c. &c. recommended

of the Confederate States, and as furnishing to the world the evidence of their firm and immovable determination to incur every sacrifice, and to omit no effort that may be necessary to the success of that holy cause.

No. 16.—Resolutions authorizing the County and Corporation Courts to prepare and preserve a durable Record of the Names and Deeds of Conspicuous Merit of all who have or shall have served honorably in our armies in the present war.

Adopted March 19, 1863.

Record to be kept of persons serving honorably in the war

1. Resolved by the general assembly, that the court of any county and corporation of this state shall be authorized to purchase and preserve among its archives a suitable book, wherein, under the superintendence and direction of such court, shall be inscribed the names of all persons belonging to such county or corporation, who have, or shall have, in any capacity, served honorably in the armies of the Confederate States or of this state, in the present war; and also, in a form to be approved by, and on proofs satisfactory to all the members of any such court, sitting as such, a concise record of any acts of conspicuous merit that shall have been performed by any such person.

Plan, &c. to be prepared and furnished by adjutant general

2. That a plan of such book, tabulated in the manner of the army rolls, but with such changes as may be deemed advisable, shall be prepared by the adjutant general, subject to the approval of the governor; and when so approved, books, prepared in conformity thereto, shall, as applied for by any such county or corporation court, be furnished, at its expense, to any such court, by the adjutant general, together with lists, extracted from the army rolls in his possession, of all persons found listed therein as belonging to such county or corporation.

No. 17.—Resolutions authorizing the disbanding of the State Line, &c.

Adopted March 24, 1863.

Disbanded

1. Resolved by the senate and house of delegates, that the forces heretofore known as the "state line" and "partizan rangers," be and they are hereby disbanded on and after the first day of April eighteen hundred and sixty-three.

State arms, &c. to be collected and transferred to confederate government

2. Resolved, that the governor be instructed to use all proper diligence in collecting the state arms and other public property in their possession, and to proceed, as far as can be done under existing circumstances, to execute the provisions of the act of assembly, by transferring the arms and other public property to the confederate government:

Proviso

provided, that all persons belonging thereto may volunteer, or if subject to conscription, may be conscripted into the military service of the Confederate States at any time prior to said date.

SEPARATE ELECTION PRECINCTS.

Accomack—Court-house; Chingoteague; New Church; Corbin and Fletcher's; Mapp's; Guilford;. Newstown; Onancock; Pungoteague.

Albemarle—Court-house; Lindsay's Turnout; Everettsville; Stony Point; Earleysville; Blackwell's; Free Union; Whitehall; Woodville; Batesville; Hillsborough; Crossroads; Covesville; Porter's; Warren; Wingfield's; Milton; Scottsville; Monticello House; Howardsville.

Alexandria—Five districts—Identical with magisterial districts.

Alleghany—Court-house; Robert Skeen's Hotel; John O. Taylor's; George Stull's; Clifton Forge; Jabez Johnston's; Griffith's Mill; Fork Run.

Amelia—At the same place as magisterial elections.

Amherst—New Glasgow; New Hope; Oronoco; Chestnut Grove; Folly; Temperance; Pedlar Mills; Elon; Court-house; Buffalo Springs.

Appomattox—Court-house; Union Academy; Wesley Chapel; Hamner's; Spout Spring; Oakville.

Augusta—Court-house; Waynesborough; Middlebrook; Spring Hill; Mt. Meridian; Greenesville; District No. 2, Staunton; Mt. Sidney; Stuart's Draft; Fishersville; Churchville; New Hope; Craigsville; Deerfield; Mt. Solon; Swoop's Mill; Midway; Newport.

Barbour—Court-house; Burner's; Nutter's; Bartlett's; Mitchell's; Yeager's; Glady Creek; Holtsberry's; Coal Precinct.

Bath—Court-house; Cedar Creek; Hamilton's; Cleek's Mill; Williamsville; Milton; Green Valley.

Berkeley—Court-house; Billingre's Hotel; Mill Creek; Hedgesville; Falling Waters; Robinson's Mill; Gerrardstown; Oak Grove; Glen Spring; Crossroads.

Boone—Court-house; Adkins' on Mud river; Adkins' on Big Coal; Lawrence's; Curtiss'; Daniel Laurel's; Thompson's Mill; Miller's.

Botetourt—Court-house; Mountain Union; Carver's; Buchanan; Rocky Point Mills; Jackson; Junction Store; Dibrell's Spring; Amsterdam.

Braxton—Court-house; Triplett's; Rilney's; Cool's; John Crite's former Residence; Christian Moda's former Residence; Haymond's Mill; Cunningham's; Saulsberry; Stonestreet; Jacob P. Conrad's.

Brooke—At same place as magisterial elections; Goodwill School-house.

Brunswick—Court-house; Benton Precinct; Trotty's Store; Oak Grove; Lucy's Store; Smoky Ordinary; Nicholson's Precinct.

Buckingham—Court-house; Stanton's Shop; New Store; Wright's; Curdsville; Allen's

Cabell—Court-house; Guyandotte; Laidley's Store; Spurlock's; Doolittle's Mill; Barrett's Precinct; McComas'; Falls of Guyandotte; Killgore's Precinct; Peter Buffington's.

Campbell—Places the same as for magisterial elections.

Caroline—Court-house; Reedy Church; Oakley's; Needwood; Sparta; Pitts'; Port Royal; Sycamore; Golansville; Madison's.

Carroll—Court-house; Polly Quesenberry's; Thomas Quesenberry's; Laurel Fork; Kinney's; Easter's; Newman's; Sulphur Springs; Richard Haynes'; Nathaniel Haynes'.

Charles City—Court house; Delarue's; Ladd's; Waddell's; Apperson's; Vaiden's.

Charlotte—Court-house; Keysville; Smith's Tavern; Clement's; Wyliesburg; Roby's Shop; Hawrey's Store; Matthews & Smith's Store.

Chesterfield—Court-house; Britton's Shop; Shell's Tavern; Manchester; Robinson's Store; Clover Hill.

Clarke—Court-house; Russell's Tavern; White Post; Millwood; Royston's Tavern; Collier's Toll-gate.

Craig—Court-house; Carper's Tavern; Walker's Store; Scott's Tavern; Martin Huffman's; George Sarver's.

Culpeper—Court-house; Rixyville; Colvin's; Stevensburg; Pottsville; Gathright's; Wellsborough; Griffinsburg.

Cumberland—Court-house; Tavern Precinct; Oak Forest; Irwin's.

Dinwiddie—Court-house; Billups'; Goodwynsville; Williams' Shop; Darvill's; Williams'; Sutherland's.

Doddridge—Court-house; Allen's; Bond's; Key's; Davis'.

Elizabeth City—Court-house; Liveley's Ordinary; Fox Hill.

Essex—Court-house; Occupacion; Lloyd's; Miller's; Bestland; Centre Cross.

Fairfax—Court-house; Crossroads; Arundel's; Sangster; Ross'; Dranesville; Anandale; West End; Accotink; Centreville; Falls Church; Fars; Bayless; Pulman's.

Fauquier—Court-house; Plains; Salem; White Ridge; Farrowsville; Orleans; Liberty; Morrisville; Paris; New Baltimore; Rectortown; Weaversville; Upperville.

Fayette—Court-house; Blake's; Gauley Bridge; Fleshman's; Lewis'; Keeney's; Terry's; Coleman's.

Fluvanna—Court-house; Howard's Store; Columbia; Morris' Store; Kent's Store; Haden's Store; Bashan and Snead's; Bledsoe's; Union Grove.

Franklin—Court-house; Allen's; Union Hall; Booth's Store; McVey's Tanyard; Helm's; Dickerson's; Kinsey's; Richland Grove; Bush's Store; Sydnorsville; Snow Creek; Aldridge's Store.

Frederick—Court-house; Engine-house; Gwinn's Tavern; Hoover's Tavern; Newtown; Middletown; Russell's; Anderson's; Brucetown; Swhier's; Cole's School-house; Pughtown.

Giles—At the same places as magisterial elections; Howe's Hotel.

Gilmer—Court-house; Jerkland; Burke's; Widow Stump's; De Kalb's; Peregrine Hays'; Knott's; Hewett's; Troy.

Goochland—Court-house; Little Store; Perkinsville; Smith's Shop; Mills'; Holland's; Poor's; Jennings'.

Gloucester—Places the same as for magisterial elections.

Greenbrier—Court house; Blue Sulphur Springs; Lick Creek; Anthony's Creek; Spring Creek; Southside; Lewisburg; White Sulphur; Miller's; Irish Corner; Williamsburg; Frankfort.

Greene—Court-house; Ruckersville; Terrill Shiflett's; McMullansville.

Greenesville—Court-house; Ryland's Depot; Blunt's Mill; Poplar Mount.

Halifax—Court-house; Meadesville; Mount Carmel; Halifax Springs; High Hill; Hudson's; Garrett's Store; Whiteville; Republican Grove; Brooklyn.

Hampshire—Court-house; John Liller's; Miers'; Burlington; Taylor's; Doyles'; Thompson's; Lupton's; Kisner's; Lovett's; Mrs. Offutt's; Stump's; Fority; Sherrard's School-house; Hash's; Blair's; Arnold's; Piedmont.

Hancock—Court-house; Holliday's Cove; New Manchester; Aton's School-house.

Hanover—Court-house; Hughes'; Jones' Crossroads; Negrofoot; Dentonsville; Cold Harbor; Ashland.

Harrison—Court-house; Shinnston; Union Meeting-house; West Milford; Lumberport; Bridgeport; Davis'; Lynch's; Sardis; Swisher's Mills.

Henrico—Court-house; Kidd's; Sweeney's; Alley's; Lovingsteine's; Dickman's; Hughes'; Walkerton; Hungary.

Henry—Court-house; Rough and Ready; Irisburg; Oak Level; Leatherwood; Ridgway; Horse Pasture.

Highland—Monterey; Ruckmansville; Wiley's; Crab Bottom; Doe Hill; McDowell; Pullins' School house; Gwin's.

Jackson—Ripley; Click's; Jones'; Range's; California; Depue's; Three forks of Reedy; Trumansville; Ravenswood; Squire Slaven's; Murrayville; Moor's Mill; MoGrew's Mill.

James City—Court-house; Burnt Ordinary; York River.

Jefferson—Eight districts—Places the same as for magisterial elections.

Kanawha—Court-house; Fleetwood's; Richards'; Bradley Low's; Atkinson's Mill; Altzs'; Couts' Month; Dog Creek; Givens'; Malden; Fork Coal; Harper's; Gatewood's; Mouth Sandy; Brooks' Store.

King George—Court-house; Hampstead; Clifton; Shiloh.

King & Queen—Court-house; Clark's Store; Stevensville; Newtown; Centreville.

King William—Court-house; Plain Dealing; Aylett's; Lanesville.

Lancaster—Court-house; Litwalton; Kilmanock; White Stone.

Lewis—Court-house; McLaughlin's Store; Jane Lew; Freeman's Creek; Skin Creek; Hall's Store; Leading Creek; Collins' Settlement.

Logan—Same places as for magisterial elections.

Loudoun—Court-house; Waterford; Lovetsville; Hillsborough; Waters'; Purcell's Store; Snickersville; Union; Middleburg; Mt. Gilead; Gum Spring; Whaley's; Goresville.

Louisa—Court-house; Free Union; Hopkins' Mill; Trevilian's; Bell's Crossroads; Walton's Tavern; Terrell's Store; Parrish's Store; Frederickshall; Bumpass' Turnout; Thompson's Crossroads; Isbell's Store; Hope's Tavern; Gentry's Store; Cosby's Tavern.

Lunenburg—Court-house; Brown's Store; Pleasant Grove; Knight and Oliver's Mill; Lochlomond; Bagley's Store; Jordan's Store.

Madison—Court-house; Stony Hill; Criglersville; Huffman's Mill; Graves' Mill; Rapidan Meeting house; Fleshman's Shop; Locust Dale.

Marion—Places the same as those for magisterial elections, and at Glover's Gap.

Marshall—Court-house; Pleasant Hill; Jones' Hotel; Bleak's School-house; Parsons' Precinct; Mouth of Fish Creek; Sand Hill; Crossroads; Smart's School-house; Burley's; Terrill's School-house; Big Run; Fair View; Linn Camp.

Mason—Court-house; Berriage Precinct; Love Precinct; Barnett Precinct; West Columbia; Neaso Precinct; Eighteen Mile Precinct; Grigg's; Sixteen Mile Precinct; Thirteen Mile Precinct.

Matthews—Same places as for magisterial elections.

Mecklenburg—Court-house; Jones'; Edmundson's; Clarkesville; Reeke's; Overby's; Wright's; Harwell's; Christiansville; Gillespie's.

Middlesex—Jamaica; Saludo; Sandy Bottom.

Monongalia—Court-house; Guseman's; Jones'; Osburn's; Ross'; Lofter's; Cassville; Cristiman's; Laurel Point; Cox's; Moore's River; Tenant's; Dowall's; Warren.

Monroe—Court-house; Dickson's; Miller's Store; Rollinsburg; Mrs. Peck's; Red Sulphur; Haynes'; Centreville.

Montgomery—Court-house; Guerrant's; Peterman's; Price's Forks; Keister's; Crumpacker's; Lafayette; Kent and McConkey's; Rough and Ready; Lovely Mount.

Morgan—Court-house; Lowe's; Baker's; Unger's; Hume's; Swann's; Miller's.

Nansemond—Court-house; Hargrove's Tavern; Harrison's Shop; Holyneck; Chuckatuck; Somerton; Darden's Store; Cypress Chapel.

Nelson—Fortune's; New Market; Faber's Mill; Greenfield; Massie's Mill; Roberts'.

New Kent—Court-house; Barhamsville; Chandler's Store; Ratcliff's Tavern.

Nicholas—Court-house; Taylor's; Brown's; Neil's; Dunbar's; Nutter's; Sawyer's; Pierson's.

Norfolk City—Four Wards.

Norfolk County—Court-house; Glebe School-house; Sycamore's; Deep Creek; School-house, District No. 2; School-house in Providence; Pleasant Grove School-house; Butts' Road School-house.

Northampton—Court-house; Bay View; Franktown; Johnsontown; Capeville.

Northumberland—Court-house; Lottsburg; Burgess' Store; Wicomico.

Nottoway—Court-house; Jennings' Ordinary; Wilson and Jones'; Blackfare.

Orange—Court-house; Barboursville; Thomas Smith's; Thomas Rhoade's; Locust Grove.

Page—Court-house; Honeyville; Oakham; George Price's Mill; Springfield; Mohler's Mill; Rileysville; Prunty's Mill.

SEPARATE ELECTION PRECINCTS. 135

Patrick—Court-house; Robertson's; Aldridge's and Lee's; Penn's Store; Carter's Store; Hancock's; Elamsville; Slusher's; Connor's; Shilor's; Gates'; Mankin's.

Pendleton—Franklin; Harper's; Kiser's; Vint's; Cowyer's Mill; Mallow's; Seneca; Circleville.

Petersburg—Centre Ward; East Ward; South Ward; West Ward.

Pittsylvania—Court-house; Danville; Spring Garden; Whitmell; Cascade; Smith's; Beaver's; Riceville; Rorer's; Strail's Store; White's; Laurel Grove; Chalk Level; Mooman's.

Pleasants—Court-house; Spring Run; Sugar Creek; Pine Grove; Hale's Mill.

Pocahontus—Four districts—Places of election the same as for magistrates.

Powhatan—Court-house; Clarke's Mill; Macon; Sublett's.

Preston—Brandonville; Miller's; Burnel's; Feather's; Summit School-house; Germany; Graham's; Huddlesin's; Kingwood; Martin's; Independence; Evansville; Nine's; Funk's

Princess Anne—Court-house; Kempsville; London Bridge; Capp's Shop; Creed's Bridge; Blackwater.

Prince Edward—Court-house; Marble Hill; Spring Creek; Prospect; Farmville; Sandy River.

Prince George—Court-house; City Point; Lilley's School-house; Tuttle's Precinct; Harrison's Store; Templeton.

Prince William—Dumfries; Cole's; Occoquan; Reeve's; Brentsville; Kinchelon's; Haymarket; Ludley.

Pulaski—Court-house; Brown's; Galbreath's; Ruper's; Thorn Spring Camp.

Putnam—Court-house; Bailey's; Pocatalico; Alexander's; Red House; Jones'; Hurricane Bridge; Wheeler's; Buffalo; Eighteen Mile Precinct.

Raleigh—Same places as magisterial elections.

Randolph—Court-house; Pennington's; Minear's; Taylor's; Kemp's; Lee.

Rappahannock—Washington; Sperryville; Yates'; Amissville; Catherine Deatheridge.

Richmond City—Jefferson Ward; Madison Ward; Monroe Ward.

Richmond County—Court-house; Stony Hill; Tavern-House; Farnham Church; Lyell's Store.

Ritchie—Harrisville; Skelton's; Leedan's; Ireland's; Deems'; Rawson's; Tebbs'; Murphy's.

Roanoke—Court-house; Big Lick; Cave Spring; Barnett's.

Rockbridge—Court-house; Brownsburg; Fairfield; Natural Bridge; Collierstown; Kerr's Creek; Trevey's; Hamilton's School-house; Paxton's School-house; Wilson's Shop; Broad Creek; Goshen.

Rockingham—Harrisonburg; Keezletown; McGaheysville; Conrad's Store; Spartapolis; Henton's Mills; Gordon's Store; Bowman's Mill; Timberville; Menonite School-house; Bridgewater; Ottobine; Wittig's Store; Sprinkle's Store; Taliaferro's Store; Port Republic; Mount Crawford; Samuel Coots'.

Russell—Court-house; Grizle's; Pound; Holly Creek; Guest's Mountain; Castlewood's; Fugate's; Hanson's; Aston's Store; Cook's Mills; Dorton's; Baylor's Store; Gibson's; Hendrick's Store.

Scott—Court-house; Winegar's; Hart's; Smith's; Puilleng's; Nickelsville; Alley's; Osborne's Ford; Stony Creek; Peters'; Rye Cove; Carter's; Neil's; Roller's.

Shenandoah—Court-house; Strasburg; Crossroads Meeting-house; Conner's Church; Town Hall; Keller's School-house; Edinburg; Columbia Furnace; Mount Jackson; Crossroads School-house; New Market; Forrestville.

Smyth—Court-house; Broad Ford; Hays'; Sanders'; St. Clair's Bottom; Burton's Store; Ashlin's; Atkins'.

Spotsylvania—Court-house; Fredericksburg; Mount Pleasant; Andrews'; Chancellor's.

Stafford—Court-house; White Oak; Master's; Tackett's Mill; Falmouth; Coakley's; Harwood's; Acquia.

Southampton—Court-house; Drewrysville; Crosskeys; Joyner's; Murfee's; Black Creek Church; Berlin; Faison's Store.

Surry—Four districts—At the same places as for election of magistrates.

Sussex—Court-house; Conunn's Mill; Henry; Stony Creek; Newville; Owen's Store.

Taylor—Court-house; Mahaney; Reed's; Claysville; Knottsville; Haymond's; Fetterman; Grafton.

Tazewell—Court-house; Repass; Tiffany's; Mouth of Slate; Gibson's; Crabtree's; Litzeville; Liberty Hill; Tugg.

Tyler—Court-house; Centreville; David John's; Hammond's; Underwood's; Dancer's; Sistersville; Pleasant Mills.

Upshur—Court-house; Reedy Mills; Simpson's Mill; Posty; Marples; Marshall's; Chesney's.

Warren—Court house; Boyd's Mill; Bentonville; Leary's School-house; Cedarville; Howellsville.

Warwick—Three precincts—The same as for election of magistrates.

Washington—Court house; Clark's; Davis'; Waterman's; Merchant's; Gobble's; Mills'; Worley's; Williams'; Morell's; Fullen's School-house; Clark's; Kelly's School-house; Dolusko Mills; Ons'; Miller's; Good Hope; Green Spring.

Wayne—William Crum's. (No other returned.)

Westmoreland—Court-house; Hague; Warrensville; Oak Grove.

Wetzel—Court-house; Forks of Proctor; Knob Fork; Church's; Cohorn's; Ice's; Willey's School house.

Williamsburg—Court-house.

Wirt—Court-house; Foster's; Petty's.

Wood—Precincts at the same places as election for magistrates.

Wyoming—Court house; Gad's; Rhineheart's; McKinney's; Bailey's; Lester's.

Wythe—Eight districts—Precincts at same places as for election of magistrates.

York—Three districts—Precincts at the same places as for election of magistrates.

TABLE

Showing the Times for the Commencement of the Regular Terms of each Circuit, County and Corporation Court.

Counties and corporations.	Circuit courts. When terms commence.	County and corporation courts. Monthly terms.	County and corporation courts. Quarterly terms.
	Circuits.		
Accomack,	5. 1st Monday in May and 1st day of November,	Last Monday,	March, May, August, Novem.
Albemarle,	10. 2d Monday in May and Oct	First Monday,	Do. June, do. do.
Alexandria,	9. 3d Monday in May and 2d Monday in November,	Fourth Monday,	Feb'y, May, do. do.
Alleghany,	14. 13th April and September,	Third Monday,	March, June, do. do.
Amelia,	2. 25th April and 20th Oct'r,	Fourth Thursday,	Do. May, do. do.
Amherst,	10 22d March and August,	Third Monday,	Do. June, do. do.
Appomattox,	3. 21st April and September,	Thursday after 1st Monday,	Do. May, do. do.
Augusta,	11. 1st June and November,	Fourth Monday,	Do. do. do. Octo'r.
Barbour,	21. 8th May and October,	First Monday,	Do. June, do. Novem.
Bath,	11. 15th May and October,	Second Monday,	Do. do. do. do.
Bedford,	4. 25th April and September,	Fourth Monday,	Feb'y, May, July, do.
Berkeley,	13. 24th April and September,	Second Monday,	March, June, August, do.
Boone,	15. 2d Monday after 4th Monday in April and Sept'r,	Wednesday after 2d Monday,	Do. do. do. do.
Botetourt,	14. 1st April and September,	Second Monday,	Do. do. do. do.
Braxton,	19. 27th April and September,	First Tuesday,	Do. do. do. do.
Brooke,	20. 18th March and August,	Last Monday,	Feb'y, May, July, do.
Brunswick,	2. 27th March and 2d Oct'r,	Fourth Monday,	March, do. August, do.
Buckingham,	3. 5th April and September,	Second Monday,	Do. do. do. do.
Cabell,	18. 27th March and August,	Fourth Monday,	Do. June, do. do.
Calhoun,	19. 12th April and September,	First Tuesday after 4th Monday,	Do. do. do. do.
Campbell,	3 18th May and October,	Second Monday,	Do. do. do. do.
Caroline,	8 1st March and 18th Sept'r,	Second Monday,	Feb'y, May, do. do.
Carroll,	16. Monday before last Monday in March and August,	First Monday,	March, June, do. do.
Charles City,	6. 18th May and November,	Third Thursday,	Do. May, do. do.
Charlotte,	3. 25th March and August,	First Monday,	Do. June, do. do.
Chesterfield,	2 7th May and 12th Nov'r,	Second Monday,	Do. do. do. do.
Clarke,	13. 12th May and October,	Second Monday in June and 4th in other months,	Feb'y, May, July, Octo'r.
Clay,	15. 1st April and September,	Second Monday,	March, June, August, Novem.
Craig,	14 15th March and August,	Fourth Monday,	Do. do. do. do.
Culpeper,	10. 1st Monday June and Nov.	Third Monday,	Do. May, do. do.
Cumberland,	3. 5th March and August,	Fourth Monday,	Feb'y, do. July, Octo'r.
Danville,	3. 22d March and August,	Thursday after 2d Monday,	March, June, August, Novem.
Dinwiddie,	2. 20th March and 26th Sept.	Third Monday,	Do. May, do. do.
Doddridge,	19. 22d May and October,	Fourth Monday,	Do. June, do. do.
Elizabeth City,	6. 15th March and September,	Fourth Thursday,	Do. May, do. do.
Essex,	8. 25th April and 12th Nov'r,	Third Monday,	Do. do. do. do.
Fairfax,	9. 1st Monday June and Nov.	Third Monday,	Do. June, do. do.
Fauquier,	9. Tuesday after 1st Monday in April and September,	Fourth Monday,	Do. May, do. do.
Fayette,	15 7th June and November,	Thursday after 2d Tuesday,	Do. June, do. do.
Floyd,	16. 1st Monday April and Sept	Thursday after 3d Monday,	Do. do. do. do.
Fluvanna,	10. 10th April and September,	Fourth Monday,	Do. May, do. do.
Franklin,	4. 15th May and October,	First Monday,	Do. June, do. do.
Frederick,	13. 10th June and November,	Monday before 1st Tuesday,	Do. do. do. do.
Fredericksburg,	- - -	Second Thursday,	Do. do. Octo'r, Decem.
Giles,	15 20th May and October,	Second Monday,	Do. do. August, Novem.
Gilmer,	19. 19th April and September,	Tuesday after 3d Monday,	Feb'y, do. do. do.
Gloucester,	6. 13th April and October,	First Monday,	March, May, do. do.
Goochland,	10 1st April and September,	Third Monday,	Do. do. do. do.
Grayson,	16. 4th Monday April and Sept.	Fourth Monday,	Feb'y, do. July, do.
Greenbrier,	14. 1st May and October,	Fourth Monday,	March, June, August, do.
Greene,	10. 3d Monday June and Nov.	Wednesday after 2d Monday,	Do. do. do. Octo'r.
Greenesville,	1. 28th April and 2d Nov'r,	First Monday,	Do. May, do. Octo'r.

TIMES AND PLACES OF COURTS.

Counties and corporations.	Circuit courts. When terms commence.	County and corporation courts. Monthly terms.	County and corporation courts. Quarterly terms.
	Circuits.		
Halifax,	3. 1st May and October,	Fourth Monday,	March, June, Aug't, Novem.
Hampshire,	13. 1st April and September,	Fourth Monday,	Do. do. do. do.
Hancock,	20. 10th March and August,	Tuesday after 2d Monday,	Jan'y, April, June, October.
Hanover,	8. 10th March and 26th Sept.	Fourth Tuesday,	Feb'y, April, July, Novem'r.
Harrison,	21. 15th April and September,	First Monday,	March, June, August, do.
Hardy,	12. 20th April and September,	Monday before 1st Tuesday,	Do. do. do. do.
Henrico,	6. 23d April and October,	First Monday,	Do. May, do. do.
Henry,	4. 1st April and September,	Second Monday,	Do. June, do. do.
Highland,	12. 2d May and October,	Thursday after 3d Monday,	Do. May, do. Octo'r.
Isle of Wight,	1. 16th May and 18th October,	First Monday,	Do. June, do. Novem.
Jackson,	18. 2d May and October,	Second Monday,	Feb'y. do. do. do.
James City and Williamsburg,	6. 25th May and November,	Second Monday,	March, do. do. Octo'r.
Jefferson,	13. 20th May and October,	Second Monday in June and October, 3d in other months,	Do. do. do. do.
Kanawha,	18. 27th May and October,	Third Monday,	Feb'y. do. do. Novem.
King George,	8. 23d March and 12th Sept.	First Thursday,	March, do. do. do.
King & Queen,	8. 2d May and 19th Nov'r,	First Thursday,	Do. May, do. do.
King William,	8. 13th May and 25th Nov'r,	Fourth Monday,	Do. do. do. do.
Lancaster,	8. 15th April and 2d Nov'r,	Third Monday,	Do do. do. do.
Lee,	17. 2d Monday after 4th Monday in April and Sept'r,	— —	Do. June, do. do.
Lewis,	19. 8th May and October,	Second Monday,	April, do. do. Septem.
Logan,	15. 1st Monday after 4th Monday in April and Sept'r,	Third Monday,	March, do. do. Novem.
Loudoun,	9. 4th Monday in April and 3d Monday in October,	Second Monday,	Do. do. do. do.
Louisa,	10. 20th April and September,	Second Monday,	Do. do. do. do.
Lunenburg,	2. 13th April and 8th Oct'r,	Second Monday,	Do. May, do. do.
Lynchburg,	3. 3d June and November,	First Monday,	Do. June, do. Octo'r.
Madison,	10. 1st Monday Mar. and Aug.	Fourth Thursday,	Feb'y, do. do. do.
Marion,	21. 10th June and November,	First Monday,	March, do. do. Novem.
Marshall,	20. 1st May and October,	Third Monday,	Do. do. do. do.
Matthews,	6. 6th April and September,	Second Monday,	Do. May, do. do.
Mason,	18. 18th April and September,	First Monday,	Feb'y, June, do. do.
Mecklenburg,	2. 2d April and 15th Sept'r,	Third Monday,	Do. May, do. do.
Mercer,	15. 27th May and October,	Thursday after 2d Monday,	March, June, do. do.
McDowell,	17. 1st Monday Mar. and Aug.	Second Monday,	Do. do. do. do.
Middlesex,	6. 1st April and October,	Fourth Wednesday,	Do. May, do. do.
Monongalia,	20. 1st April and September,	Fourth Monday,	Do. June, do. do.
Monroe,	14. 12th May and October,	Third Monday,	Do. do. do. do.
Montgomery,	16. 2d Monday in Ap'l and Sep.	First Monday,	Do. do. do. do.
Morgan,	13. 6th May and October,	Fourth Monday,	Do. do. Sept. do.
Nansemond,	15. 16th April and 12th Oct'r,	Second Monday,	Do. do. Aug. do.
Nelson,	10. 27th April and September,	Fourth Monday,	Feb'y, May, July, do.
New Kent,	6. 10th May and November,	Second Thursday,	March, do. Aug. do.
Nicholas,	15. 6th April and September,	Monday before 2d Tuesday,	Do. June, do. do.
Norfolk city,	1. 1st June and 15th Nov'r,	Fourth Monday,	Feb'y, April, July, October.
Norfolk county,	1. 1st April and 28th Sept'r,	Third Monday,	March, June, Aug't, Novem.
Northampton,	5. 3d Monday in Ap'l and Sep.	Second Monday,	Do. do. Sept. do.
Northumberland,	8. 9th April and 28th Oct'r,	Second Monday,	Do. May, Aug. do.
Nottoway,	2. 20th April and 15th Oct'r,	First Thursday,	Do. do. do. do.
Ohio,	20. 10th May and October,	First Monday,	Feb'y, July, Sept'r, Decem.
Orange,	10. 1st May and October,	Fourth Monday,	March, May, Aug't, Decem.
Page,	12. 11th April and September,	Fourth Monday,	Feb'y, do. July, do.
Patrick,	4. 12th April and September,	Fourth Monday,	Do. do. do. do.
Pendleton,	12. 27th April and September,	Thursday after 1st Tuesday,	March, June, Sept'r, do.
Petersburg,	2. 22d May, 16th November,	Third Thursday,	Do. do. Decem.
Pittsylvania,	4. 28th May and October,	Third Monday,	Do. do. Aug. Novem.
Pleasants,	19. 30th May and October,	Thursday after 2d Monday,	Feb'y, May, July, October.
Pocahontas,	14. 23d April and September,	First Tuesday,	March, June, Aug't, Novem.
Powhatan,	2. 2d May and 27th October,	First Wednesday,	Do. do. do. Octo'r.
Preston,	21. 18th March and August,	Second Monday,	Feb'y, May, July, Novem.
Princess Anne,	1. 25th May and 22d Sept'r,	First Monday,	March, June, Aug. do.
Prince Edward,	3. 15th March and August,	Third Monday,	Feb'y, May, July, do.
Prince George,	2. 17th May and 12th Nov'r,	Second Thursday,	March, do. Aug't, do.
Prince William,	9. 2d Monday in May and Oct.	First Monday,	Do. June, do. do.
Pulaski,	16. 3d Monday April and Sep.	Thursday after 1st Monday,	Do. do. do. do.
Putnam,	18. 8th April and September,	Fourth Monday,	Do. do. do. do.
Raleigh,	15. 3d Monday April and Sep.	First Monday,	Do. do. do. do.
Randolph,	21. 26th May and October,	Fourth Monday,	Do. do. do. do.

TIMES AND PLACES OF COURTS. 139

Counties and corporations.	Circuit courts. When terms commence.	County and corporation courts. Monthly terms.	County and corporation courts. Quarterly terms.
	Circuits.		
Rappahannock,	9. 3d Monday in March and 1st Monday in October,	Second Monday,	March, May, August, Novem.
Richmond city,	7. 1st May and November,	Second Monday,	Jan'y, Ap'l, July, Octo'r.
Richmond co.	8. 3d April and 23d October,	First Monday,	March, May, August, Novem.
Ritchie,	19. 15th April and September,	Tuesday after 1st Monday,	Feb'y, June, do. do.
Roane,	18. 17th May and October,	First Monday,	Jan'y, Ap'l, July, Sept'r.
Roanoke,	14. 22d March and August,	Third Monday,	March, June, Aug't, Novem.
Rockbridge,	11. 12th April and September,	Monday before 1st Tuesday,	Do. do. do. do.
Rockingham,	12. 11th May and October,	Third Monday,	Feb'y, May, do. do.
Russell,	17. 4th Monday April and Sep.	Tuesday after 1st Monday,	March, June, do. do.
Scott,	17. 3d Monday after 4th Monday April and Sept'r,	Tuesday after 2d Monday,	Do. do. do. do.
Shenandoah,	12. 30th March and August,	Monday before 2d Tuesday,	Do. do. do. do.
Smyth,	17. 1st Monday April and Sep.	Tuesday after 1st Monday,	Do. do. do. do.
Southampton,	1. 2d May and 7th October,	Third Monday,	Do. do. do. do.
Spotsylvania,	8. 20th May and 6th October,	First Monday,	Do. do. do. do.
Stafford,	9. 4th Monday Mar. and Sept.	Third Wednesday,	Do. do. do. do.
Staunton.	- - -	Wednesday after 1st Monday,	Feb'y, May, July, Octo'r.
Surry,	1. 10th May and 25th Oct'r,	Fourth Monday,	March, do. August, Novem.
Sussex,	1. 24th April and 29th Oct'r,	First Thursday,	Do. do. do. Octo'r.
Taylor,	21. 4th March and August,	Fourth Monday,	Do. June, do. Novem.
Tazewell,	17. Last Monday Mar. and Aug.	Wednesday after 1st Monday,	Feb'y, May, July, Octo'r.
Tucker,	21. 23d May and October,	Third Monday,	March, June, Aug't, Novem.
Tyler,	20. 22d April and September,	Second Monday,	Do. do. do. do.
Upshur,	21. 4th April and September,	Third Monday,	Do. do. do. do.
Warren,	12. 25th March and August,	Third Monday,	Do. May, do. do.
Warwick,	6. 21st March and September,	Second Monday,	Do. June, do. Decem.
Washington,	17. 9d Monday April and Sep.	Fourth Monday,	Do. do. do. Novem.
Wayne,	18. 20th March and August,	Tuesday after 1st Monday,	Do. do. do. do.
Webster,	15. 14th April and September,	Fourth Tuesday,	Do. do. do. do.
Westmoreland,	8. 28th March and 18th Oct'r,	Fourth Monday,	April, May, do. do.
Wetzel,	20. 12th April and September,	Tuesday after 1st Monday,	Feb'y, do. July, Octo'r.
Williamsburg,	6. 25th May and November,	Fourth Monday,	March, June, Aug't, Novem.
Winchester,	- - -	First Saturday,	Do. May, do. do.
Wirt,	19. 3d April and September,	Tuesday after 4th Monday,	Feb'y, June, do. do.
Wise,	17. 1st Monday after 4th Monday in April and Sept'r,	Fourth Monday,	March, do. do. do.
Wood,	19. 5th June and November,	Third Monday,	Feb'y, do. do. do.
Wyoming,	15. 4th Monday April and Sep.	Friday after 3d Monday,	March, do. do. do.
Wythe,	16. 1st Monday May and Oct'r,	Second Monday,	Do. do. do. do.
York,	6. 26th March and September,	Third Monday,	Do. May, do. Octo'r.

RECEIPTS.

1861.			
Oct.	1, To balance, per last annual report,		138,214 84
	31, To receipts in October 1861,		231,864 93
Nov.	30, To do. in November 1861,		408,246 10
Dec.	31, To do. in December 1861,		1,245,184 02
			$ 2,023,509 89
1862.			
Jan.	1, To balance brought down,		717,911 69
	31, To receipts in January 1862,		252,149 81
Feb.	28, To do. in February 1862,		1,094,432 67
Mar.	31, To do. in March 1862,		492,603 06
			$ 2,557,097 23
April	1, To balance brought down,		1,017,810 32
	30, To receipts in April 1862,		2,036,122 05
May	31, To do. in May 1862,		222,341 30
June	30, To do. in June 1862,		155,125 30
			$ 3,431,398 97
July	1, To balance brought down,		482,839 78
	31, To receipts in July 1862,		278,449 08
Aug.	30, To do. in August 1862,		1,406,159 36
Sep.	30, To do. in September 1862,		1,132,155 44
			$ 3,299,603 66
Oct.	1. To balance against the treasurer this day, exclusive of the funds under the direction of the second auditor,		$ 434,778 96

DISBURSEMENTS.

By amount of warrants paid in October 1861,			·	·	·	284,274 65
By do. do. November 1861,			·	·	·	280,990 97
By do. do. December 1861,			·	·	·	740,332 58
Balance 31st December 1861,				·	·	717,911 69
						$2,023,509 89

By amount of warrants paid in January 1862,			·	·	·	284,632 56
By do. do. February 1862,			·	·	·	1,123,355 95
By do. do. March 1862,			·	·	·	131,308 40
Balance 30th March 1862,				·	·	1,017,810 32
						$2,557,097 23

By amount of warrants paid in April 1862,			·	·	·	2,279,868 57
By do. do. May 1862,			·	·	·	129,553 69
By do. do. June 1862,			·	·	·	539,136 93
Balance 30th June 1862,				·	·	482,839 78
						$3,431,398 97

By amount of warrants paid in July 1862,			·	·	·	190,838 34
By do. do. August 1862,			·	·	·	1,698,358 97
By do. do. September 1862,			·	·	·	975,627 39
Balance 30th September 1862,				·	·	434,778 96
						$3,299,603 66

Total amount of warrants issued by the auditor from the 1st October 1861
to the 30th September 1862, inclusive,   ·   ·   ·   8,658,846 52

Add warrants No. 8316, $18 00 ⎫
                8317,   84 25 ⎬ Issued prior to the 1st October 1861,
                8327,   55 00   and paid since that day,   ·   182 25
           11472,   25 00 ⎭

                                                                                                             8,659,028 77

Deduct warrants No. 1806, $5 12 ⎫
                    4259,   24 70 ⎪
                    6559,   19 00 ⎪
                    6625,   520 99 ⎪ Issued prior to the 1st October
                    6638,   21 00 ⎬ 1862, and unpaid on the morn-
                    6687,   25 00   ing of that day,   ·   ·   759 77
                    6752,   15 96 ⎪
                    6791,   100 00 ⎪
                    6847,   28 00 ⎭

                      Paid by the treasurer in the fiscal year 1861–62, $8,658,269 00

Auditor's Office, Dec. 16, 1862.

APPROPRIATIONS.

General appropriations for fiscal year ending September 30, 1863:

Direct appropriations,	8,954,798 71
Estimated amount not specified,	2,500 00
Amount included in general appropriations,	8,957,298 71
Salt,	1,000,000 00
Other appropriations,	2,980 44
Total,	$ 9,960,279 15

This does not include money refunded under acts for refunding money received for exemption from military duty.

INDEX.

ADMINISTRATIONS.
See Wills, &c.   10

AGENCY FOR RECEIVING AND FORWARDING SUPPLIES TO VIRGINIA SOLDIERS.
Act establishing,   50
Agent, how appointed,   50
Depot, how provided,   50-51
Transportation,   51
Duty of agent as to advertising,   51
Salary of agent,   51
Clerks,   51
Soldiers, when detailed,   51
Bond, how given,   51
Remedy against agent,   51
Appropriation,   51

AGENTS FOR RENTING HOUSES.
License to,   18

AGENTS FOR HIRING NEGROES.
License to,   18

AGRICULTURAL PRODUCTIONS.
When taxed,   26-7

AGRICULTURAL PRODUCTIONS AND SUPPLIES.
Preamble and resolution advising as to increase of, &c.   129-30

AIDS OF GOVERNOR.
Ordinance as to, amended,   50
Number of aids governor may appoint,   50
Who to receive pay,   50

ALCOHOL.
Act of 1862 repealed,   87

ALDERSON, J. M.
Act for relief of representative of,   113
Militia fines to be delivered to collector,   113
Sheriff to give receipts,   113
Auditor to charge sheriff with amount,   113

ALIENS.
License, when to issue to,   34

APPROPRIATIONS.
Salary of clerk of sinking fund,   35
General assembly,   35
Elections,   35
Judges,   35
Prisoners, jurors, &c.   35
Slaves condemned,   35
Expenses of penitentiary,   35

J. W. Hancock,   35
Convicts, &c.   35
Mileage to officers and guards,   35
Penitentiary,   35
Records court of appeals,   35
Contingent expenses of courts,   35
Militia,   35
Adjutant general,   35
Annuity to Virginia military institute,   35
Military contingent fund,   35
Public guard,   35-6
Interior guard at penitentiary,   36
Transportation of arms,   36
Commissioners of revenue,   36
Central lunatic asylum,   36
Eastern lunatic asylum,   36
Robert Saunders, &c.   36
Wm. M. Hume,   36
Lunatics in county jails,   36
Deaf, dumb and blind,   36
Pensions,   36
Civil prosecutions,   36
Public warehouses,   36
Governor's house,   36
Capitol,   36
Grattan's Reports,   36
Leigh's Reports,   36
Vaccine agent,   37
Messenger in auditor's office,   37
Registration of marriages, &c.   37
Printing,   37
Temporary clerks in auditor's office,   37
Commissions to sheriffs,   37
New river navigation company,   37
Pages,   37
Clerk joint committee on salt,   37
Porter of senate,   37
Fires, furnaces, &c.   37
Temporary loans,   37
Interest on loans for war tax,   37
Interest bearing treasury notes,   37
Naval officers,   37
Military expenses,   37
Auditing board,   37
Virginia state line,   38
Penitentiary, raw material for,   38
Kean, Patrick,   38
Hoyer & Ludwig,   38
J. D. Pendleton and John Burwell,   38
General fund,   38
How disposed of,   38
Limitation of power of auditor,   38
Payments, when made,   38
Table showing, at adjourned session,   142

ARDENT SPIRITS.
License to distill or rectify,   13-14

Prohibition of sale of, 27
ATTACHMENTS AGAINST NON-RESIDENTS.
Act to enlarge powers of circuit courts in, 77
Sale of slaves, how ordered, 77
How made, 77

ATTORNEYS AT LAW.
Tax on license to, 20

BAGATELLE TABLES.
Tax on license to, 13

BANKS.
Act to authorize conversion of Confederate treasury notes into other securities, 82
Code amended, 82
When bank may loan money, 82
Interest, 82
Loans, how regulated, 82
Proviso as to treasury notes, 82

BANKS (RELIEF OF).
Act to amend act for, 83
Act 1861 amended, 83
Forfeiture of charter suspended, 83
Charter to remain in force, 83
Proviso, 83

BANKS (CONTINGENT FUND OF).
Act to authorize banks to increase contingent funds, 58
Code amended, 58
Rate of dividends, 58
Surplus fund, 58
Limitation of surplus fund, 58

BANK CHARTERS.
Tax on, 10

BANK DIVIDENDS.
Tax on, 4

BANK OF ROCKINGHAM.
Act authorizing, to increase contingent fund, 104
Act to amend charter of, 104
Charter amended, 105
When charter to expire, 105
Treasurer to transfer certificates, 105
Bond and security, how given, 105
When execution may issue, 105
Denomination of notes, 105
Quarterly statements, 105
Board of directors, 105
Proviso as to small notes, 105

BARBERS.
Tax on license to, 21

BILLIARD TABLES.
Tax on license to, 12-13

BIRTHS AND DEATHS.
Act to amend section 22 of chapter 103 of Code, 58
Code amended, 58
Duty of commissioner, 59

Compensation, 59
Duty of auditor in certain cases, 59

BONDS OF SHERIFFS.
See Sheriffs' bonds.

BOOK AGENTS.
Tax on license to, 17

BOWLING ALLEYS.
Tax on license to, 12

BRAGG, E. W.
See Canfield.

BROKERS.
Tax on license to, 19

BUILDING FUND ASSOCIATIONS.
Act allowing, to purchase stock, 111
Power to purchase stock, 111

BURWELL, JOHN.
Appropriation to, 38

CANFIELD, E. W. AND C. D. BRAGG.
Act for relief of, 119

CARRIAGES, BUGGIES AND OTHER VEHICLES.
Tax on license to sell, 20

CENTRAL LUNATIC ASYLUM.
Act making appropriation to, 89-90

CERTIFICATES OF STOCK.
See Chartered companies.

CHAMBERS, GEO. W.
Act for relief of, 116
Preamble, 116
Amount appropriated, 116

CHANGE OF FIRM.
Effect of, 27

CHARTERED COMPANIES.
Act to authorize transfer and issue of new certificates of stock in, 89
When property sold or sequestered, 89
New certificates, how granted, 89
Old certificates destroyed, 89
When to report to auditor, 29

CHANGES IN CODE.
See Freight on rail roads.
See Tobacco inspectors.
See Banks, contingent funds of.
See Births and deaths.
See Contested elections.
See Virginia military institute.
See Printer to senate.
See Interior guard at penitentiary.
See Officers of penitentiary.
See Sheriffs' bonds.
See Clerks of courts.
See Compensation of clerks of courts.
See Hospitals (lands, how condemned for).
See Circuit courts, special terms of.

CIRCUIT COURTS (SPECIAL TERMS OF).

Act to enlarge powers of,	69
Code amended,	69
Trial of prisoner,	69
Special term,	69
Trial of prisoner at special term,	69

CLERKS OF COURTS.

Act to amend Code as to compensation of, for public services,	63
Code amended,	63
Compensation for public services,	63
Corporation of Richmond,	63

CLERK OF HUSTINGS COURT OF RICHMOND.

Act for relief of,	116–17

COLLATERAL INHERITANCES.

Tax on,	7

COLLINS, C. A. J.

Preamble and resolutions for demand of, from confederate government,	124–25

COMMISSION MERCHANTS.

Tax on license to,	15

COMMISSIONS TO SHERIFFS AND COLLECTORS.

On licenses,	32

COMMISSIONERS OF ELECTION.

Resolution giving power to justices to appoint, in certain cases,	124

COMMISSIONERS' COMPENSATION.

Other than fees,	31

COMMON CRIER.

Tax on,	16–17

COMPENSATION OF CLERKS OF COURTS.

Act increasing, during war,	63
Code amended,	63
Clerk of county or corporation court.	
Fee for recordation of writing,	63
Recordation of plat,	64
Courses,	64
In deed book,	64
Deed of trust or mortgage, recordation of,	64
Swearing witnesses,	64
Recordation of will,	64
Order as to decedent's estates,	64
Swearing personal representative,	64
One fee where more than one,	64
Licenses for,	64
Marriage license,	64
Search,	64
Certificate,	65
Injunction bond,	65
Any other bond,	65
Writ of ad quod damnum,	65
Caveat,	65
Summons to answer bill,	65
Any other summons,	65
Copy of process,	65
Notary,	65

Postage,	65
Appearance,	65
Filing and endorsing petition,	65
Depositions,	65
Filing papers for plaintiff,	65
Filing papers for defendant,	65
Issuing an attachment,	65
Scire facias,	65
Rules,	65
Docketing,	65
Swearing jury and witnesses,	66
In case no jury is sworn,	66
Swearing witnesses during attendance,	65
Administering oath,	65
Judgments, decrees, &c.	65
Docketing judgments,	65
Taxing costs,	65
Execution returned by constable,	65
Execution, entry of,	63
Transcript of record,	65
Copy,	67
Annexing seal,	67
Code amended,	67
Clerk of a circuit court.	
Fee for writ of supersedeas,	67
Bond,	67
Endorsing writ,	67
Filing record,	67
Fees, when clerk of court of appeals.	
Issuing process,	67
Docketing, &c.	67
Judgments, decrees, &c.	67
Orders, issuing execution, &c.	67
Damages, taxing,	68
Fees in chancery cases,	68
For issuing attachments in,	68
Process,	68
Exhibits,	68
Exhibits with commissioner's report,	68
Filing papers,	68
Rules,	68
Executions,	68
Continuation of act,	68

COMPENSATION OF FIDUCIARIES.

Act to provide against forfeiture of,	82

CONFEDERATE INSURANCE COMPANY.

Company incorporated,	98
Insurance, how made,	99
Money received on deposit,	99
Funds to be invested or loaned,	99
Power to purchase and hold lands,	99
Capital,	99
How payable,	99
Management of company,	99
Directors, how elected,	99
President, how chosen,	99
Term of office,	99
Vacancy, how filled,	99
Secretary, how appointed,	100
Compensation of officers,	100
Power to appoint agents,	100
Scale of voting,	100
Power to transfer stock,	100
Dividends,	100
To make and publish report,	100
Liability of members,	100
Books of subscription, how opened,	100

146 INDEX.

Board to give notice, 101
Act to amend 4th section of act of incorporation, 101
Funds, how invested, 101
Real or personal estate, 101

CONFEDERATE STATES TREASURY NOTES.
What, receivable in taxes, 33
See Banks.

CONFEDERATE STATES WAR TAX.
Act authorizing payment of interest on bonds given for, 39
When to bear interest, 39
When holders entitled to interest, 39
When auditor to issue warrant, 39
Rate of interest, 39

CONTESTED ELECTIONS.
Act to extend time for filing complaint in, 59
Code amended, 59
Returns, how enquired into, 59
Complaint, how made, 59
Duty of courts, 59
Time when complaint to be filed, 60
Duty of clerk, 60
Proviso in case of justice of peace, 60

CONTINGENT FUNDS.
See Banks.

CONTRACT FOR SUPPLY OF SALT.
See Stuart, Buchanan & Co.

COOK SHOPS, &c.
Tax on license to, 12

COOLEY, B. B. & J. W.
Act authorizing governor to deliver infant slave to, 115
Act authorizing sum of money to be paid to, for slave condemned, 115
Amount appropriated, 115

CORPORATIONS.
Tax on charters of, 23

COUNCIL OF LYNCHBURG.
Act to enlarge powers of, 107
Powers of council enlarged, 107
Council may enact ordinances, 107
Persons, when to be arrested, 107
Power of officers, 107
Armed police, 107

COUNCIL OF RICHMOND.
Act to enlarge powers of, 106
Powers enlarged, 106
Council to enact ordinances, 107
Persons to be arrested for violating ordinances, 107
Powers of officers, 107
Armed police organized, 107

COUNTY COURTS.
Act to extend jurisdiction of, 78
Act of 1862 amended, 78
Ordinance amended, 79
Jurisdiction of courts, 79

Recordation, 79
When no tax to be charged, 79
Duty of clerk of circuit court of Richmond, 79
Penalty, 79
Fees and postage, 79

COUNTY OFFICERS (ELECTION OF).
Act to provide for, 76
When county prevented from holding elections for, 76
Court may order election, 77
For unexpired terms, 77

COURT OF APPEALS.
Act as to sessions of, 80
Place of session may be changed, 80
Notice of removal, how given, 80
Removal of library, &c. 80

COURTS OF COUNTIES IN POSSESSION OF ENEMY.
See County courts.

DAGUERREIAN ARTISTS.
Tax on license to, 20

DEDUCTION FROM COMPENSATION OF COMMISSIONER.
When made, 25

DEEDS.
Tax on, 10

DEPUTY COLLECTORS.
How appointed, 33

DISBURSEMENTS.
Tables showing, 141

DISCHARGE FROM ACTIVE MILITARY SERVICE.
Act to provide for, of persons who have furnished substitutes, 41
When person who has furnished substitute exempt, 41
When entitled to discharge, 41
Question of exemption, how determined, 41

DISTILLATION.
See Spirituous and malt liquors.

DISTILLATION OF FRUIT.
Act for relief of persons engaged in, 87
When person may appear, 87
When court satisfied as to failure to obtain license, 87
Auditor to issue warrant, 87-8
Duty of sheriff, 88
Duty of attorney for commonwealth, 88

DISTRESS FOR RENT PAYABLE IN MONEY.
Act to amend act amending Code so as to exempt the property of persons in the military service from, 56
Act of 1862 amended, 56
No legal proceedings against persons in military service, 56
Exception as to criminal cases, 56

INDEX. 147

Exceptions, 56

DISTRESS FOR TAXES.
When taxes may be distrained for, 33

DISTRICT SCHOOL HOUSES IN HENRY.
Act authorizing sale of, 110
Sale authorized, 110
Power of court, 110
Proceeds of sale, how disposed of, 110
Court to appoint commissioners, 110
Bond and security to be given, 110

DIVIDENDS OF COMPANIES NOT INCORPORATED BY THE STATE.
Tax on, 5

DIVIDENDS OF STEAM BOAT AND SUCH LIKE COMPANIES.
Tax on, 5

DOMESTIC MANUFACTURES.
How taxed, 27

DOUBLE TAX.
When to be imposed, 25

DURATION OF SESSION.
Resolution as to, 123

ELECTION LAWS.
Act to provide for voting by persons in military service, &c. 71–75
Where persons in camp may vote, 72
Commissioners, how appointed, 72
Polls for members of congress, &c. 72
Polls for governor, &c. 72
Duty of commissioners, 72
Polls, where sent, 72
Refugees, where to vote, 72
Oath to be taken, 73
Poll books, how transmitted, 73
Code amended, 73
Duty of commissioners, 73
Certificate, how written, 73
When officers to meet, 73
Returns, how compared, 73
Notice given, 73
Special elections, 73
Certified statement to secretary of commonwealth, 73–4
Duty of secretary of commonwealth, 74
In case of tie, governor to decide, 74
Duties of governor under ordinance, 74
Proclamation of governor, how made, 74
Request to president, 74
Result of vote, how forwarded, 74
See Elections of senators, &c.
See Representation for counties.

ELECTIONS OF SENATORS AND DELEGATES.
Act to prescribe mode of certifying, &c. of 75
When commissioners to meet, 75
Code suspended, 75

ELECTION OF COUNTY OFFICERS.
See County officers.

EXCHANGE BANK.
Act authorizing branch of, at Richmond to declare a dividend, 83
Contribution from other branches, 83

EXEMPTION FROM MILITARY DUTY
See Money received for.
See Discharge from active service.

EXPRESS COMPANIES.
Tax on, 8–9

FARMVILLE INSURANCE COMPANY.
Act to incorporate, 93–95
Company incorporated, 93
Insurance, how and upon what made, 93
Money received on deposit, 93
Investments, how made, 93
Capital stock, 94
How payable, 94
Affairs of company, how managed, 94
Officers, how appointed, 94
Agents, 94
Scale of voting, 94
Dividends, how declared, 94
Responsibility of stockholders, 95
Commissioners, 95
Restriction as to bank notes, 95

FEES.
See Jailors' fees, and Compensation of clerks

FENCE LAW.
Act of 1862 amended, 90
First section amended, 90
Second section amended, 90
Power of courts, 90
Acts of county courts legalized, 90

FIDUCIARIES.
Act authorizing, to invest funds in certain cases, 81
When fiduciary may invest funds, 81
In what funds may be invested, 81
As to joint fiduciaries, 81
Continuance of act, 81
See Compensation of.

FLOYD, MAJ. GEN. J. B.
Thanks to Gen. Floyd, 125
Thanks to officers and men, 125

FORMS FOR TAX PAYERS.
When to be furnished, 24

FREIGHTS ON RAIL ROADS.
Act requiring rail road companies to give receipts showing weight of, 57
Code amended, 57
Rates of transportation on persons and produce, 57
Rates when articles weigh less than four pounds, 57
Receipts, how given, 57
Weight shown, 57
Charge, for what made, 57

FREE NEGROES.
Taxes on, 4

INDEX.

GAS LIGHT AND OTHER COMPANIES.
Tax on charters of, 11

GENERAL ASSEMBLY.
Act to secure representation in, 71
When senators or delegates may be admitted, 71
When writ to be issued, 71
See Elections of senators and delegates.
See Representation for counties when courthouses in possession of public enemy.

GENERAL AUCTIONEERS.
Taxes on license to, 15

GLEE CLUB.
See Harmonic association.

GORDON & BROTHER.
Act for relief of, 115

GRAZIERS BANK.
See Northwestern Bank.

HANCOCK, J. W.
Appropriation to, 35

HARMONIC ASSOCIATION.
Act incorporating, 111
Company incorporated, 111
Rights, powers, &c. 112
Property to be held, 112

HASKINS, JOHN, SEN.
Act concerning estate of, 117
Act of 1859 amended; stock how sold, 117
Investments, how made, 118

HAWKERS AND PEDDLERS.
Tax on license to, 35

HENRY COUNTY.
See District school houses.

HOME GUARD.
Act of 1862 as to, amended, 47
Guard duty of, 47
Deserters, how arrested, 47
When major may be elected, 47
Proviso as to troops being sent out of county, 47

HORSES AND MULES, SOLD FOR PROFIT.
Tax on license, 20

HOSPITALS (LAND, HOW CONDEMNED FOR).
Act authorizing county courts to condemn land for, 60
Code amended, 60
Powers of court or council, 60
Lands and houses, how condemned, 60
Limitation, 60
Proviso as to dwelling houses, 60

HOYER & LUDWIG.
Appropriation to, 35

HUME, W. M.
Act for relief of, 118
Appropriation, 118
Amount, 118
Appropriation to, 36

IMPRESSMENT.
Preamble and resolution of instruction to senators as to, 123-4

IMPRESSMENT OF SLAVES.
See Public defence, and 43-7

INCOME.
Tax on, 5-6

INSOLVENTS.
Taxes of, how collected, 23

INSPECTION OF FLOUR.
Established at Danville, 91

INSPECTOR OF SALT.
Act to authorize appointment of, 55-6
Inspector, how appointed, 55
Salt to be inspected, 55
Rules and regulations, how prescribed, 55
Deputies, how appointed, 56
Repealing clause, 56

INSPECTION OF TOBACCO.
Established at Danville, 91

INSURANCE COMPANIES.
Tax on license to, 20

INSURANCE AND SAVINGS SOCIETY OF PETERSBURG.
Act to incorporate, 95
Company incorporated, 95
Privileges of company, 95
Capital stock, 95
How paid, 96
Meeting, when called, 95
President and directors, how appointed, 95
Management, 95
Vacancies, how filled, 95
Quorum in meetings of, 95
Compensation of president, 97
Secretary and officers, how appointed, 97
Bond and security to be given, 97
Assignment of stock, 97
Authority to make insurance, 97
Money received on deposit, 97
Proviso as to bank notes, 97
Effect of policies of insurance, 97
Dividends, how declared, 97
General meetings, 94
Agents, how appointed, 98
Corporation subject to repeal, 98

INTERIOR GUARD AT PENITENTIARY.
Act increasing compensation of, 61
Code amended, 61
Compensation of guard, 61

INTERNAL IMPROVEMENTS.
Tax on, 7-8

JAILORS' FEES.
Act concerning, 80
Act of 1852 amended, 80
Jailors' fees, 80
Powers of courts, 80

JAILS OF THE STATE.
Act as to use of, by confederate government, 51
When persons arrested under confederate laws may be committed, 51-2
Proviso, 52
Fees of jailors, 52
Duty of jailors, 52
Continuance of act, 52

JUDICIAL CIRCUIT (FOURTEENTH).
Act changing terms of courts in, 77
Act of 1854 amended, 77
Terms of courts, 77

JUNIOR MAJORS.
Act for payment of, 49
When to be paid, 49-50

KEAN, PATRICK.
Appropriation to, 38

LAIDLEY, JAMES M. & AL.
Act for relief of, 113
Auditor authorized to make settlement, 113
Damages released, 113
Auditor, when to refund, 113

LANDS AND LOTS.
Taxes on, 3

LICENSES.
To whom not to issue, 21
How granted, 27
Prohibition of sale of ardent spirits, &c. 27

LICENSED PRIVILEGE.
Where exercised, 21

LIMITATION OF LICENSE.
License, how limited, 24

LITTLETON, THOMAS.
Act for relief of, 116
Preamble, 116
Auditor to pay account, 116

LISTS.
How made out, and for whom, 31

LIVELY, E. H.
Appropriation to, 36

LIVERY STABLES.
Tax on license to, 13

LYBROOK, S. E.
Act for relief of, 119

LYNCHBURG.
See Council of.

MAJOR.
Act allowing but one to a regiment, 49

Officers of separate military organization, 49
See Junior majors.

MANUFACTURING COMPANIES.
Tax on charters of, 10-11

MANUFACTURERS OF PORTER, ALE AND BEER.
Tax on license to, 13

MATTHEWS, T S. A.
See Laidley, James M.

MEDICINES.
License for sale of, 17

MERCHANTS.
License to sell ardent spirits, 14-15

MERCHANT WHO IS A BEGINNER.
Tax on license to, 8-9

MERCHANT TAILORS.
Tax on license to, 15

MILL SWAMP PRECINCT.
Act establishing, in Isle of Wight, 119

MINERS AND MANUFACTURERS.
License to, and tax on, 21-23

MISDEMEANORS.
Act to extend time for prosecution of, in certain cases, 78

MONEY RECEIVED FOR EXEMPTION FROM MILITARY DUTY.
Act to refund, 47
Preamble, 47
When money to be refunded, 47-8
When sheriff may refund, 48
Act of 1863 amended, 48
When auditor to issue warrant, 48
Costs, 48
Act of 1833 amended, 49
When warrant to issue, 49

NEGRO AUCTIONEERS.
Tax on license to, 16

NORTHWESTERN BANK AT JEFFERSONVILLE.
Act amending act converting, into separate bank, 84
Act of 1852 amended, 84
When loyal stockholder may demand transfer, 84
Certificate of stock, how returned and assigned, 84

OATH TO SUPPORT USURPED GOVERNMENT.
Act concerning officers of state who have taken, 88
What, when oath taken by officer, 88
Acts to be void, 88
To whom act applies, 88
Oath or affirmation, how taken, 89
Record evidence not required, 89

INDEX.

OFFICERS OF PENITENTIARY.
Act increasing salaries of certain, 61
Code amended, 61
Salary of superintendent, 61
Salary of assistants, 61-2
Salary of surgeon, 62
Directors, 62
Clerk, salary of, 62
Time act continues, 62

ORDINARIES.
Tax on license to, 12

OUTLINE OF TAX BILL.
Resolution directing auditor to prepare, 126

PARIS, WILLIAM.
Act for relief of securities of, 114
Act amending act, 114
Relief to securities; damages refunded, 114
Act, how construed, 114
Money, how refunded, 114

PASSPORTS FOR MEMBERS.
Resolution requesting governor to apply for, 123
Governor requested to apply for passports for state officers, 123

PATENT RIGHTS.
Tax on license to sell, 17

PENALTIES.
For failure to obtain license, 24
How recoverable, 32

PENDLETON, J. D.
Appropriation to, 38

PERSONAL PROPERTY.
Taxes on, 3-4
What exempt from taxation, 29-30

PHYSICIANS AND OTHERS.
Tax on license to, 20

PIERCE, W. H.
Appropriation to, 36

POPULATION OF COUNTIES, CITIES AND TOWNS.
How estimated, 29

PRINTER TO SENATE.
Act amending Code, to compensate, 61
Code amended, 61
Annual salary of printer, 61
Extra work, when paid for, 61

PRIVATE CORPORATIONS.
Tax on, 11

PRIVATE ENTERTAINMENT.
Tax on license for, 11

PROFITS.
Tax on, 6-7

PROSPECT TAN-YARD COMPANY.
Act to incorporate, 104

Company incorporated, 104
Name of company, 104
Rights and privileges, 104
Power to purchase real estate, 104
Capital, 104

PUBLIC BONDS.
Taxes on, 4

PUBLIC DEFENCE (SLAVES).
Act to provide for, 42-46
Act of 1862 amended, 42
Slaves, how called into service of Confederate States, 42
Time of service, 42
How apportioned, 42
When governor may exempt counties, 42
Persons, how exempted, 42
Monthly allowance for slaves, 42
Value of, when paid by confederate government, 42
Compensation for injuries, 42-3
Burden of proof, 43
Hired slaves, how regarded, 43
Notice of requisition, 43
Duty of clerks of courts, 43
Duty of sheriffs, 43
Number of slaves subject to requisition, how ascertained, 43
Apportionment, how made, 43
Proviso as to soldiers and widows, 43
When slaveholder not exempted, 43
How slaves delivered, 44
When returned, 44
How seized, and when, 44
Expenses, how paid, 44
Fine for withholding slaves, 44
Sheriff to report delinquents, 44
Fine and execution therefor, 44
Detail of slaves, how made, 44
Clerk and sheriff to attend court, 44
Duty of clerk, 44
Duty of governor, 45
Number of slaves, 45
Receipts, how given, 45
Fee of sheriff, 45
Requisition to be equalized, 45
When number and time of service to be forwarded, 45
Slaves to be in charge of overseer or agent, 45
How discharged, 46
Subsistence, 46
Slaves sent voluntarily, 46
Act to be communicated to president, 46
Twelfth section of act amended, 46
How amended, 46
As to impressments, 46
Title amended, 46-7
Resolutions suspending act of 1862 as to certain counties, 122

PUBLIC POUND IN HENRICO.
Act authorizing establishment of, 110
Court to establish public pound, 110
What animals to be confined, 110
Keepers to be appointed, 110
Expenses, how defrayed, 110
Fines imposed, 110
When stock to be sold, 111

Where to be sold,	111
How bills of expenses to be assessed,	111
What amount to be paid owners,	111
Proviso,	111

PUBLIC SHOWS, &c.
Tax on license to,	19

RANDOLPH MACON COLLEGE.
Act amending act authorizing a military school at,'	109
Act amended; section as amended,	109

REAL ESTATE AUCTIONEERS.
Tax on license to,	16

RECEIPTS IN TREASURY.
Tables showing,	140

RECORD OF NAMES AND DEEDS OF CONSPICUOUS MERIT OF VIRGINIANS IN MILITARY SERVICE.
Resolutions authorizing county courts to prepare,	130
Court authorized to purchase and preserve book of record,	130
Adjutant general to prepare books,	130

REDRESS AGAINST NEW ASSESSMENTS.
See	26

REFRESHMENTS IN THEATRES.
Tax on license for sale of,	18

REPORTS OF CHARTERED COMPANIES.
When to be made to auditor,	29

REPRESENTATION FOR COUNTIES, COURTHOUSES BEING IN POSSESSION OF THE ENEMY.
Act to provide,	75–6
Where districts partially in power of enemy,	75
When elections cannot be held at courthouses, what,	76
Duty of conductor,	76
Duty of secretary of commonwealth,	76
Time within which to perform duties,	76

RICHMOND.
See Council of.

RICHMOND IMPORTING AND EXPORTING COMPANY.
Act to incorporate,	102
Company incorporated,	102
Corporate name,	102
Capital,	102
Affairs of company, how managed,	102
Proviso,	102
Act amending act,	103
Company incorporated,	103
Corporate name; powers,	103
Capital,	103
Affairs, how managed,	103

ROANOKE VALLEY RAIL ROAD.
Act for sale of,	85

Power to sell,	85
Notice of sale,	85
Sale subject to approval of board of public works,	85
Proviso as to validity of sale,	85
Proceeds of sale,	85

ROCKBRIDGE INSURANCE COMPANY.
Act to amend charter of,	101
Act of 1861 amended,	101
Twelfth section amended,	102

SALE OF ARDENT SPIRITS IN THEATRES.
Tax on license for,	18–19

SALE OF PORTER, ALE AND BEER.
Tax on license for,	19

SALT (PRODUCTION AND DISTRIBUTION OF).
Act to provide for,	52–55
Superintendent of salt works,	52
How elected,	52
How removable,	52
Bond, how given,	52
In case of vacancy,	52
Duties of superintendent,	52–3
Powers of,	53
Board of supervisors,	53
Leases, how confirmed and continued,	53
Exception,	53
Other furnaces,	53
Assistants, how appointed,	53
Salaries of,	53
Control of transportation,	53
Salt, how distributed,	53
Value of impressed property, how ascertained,	53–4
Duty of assessors,	54
How, in case owner refuse to appoint assessor,	54
Assessors of real property, how appointed,	54
Appeal, when allowed,	54
No injunction to be granted,	54
Valuation, how paid,	54
Salt, how sold and delivered,	54
Price, how fixed,	54
Surplus, how disposed of,	55
Monthly reports of superintendent,	55
Monthly reports of board of supervisors,	55
Amount appropriated,	55
Repealing clause,	55

SAMPLE MERCHANTS.
Tax on license to,	17

SAVINGS BANKS AND INSURANCE COMPANIES.
Taxes on,	5

SAVINGS INSTITUTIONS.
Tax on charters of,	11

SAUNDERS, ROBERT.
Appropriation to,	36

152 INDEX.

SEALS.
Tax on, 2-10

SENATORS AND DELEGATES.
See Election of.

SEPARATE ELECTION PRECINCTS.
See Table of, 131-3

SEQUESTRATION LAWS.
Tax on estates passing under, 7

SERGEANTS OF RICHMOND AND PETERSBURG.
Act for relief of, 117
Relief granted, 117
Amount appropriated, 117
Proviso, 117

SHERIFFS' BONDS.
Act concerning, 62
Code amended, 62
Bonds of sheriffs, &c. 62
Amount of bond, 62
When security deemed insufficient, 62
Auditor may petition, 62
New bond, 63
When court to remove officer, 63

SHERIFFS' COMMISSIONS.
On taxes other than licenses, 30-31

SLAVES.
Bought or sold for profit, 21
Number of, escaping to enemy, how ascertained, 34
See Public defence.

SLAVES AND SIMILAR SUBJECTS.
How taxed, 25

SOUTHERN FEMALE COLLEGE OF PETERSBURG.
Act to incorporate, 108
Institution incorporated, 108
Trustees to hold property, 108
How managed, 108
Quorum, 108
How vacancy fill'd, 108
Treasurer to receive moneys, 108
To give bond, 109
Amount of joint stock subscription, 109
Dividends, 109
Power to collect subscriptions, 109

SOUTH SIDE RAIL ROAD COMPANY.
Act to convert into stock interest due by, to state, 85
Amount of interest to be converted, 85
Proviso as to preferred stock, 85
Time of commencement and completion of work, 85

SPIRITUOUS AND MALT LIQUORS.
Act to amend act of 1852, 85
Distillation prohibited, 85
Penalties, 87
Proviso as to existing contracts, 87
See Alcohol.

SPOTSYLVANIA COUNTY.
Act to legalize proceedings of court of, 105
Preamble, 105
Proceedings legalized, 106

STATE TROOPS AND RANGERS.
Act transferring, to confederate government, 39-41
Governor directed to transfer, 39
Under what acts, 39
When rangers may elect major, 39
Company officers how elected, 40
Battalions and regiments, how formed, 40
Field officers, how chosen, 40
Battalions, when formed, 40
What field officers discharged, 40
How regiments, &c. mustered into service, 40
How received, 40
Who may be discharged, 40
Inventory of arms, &c., how taken, 40
How transferred to confederate government, 40
Staff officers, how appointed, 40
Arms, &c., how valued, 40
Valuation, how paid by confederate government, 41
Enlistments, when to cease, 41
Payments of troops not allowed after transfer, 41
When pay and rations not to be received, 41

STALLIONS.
Tax on license to owners of, 18

STATEMENT OF RAIL ROAD OFFICERS.
How made, 8

STUART, BUCHANAN & CO. (SALT).
Resolution confirming contract with, 126
Contract, 127-29
Parties, 127
Term of lease, 127
Description of real property, 127
Furnaces, 127
Salt water, 128
Personal property, 128
Ways to furnaces, 128
Arbitration, 128
Payments, how made, 128
Signatures, 129
Contract confirmed, 129

SUBSTITUTES.
See Discharge from active military service.

SUITS.
Tax on, 9

SUTLERS.
Tax on license to, 23

TAXES.
Act imposing, 3-31
On persons and property.
Bank charters, tax on, 10
Bank dividends, " 4
Bonds, public, " 4
Charters of gas companies, &c., tax on, 11

Charters of manufacturing companies, tax on,	10-11
Charters of private corporations, tax on,	11
Charters of savings banks, "	11
Collateral inheritances, "	7
Deeds, "	10
Dividends of companies not incorporated by this state, tax on,	5
Dividends of steam boat and such like companies, tax on,	4-5
Estates sequestered, tax on,	7
Express companies, "	8-9
Free negroes, "	4
Income, "	5-6
Internal improvement companies, tax on,	7-8
See Statement of rail road officers.	
Lands and lots, taxes on,	3
Personal property, "	3-4
Profits, "	6-7
Rate of taxes on profits,	6-7
Redress against erroneous assessment,	6
Savings banks and insurance companies, taxes on,	5
Seals,	9-10
Suits,	9
Statement of rail road officers,	8
Toll bridges and ferries, taxes on,	7
Transfer of state stock, "	10
Unorganized companies, "	11
White males, "	4
Wills and administrations, "	10
Licenses.	
Agents, book,	17
Agents for hiring negroes,	18
Agents for renting houses,	18
Ardent spirits, to distill or rectify,	13-14
Attorneys at law—See Physicians.	
Auctioneers, general,	15-16
Auctioneers of negroes,	16
Auctioneers of real estate,	16
Auditor, power of, to reform assessments,	23
See Miners and manufacturers.	
Bagatelle tables,	13
Barbers,	21
Billiard tables,	12-13
Bowling alleys,	12
Brokers,	19
Carriages, buggies, &c.	20
Certificate of commissioner, when license,	23
Commission merchants,	15
Commissioner to return obligations to auditor, when,	22-3
Commissioner, when liable,	23
See Miners and manufacturers.	
Common crier,	16
Cook shops and eating houses,	12
Daguerreian artists,	20
Hawkers and peddlers,	21
Horses, mules, &c. sold for profit,	20
Insurance companies,	20
License, to whom not to be issued,	21
License to commence business as manufacturer,	22-3
Livery stables,	13
Manufacture of porter, &c.	19
Medicines,	17
Merchants,	14
Merchant's commission.	
Merchant's license to sell ardent spirits,	14-15
Merchants, sample,	17
Merchant tailors,	15
Miners and manufacturers,	21-2
Penalty for failure to obtain license,	22
Rate of taxation on,	22
License to commence business,	22
How enforced,	23
Certificate, when license,	23
Tax, when quadrupled,	23
Assessment, how reformed,	23
Commissioner liable for false certificate,	23
Ordinaries,	12
Patent rights,	17
Penalties on manufacturers for failing to obtain license,	22
Physicians, attorneys at law, &c.	20
Private entertainments,	12
Public shows, &c.	17
Rate of taxation on manufactures,	22
Refreshments in theatres,	18
Sales of ardent spirits in theatres,	18
Sale of porter, ale and beer,	19
Slaves bought or sold for profit,	21
Stallions,	18
Telegraph companies,	20-21
Theatrical performances,	17
General provisions.	
Agricultural productions, when taxed,	26-7
Aliens, how licenses may issue to,	31
Auditor to publish section of act,	33
Banks and insurance companies to report to auditor,	29
Commissions to sheriffs and collectors on license tax,	32
Commissions to sheriffs,	30-31
Commissioner's compensation,	31
Confederate States treasury notes, what receivable,	33
Corporation tax on,	23
Deduction from commissioner's compensation,	25
Deputy collectors, how appointed,	33
Domestic manufactures, how taxed,	27
Double tax, when,	25
Effect of change of firm,	27-8
Erroneous assessment,	25
Forms for tax payers,	24
Insolvents, how collected,	23
Licenses, how granted,	27
License to sutlers, &c.	23
License to merchant, a beginner,	28-9
License, where exercised,	24
Limitation of license,	24
List for auditor, clerk, &c., fees of commissioner for,	31
Market value of stocks to be taxed,	24
Number of slaves escaping to be ascertained,	31
Personal property exempt,	29-30
Penalty for failure to obtain license,	24
Penalties, how recoverable,	32-3
Population of counties, how estimated,	29
Redress against new assessment,	26
Slaves and similar subjects, how taxed,	25
Tax on corporations,	23
Tax tickets,	24
Taxes, when distrained for,	33-4
Value of lands and lots not to be changed,	25
When may be changed,	26
When agricultural productions to be taxed,	26-7

When double tax imposed, 25
When forms to be furnished, 24
When tax tickets to be made out, 24
When taxes may be distrained for, 33
Where license privilege to be exercised, 24

TAX BILL.
Resolution explanatory of, 126

TAX TICKETS.
When to be made out, 24

TELEGRAPH COMPANIES.
See Tax bill, 126
License to, 17

TERMS OF COURTS.
Tables showing, 137-39

THEATRICAL PERFORMANCES.
Tax on license for, 18

THORNTON, S. T.
Act for relief of, 112
Preamble, 112
Court to authorize removal of slaves, 112
Proviso, 112
Bond and security, 112
To report to court annually, 112
Court may require new bond, 112
Penalty for failure to give bond, 112

TOBACCO.
Act to limit production of, 70-71
Preamble, 70
Production of tobacco limited, 70
Number of plants to each hand, 70
List of field hands to be rendered on oath, 70
Proviso as to crop, 70
List, how returned, 70
Penalty for violating 1st section, 70
Amount of fine, 70
Forfeiture, how disposed of, 70
Penalty for violating 2d section, 71
Duties of judges and attorneys, 71
Duty of commissioners, 71
Continuance of act, 71

TOBACCO INSPECTORS (FEES OF).
Act increasing; Code amended, 57
Fees to inspectors, 58
Continuance of act, 58

TOLL BRIDGES.
Tax on, 7

TRANSFER OF PRISONERS.
Transfer directed, 121

TRANSFER OF STATE STOCK.
Tax on, 10

TRANSPORTATION OF SALT.
On rail roads and canals, 126

TRIAL.
See Circuit courts.

UNORGANIZED COMPANIES.
How taxed, 11

USURPED GOVERNMENT.
See Oath to support, 88

VALUE OF LANDS AND LOTS.
Not generally to be changed, 25
When may be changed, 25

VIRGINIA MILITARY INSTITUTE.
Act amending 2d and 5th sections of chapter 34 of Code, 60
Code amended, 60
Board of visitors, how appointed, 60
Board a corporation, 60
Code amended, 60
Expenses of board, 60
Preamble and resolutions as to disorderly practices at, 122
Condemnation expressed, 122
Instruction to officers, 122
Disapprobation of conduct of, 122
Requirement of officers, 122
Duty of officers, 122

VIRGINIA SOLDIERS.
See Agency for receiving and forwarding supplies to.

VOTING BY SOLDIERS.
See Election laws.

WHITE MALES.
Tax on, 4

WILLS AND ADMINISTRATIONS.
Taxes on, 10

WOMEN OF VIRGINIA.
Resolution in honor of, 121
Patriotism appreciated, 121
Regarded with highest admiration, 121
Resolution to be entered on journals, 121

ZARVONA, COL. R. T,
See Transfer of prisoners.

THE

NEW CONSTITUTION OF VIRGINIA,

WITH THE AMENDED

BILL OF RIGHTS,

AS ADOPTED BY THE

REFORM CONVENTION OF 1850-51,

AND AMENDED BY

THE CONVENTION OF 1860-61,

VIRGINIA BILL OF RIGHTS.

When, on the 15th of May 1776, the Convention of Virginia instructed their delegates in Congress to propose to that body to declare the United Colonies free and independent States, it, at the same time, appointed a committee to prepare a declaration of rights and such a plan of government as would be most likely to maintain peace and order in the Colony and secure substantial and equal liberty to the people. On subsequent days the committee was enlarged; Mr. George Mason was added to it on the 18th. The declaration of rights was on the 27th reported by Mr. Archibald Cary, the chairman of the committee, and, after being twice read, was ordered to be printed for the perusal of members. It was considered in committee of the whole on the 29th of May and the 3d, 4th, 5th and 10th of June. It was then reported to the house with amendments. On the 11th the convention considered the amendments, and having agreed thereto, ordered that the declaration (with the amendments) be fairly transcribed and read a third time. This having been done on the 12th, the declaration was then read a third time and passed nem. con. A manuscript copy of the first draft of the declaration, just as it was drawn by Mr. Mason,* is in the library of Virginia. The declaration as it passed was adopted without alteration by the Convention of 1829-30, and re-adopted with amendments by the Convention of 1850-51, and as amended is as follows: †

A Declaration of Rights made by the Representatives of the good people of VIRGINIA, *assembled in full and free Convention, which rights do pertain to them and their posterity as the basis and foundation of government.*

1. That all men are by nature equally free and independent, and have certain inherent rights, of which, when they enter into a state of society, they cannot, by any compact, deprive or divest their posterity; namely, the enjoyment of life and liberty, with the means of acquiring and possessing property, and pursuing and obtaining happiness and safety.

2. That all power is vested in, and consequently derived from, the people; that Magistrates are their trustees and servants, and at all times amenable to them.

3. That government is, or ought to be, instituted for the common benefit, protection and security of the people, nation, or community: of all the various modes and forms of government, that is best, which is capable of producing the greatest degree of happiness and safety, and is most effectually secured against the danger of mal-administration; and that, when any government shall be found inadequate or contrary to these purposes, a majority of the community hath an indubitable, unalienable, and indefensible right, to reform, alter, or abolish it, in such manner as shall be judged most conducive to the public weal.

4. That no man, or set of men, are entitled to exclusive or separate emoluments or privileges from the community, but in consideration of public services; which not being descendible, neither ought the offices of Magistrate, Legislator, or Judge, to be hereditary.

* Va. Hist. Reg. Jan. 1849, p. 29.
† See Acts 1852, p. 320-21. Sections amended are 5, 6, 8 and 11. The Bill of Rights as originally passed, is found in the Revised Code of 1819, p. 31-2, and Code of 1849, p 32, 33, 34, 1st Edition.

*5. That the legislative, executive and judicial powers should be separate and distinct; and that the members thereof may be restrained from oppression, by feeling and participating the burthens of the people, they should, at fixed periods, be reduced to a private station, return into that body from which they were originally taken, and the vacancies be supplied by frequent, certain, and regular elections, in which all, or any part of the former members, to be again eligible, or ineligible, as the laws shall direct.

†6. That all elections ought to be free: and that all men, having sufficient evidence of permanent common interest with, and attachment to, the community, have the right of suffrage, and cannot be taxed or deprived of their property for public uses, without their own consent, or that of their representatives so elected, nor bound by any law to which they have not, in like manner, assented, for the public good.

7. That all power of suspending laws, or the execution of laws, by any authority, without the consent of the representatives of the people, is injurious to their rights, and ought not to be exercised.

‡8. That, in all capital or criminal prosecutions, a man hath a right to demand the cause and nature of his accusation, to be confronted with the accusers and witnesses, to call for evidence in his favor, and to a speedy trial by an impartial jury of twelve men of his vicinage, without whose unanimous consent he cannot be found guilty; nor can he be compelled to give evidence against himself; that no man be deprived of his liberty, except by the law of the land or the judgment of his peers.

9. That excessive bail ought not to be required, nor excessive fines imposed, nor cruel and unusual punishments inflicted.

10. That general warrants, whereby an officer or messenger may be commanded to search suspected places without evidence of a fact committed, or to seize any person or persons not named, or whose offence is not particularly described and supported by evidence, are grievous and oppressive, and ought not to be granted.

11. That, in controversies respecting property, and in suits between man and man, the ancient trial by jury of twelve men is preferable to any other, and ought to be held sacred.

12. That the freedom of the press is one of the great bulwarks of liberty, and can never be restrained but by despotic governments.

13. That a well regulated militia, composed of the body of the people, trained to arms, is the proper, natural and safe defence of a free state; that standing armies, in time of peace, should be avoided, as dangerous to liberty; and that in all cases, the military should be under strict subordination to, and governed by, the civil power.

---

* Amended. Acts 1852, p. 321, § 5. The 5th section, without amendment, read: "That the legislative and executive powers of the state should be separate and distinct from the judiciary, and that the members of the two first" &c.
† Amend-d. Acts 1852, p. 321, § 6. The 6th section was: "That election of members to serve as representatives of the people in assembly" &c.
‡ Amended. Acts 1852, p. 321, § 8, 11. In the 8th and 11th sections, the words "of twelve men" inserted after the word "jury."

14. That the people have a right to uniform government; and therefore, that no government separate from, or independent of, the government of Virginia, ought to be erected or established within the limits thereof.

15. That no free government, or the blessings of liberty, can be preserved to any people, but by a firm adherence to justice, moderation, temperance, frugality, and virtue, and by a frequent recurrence to fundamental principles.

16. That religion, or the duty which we owe to our Creator, and the manner of discharging it, can be directed only by reason and conviction, not by force or violence; and therefore all men are equally entitled to the free exercise of religion, according to the dictates of conscience; and that it is the mutual duty of all to practice Christian forbearance, love, and charity towards each other.

CONSTITUTION OF VIRGINIA.

Mr. Archibald Cary, from the committee appointed for the purpose, reported on the 24th of June 1776 a plan of government for the colony. It was then read the first time, read a second time on the 26th, and considered in committee of the whole on that day and on the 27th and 28th. It was then reported to the house with amendments, which were read twice and agreed to. After being fairly transcribed, it was read a third time on the 29th and passed unanimously.*

This constitution or form of government was originally drawn up by George Mason.† Mr. Jefferson had put a draft of one into the hands of Mr. Wythe, who reached Williamsburg after the other was committed to the committee of the whole. Two or three parts of Mr. Jefferson's plan were, with little alteration, inserted in the other; and his preamble was also adopted.‡

The constitution so resolved upon may be seen in the 9th volume of Hening's Statutes at Large, page 112 to 119, and in the editions of the Code of Virginia published from 1776 to 1819. At the end of it, in the Code of 1819, will be seen a note of Mr. Leigh as to the form of the colonial government for which it was substituted. This constitution was in force until superseded by the amended constitution or form of government for Virginia, which, on the 15th of January 1830, was submitted and proposed to the people of Virginia by their delegates and representatives, in convention assembled.

This amended constitution continued in force until January 1852. A convention to form a new constitution was called. It assembled on the 14th October 1850, and the present constitution was adopted on the 1st of August 1851. It was ratified by the people on the 4th Thursday in October following. On the second Monday of the succeeding December an election was held for the legislature, governor, lieutenant governor and attorney general. The first general assembly convened on the second Monday in January (the 12th day of the month), and the first governor and lieutenant governor qualified on the 16th of January 1852. The constitution thus formed and put into operation is as follows:

ARTICLE I.
Preamble.

Bill of rights.
Sec.
1. Force of bill of rights.

ARTICLE II.
Division of powers.
1. Division of powers between departments.

ARTICLE III.
Qualification of voters.
1. Right of suffrage.
2. Cities and towns to be laid off into wards. Places for elections. Citizens to vote in their wards.
3. Exemption of voters.
4. How votes are given.

ARTICLE IV.
Legislative department.
1. Legislature, how composed.
2. House of delegates, how chosen. Number of delegates to each county, city or election district.

Sec.
3. Senate, how elected. Returning officers, when and where to meet. Senate classified. Term of service.
4. Senatorial districts.
5. Apportionment of representation. How submitted to the vote of the people.
6. How long polls to be kept open. When and how certified. Governor to communicate result to legislature. When again referred to the people. Reapportionment according to vote of people.
7. Qualification of senators and delegates. Disqualification. Removals to vacate office.
8. Legislature, how often to meet. Sessions, how long. Adjournment, how long, and where. Quorum. How attendance enforced.
9. Speaker of house and president of senate. Officers; rules; writs of election, by whom issued. Houses to judge of elections, &c. Members punished.
10. Pay of members. Ineligible to offices in certain cases.
11. Bills and resolutions, where to originate and how disposed of.
12. Journal; yeas and nays, how recorded. How bills to be read.
13. Representation in congress, how apportioned.
14. Congressional districts, how formed.
15. Habeas corpus not suspended. Legislative power restrained in certain cases. Freedom of speech or of the press. Religious liberty.

*Journal of the Convention.
† Mr. Madison's letter in Sparks' Writings of Washington, vol. 9, page 548.
‡ Mr. Wythe's letter of the 27th of July 1776 to Mr. Jefferson. Burke's Va., vol. 4, p. 150, 151.

CONSTITUTION OF VIRGINIA.

Sec.	
16.	Laws, how to be framed.
17.	Disqualification for duelling
18.	Impeachments, how presented. Extent of judgment. Senate may sit during legislative recess.
19.	How emancipated slaves forfeit their freedom.
20.	Restrictions on emancipation. Removal of free negroes.
21.	Legislature not to emancipate.
22.	Taxation to be uniform and ad valorem.
23.	Property, how exempt from tax.
24.	Capitation tax. What part applied to schools. Exemption for infirmity.
25.	Tax on incomes, salaries and licenses.
26.	How money drawn from treasury. Financial statement to be published.
27.	On what acts yeas and nays required. Majority of all requisite.
28.	Debts to state by corporations not to be released. State faith not to be pledged for corporations.
29.	Sinking fund.
30.	How state stocks may be sold.
31.	Loans, when redeemable.
32.	Charter to churches prohibited. Church property, how secured.
33.	Lotteries prohibited.
34.	New counties, how formed. Voters in election districts, where to vote.
35.	Power over divorces, names and sale of property.
36.	Registration of voters, and of births, marriages and deaths.
37.	State census. Returns thereof.
38.	Provision relative to elections and vacancies in office.

ARTICLE V.

Executive department.

1.	Governor; his term; eligibility to office.
2.	How elected. Returns of election of governor, how disposed of. Votes, when and how counted. Election, how decided. Contested elections.
3.	Who eligible to office of governor.
4.	Where to reside. His pay.
5.	His duties and powers.
6.	Power to require information from executive officers and opinions from attorney general.
7.	Commissions and grants to be in name of commonwealth. How attested.
8.	Lieutenant governor, how elected; his term and qualification.
9.	When to act as governor. Who to discharge executive functions.
10.	President of senate; his compensation.
11.	Secretary, treasurer and auditor, how elected; their terms.
12.	Record of governor's acts, how kept; when laid before legislature. Duties of secretary.
13.	Powers and duties of treasurer and auditor.
14.	Board of public works, how elected; term of office.

Sec.	
15.	Legislature to provide for election; compensation and organization of board. Board, when to meet.
16.	Officers on public works, how appointed. Duties of board.
17.	How removed from office.
18.	Board, how abolished.
19.	Appointment of militia officers.

ARTICLE VI.

Judiciary department.

1.	Judiciary: of what courts composed. Jurisdiction.
2.	Judicial divisions. Circuits.
3.	Districts.
4.	Sections.
5.	Rearrangement of judicial divisions, how made.
6.	Judges of circuit courts, how elected, their term, age and residence.
7.	Circuit courts, when held.
8.	District courts, when held and by whom.
9.	Jurisdiction.
10.	Court of appeals, how elected; term of office, age and residence.
11.	Court, how constituted. Its jurisdiction.
12.	Special court of appeals, how constituted. Its powers and duties.
13.	Reasons of decisions of court of appeals to be recorded.
14.	Judges, how commissioned; their salaries; mileage.
15.	Judges not to hold other offices.
16.	Elections of judges, when not to be held.
17.	Judges, how removed from office. Notice to be given.
18.	Officers of courts, how appointed; their duties, pay and tenure.
19.	Clerk of circuit court, how elected; term of office. Attorneys, how elected; their term, duties and pay; how removed.
20.	Vacancy in office of clerk, how filled.
21.	Pay of jurors.
22.	Attorney general, how elected; his term. How commissioned; his duties and pay; how removed.
23.	Judges and officers to remain such until successors qualified.
24.	Writs, how attested. Conclusion of indictments.
25.	County courts, how constituted, and when held.
26.	Their jurisdiction.
27.	Districts for election of justices; how elected and commissioned; their term. Presiding justice, his duty. Justices classified.
28.	Pay of justices.
29.	Powers and jurisdiction.
30.	County officers, how elected; their term.
31.	Officers, where to reside. Eligibility of sheriffs.
32.	County officers subject to indictment.
33.	Jurisdiction of corporation courts and magistrates.
34.	Corporation officers, how elected, or appointed.

Whereas the delegates and representatives of the good people of Virginia, in convention assembled, on the twenty-ninth day of June, in the year of our Lord one thousand seven hundred and seventy-six—reciting and declaring, that whereas George the Third, king of Great Britain and Ireland and elector of Hanover, before that time entrusted with the exercise of the kingly office in the government of Virginia, had endeavored to pervert the same into a detestable and insupportable tyranny, by putting his negative on laws the most wholesome and necessary for the public good; by denying his governors permission to pass laws of immediate and pressing importance, unless suspended in their operation for his assent, and when so suspended, neglecting to attend to them for many years; by refusing to pass certain other laws, unless the persons to be benefited by them would relinquish the inestimable right of representation in the legislature; by dissolving legislative assemblies repeatedly and continually, for opposing with manly firmness his invasions of the rights of the people; when dissolved, by refusing to call others for a long space of time, thereby leaving the political system without any legislative head; by endeavoring to prevent the population of our country, and for that purpose obstructing the laws for the naturalization of foreigners; by keeping among us, in time of peace, standing armies and ships of war; by affecting to render the military independent of and superior to the civil power; by combining with others to subject us to a foreign jurisdiction, giving his assent to their pretended acts of legislation, for quartering large bodies of armed troops among us, for cutting off our trade with all parts of the world, for imposing taxes on us without our consent, for depriving us of the benefits of the trial by jury, for transporting us beyond seas to be tried for pretended offences, for suspending our own legislatures, and declaring themselves invested with power to legislate for us in all cases whatsoever; by plundering our seas, ravaging our coasts, burning our towns, and destroying the lives of our people; by inciting insurrections of our fellow subjects with the allurements of forfeiture and confiscation; by prompting our negroes to rise in arms among us—those very negroes, whom, by an inhuman use of his negative, he had refused us permission to exclude by law; by endeavoring to bring on the inhabitants of our frontiers the merciless Indian savages, whose known rule of warfare is an undistinguished destruction of all ages, sexes and conditions of existence; by transporting hither a large army of foreign mercenaries to complete the work of death, desolation and tyranny, then already begun with circumstances of cruelty and perfidy unworthy the head of a civilized nation; by answering our repeated petitions for redress with a repetition of injuries; and finally, by abandoning the helm of government, and declaring us out of his allegiance and protection; by which several acts of misrule, the government of this country, as before exercised under the crown of Great Britain, was totally dissolved—did, therefore, having maturely considered the premises, and viewing with great concern the deplorable condition to which this once happy country would be reduced, unless some regular, adequate mode of civil policy should be speedily adopted, and in compliance with the recommendation of the general congress, ordain and declare a form of government of Virginia:

And whereas a convention held on the first Monday in October, in the year one thousand eight hundred and twenty-nine, did propose to the people of the commonwealth an amended constitution or form of government, which was ratified by them:

And whereas the general assembly of Virginia, by an act passed on the fourth of March, in the year one thousand eight hundred and fifty, did provide for the election, by the people, of delegates to meet in general convention, to consider, discuss and propose a new constitution, or alterations and amendments to the existing constitution of this commonwealth; and by an act passed on the thirteenth of March, in the year one thousand eight hundred and fifty-one, did further provide for submitting the same to the people for ratification or rejection:

We, therefore, the delegates of the good people of Virginia, elected and in convention assembled, in pursuance of said acts, do propose to the people the following constitution and form of government for this commonwealth:

ARTICLE I.

BILL OF RIGHTS.

The declaration of rights, as amended and prefixed to this constitution, shall have the same relation thereto as it had to the former constitution.

ARTICLE II.

DIVISION OF POWERS.

The legislative, executive and judiciary departments shall be separate and distinct, so that neither exercise the powers properly belonging to either of the others; nor shall any person exercise the powers of more than one of them at the same time, except that justices of the peace shall be eligible to either house of assembly.

ARTICLE III.

QUALIFICATION OF VOTERS.

1. Every white male citizen of the commonwealth, of the age of twenty-one years, who has been a resident of the state for two years, and of the county, city or town where he offers to vote for twelve months next preceding an election—and no other person—shall be qualified to vote for members of the general assembly and all officers elective by the people: but no person in the military, naval or marine service of the Confederate States shall be deemed a resident of this state, by reason of being stationed therein. And no person shall have the right to vote, who is of unsound mind, or a pauper, or a non-commissioned officer, soldier, seaman or marine in the service of the Confederate States, or who has been convicted of bribery in an election, or of any infamous offence.

2. The general assembly, at its first session after the adoption of this constitution, and afterwards as occasion may require, shall cause every city or town, the white population of which exceeds five thousand, to be laid off into convenient wards, and a separate place of voting to be established in each; and thereafter no inhabitant of such city or town shall be allowed to vote except in the ward in which he resides.

3. No voter, during the time for holding any election at which he is entitled to vote, shall be compelled to perform military service, except in time of war or public danger; to work upon the public roads, or to attend any court as suitor, juror or witness; and no voter shall be subject to arrest under any civil process during his attendance at elections, or in going to and returning from them.

4. In all elections votes shall be given openly, or viva voce, and not by ballot; but dumb persons entitled to suffrage may vote by ballot.

ARTICLE IV.

LEGISLATIVE DEPARTMENT.

1. The legislature shall be formed of two distinct branches, which together shall be a complete legislature, and shall be called the General Assembly of Virginia.

House of Delegates.

2. One of these shall be called the House of Delegates, and shall consist of one hundred and fifty-two members, to be chosen biennially for and by the several counties, cities and towns of the commonwealth, and distributed and apportioned as follows:

The counties of Augusta and Rockingham and the city of Richmond shall each elect three delegates; the counties of Albemarle, Bedford, Berkeley, Campbell, Fauquier, Franklin, Frederick, Halifax, Hampshire, Harrison, Jefferson, Kanawha, Loudoun, Marion, Monongalia, Monroe, Norfolk, Pittsylvania, Preston, Rockbridge, Shenandoah and Washington shall each elect two delegates; the counties of Botetourt and Craig shall together elect two delegates.

The counties of Accomack, Alexandria, Amherst, Appomattox, Barbour, Brunswick, Buckingham, Cabell, Caroline, Carroll, Charlotte, Chesterfield, Clarke, Culpeper, Dinwiddie, Fairfax, Floyd, Fluvanna, Giles, Gloucester, Goochland, Grayson, Greenbrier, Hanover, Hardy, Henrico, Henry, Highland, Isle of Wight, Jackson, King William, Lee, Lewis, Louisa, Lunenburg, Madison, Marshall, Mason, Mercer, Mecklenburg, Montgomery, Morgan, Nansemond, Nelson, Northampton, Page, Patrick, Pendleton, Pocahontas, Princess Anne, Prince Edward, Prince William, Pulaski, Putnam, Randolph, Rappahannock, Roanoke, Scott, Smyth, Southampton, Spotsylvania, Taylor, Upshur, Warren, Wayne, Wetzel, Wood and Wythe, and the cities of Norfolk and Petersburg, shall each elect one delegate.*

The counties of Lee and Scott, in addition to the delegate to be elected by each, shall together elect one delegate.

The following counties and cities shall compose election districts: Alleghany and Bath; Amelia and Nottoway; Boone, Wyoming and Logan; Braxton and Nicholas; Charles City, James City and New Kent; Cumberland and Powhatan; Doddridge and Tyler; Elizabeth City, Warwick, York, and the city of Williamsburg; Essex and King & Queen; Fayette and Raleigh; Gilmer and Wirt; Greene

---

*Since the adoption of the constitution, the following counties have been formed: The county of Calhoun constitutes a part of the election district of Gilmer and Wirt. Acts 1855-6, p. 91, ch. 108, § 10. The acts establishing the counties of Wise and Roane do not prescribe how they shall vote for members of the house of delegates. See Acts 1855-6, p. 89, § 13, 14, for Wise, and p. 94, § 15, for Roane. They will elect delegates therefore under the constitution, each part voting with the county from which it was taken. The county of Tucker votes with the county of Randolph as an election district. Id. p. 97, ch. 110, § 14. The act forming the county of McDowell has no provision for electing a delegate. The counties of McDowell and Tazewell therefore vote together. Acts 1857-8, p. 103, ch. 155, § 13. The county of Buchanan is not provided for in the act creating it, and is therefore in the same condition, and votes for a delegate with Tazewell and Russell. Id. p. 110, ch. 156, § 14. The county of Clay forms a part of the electoral district with Braxton and Nicholas. Id. p. 113, ch. 158, § 14. The county of Webster is formed out of the counties of Braxton, Nicholas and Randolph. The voters of the county of Webster are to vote as they have heretofore voted for members of the house of delegates. Acts 1859-60, p. 156, ch. 47, § 15. So much of Bland county as was taken respectively from Giles, Tazewell and Wythe, shall remain attached to the electoral, congressional and senatorial districts respectively to which the said counties from which it was taken belong, and shall vote with said counties for members of the house of delegates.

and Orange; Greenesville and Sussex; King George and Stafford; Lancaster and Northumberland; Matthews and Middlesex; Pleasants and Ritchie; Prince George and Surry; and Richmond and Westmoreland—each of which districts shall elect one delegate.

At the first general election, under this constitution, the county of Ohio shall elect three delegates, and the counties of Brooke and Hancock shall together elect one delegate; at the second general election, the county of Ohio shall elect two delegates, and the counties of Brooke and Hancock shall each elect one delegate; and so on, alternately, at succeeding general elections.

At the first general election, the county of Russell shall elect two delegates, and the county of Tazewell shall elect one delegate; at the second general election, the county of Tazewell shall elect two delegates, and the county of Russell shall elect one delegate; and so on, alternately, at succeeding general elections.*

The general assembly shall have power, upon application of a majority of the voters of the county of Campbell, to provide, that instead of the two delegates to be elected by said county, the town of Lynchburg shall elect one delegate, and the residue of the county of Campbell shall elect one delegate.

Senate.

3. The other house of the general assembly shall be called the Senate, and shall consist of fifty members, to be elected for the term of four years; for the election of whom, the counties, cities and towns shall be divided into fifty districts. Each county, city and town of the respective districts, at the time of the first election of its delegate or delegates under this constitution, shall vote for one senator; and the sheriffs or other officers holding the election for each county, city and town, within five days at farthest after the last election in the district, shall meet at the court-house of the county or city first named in the district, and from the polls so taken in their respective counties, cities and towns, return as senator the person who has received the greatest number of votes in the whole district. Upon the assembling of the senators so elected, they shall be divided in two equal classes, to be numbered by lot. The term of service of the senators of the first class shall expire with that of the delegates first elected under this constitution, and of the senators of the second class at the expiration of two years thereafter; and this alternation shall be continued, so that one-half of the senators may be chosen every second year.

4. For the election of senators—

I. The counties of Accomack and Northampton shall form one district:
II. The city of Norfolk shall be another district:
III. The counties of Norfolk and Princess Anne shall form another district:
IV. The counties of Isle of Wight, Nansemond and Surry shall form another district:
V. The counties of Sussex, Southampton and Greenesville shall form another district:
VI. The city of Petersburg and the county of Prince George shall form another district:
VII. The counties of Dinwiddie, Amelia and Brunswick shall form another district:
VIII. The counties of Powhatan, Cumberland and Chesterfield shall form another district:

* See note on page 10.

IX. The counties of Lunenburg, Nottoway and Prince Edward shall form another district:
X. The counties of Mecklenburg and Charlotte shall form another district:
XI. The county of Pittsylvania shall be another district:
XII. The county of Halifax shall be another district:
XIII. The counties of Henry, Patrick and Franklin shall form another district:
XIV. The county of Bedford shall be another district:
XV. The counties of Campbell and Appomattox shall form another district:
XVI. The city of Williamsburg and the counties of James City, Charles City, New Kent, York, Elizabeth City and Warwick shall form another district:
XVII. The counties of Henrico and Hanover shall form another district:
XVIII. The city of Richmond shall be another district:
XIX. The counties of Gloucester, Matthews and Middlesex shall form another district:
XX. The counties of Richmond, Lancaster, Northumberland and Westmoreland shall form another district:
XXI. The counties of King & Queen. King William and Essex shall form another district:
XXII. The counties of Caroline and Spotsylvania shall form another district:
XXIII. The counties of Stafford, King George and Prince William shall form another district:
XXIV. The counties of Fairfax and Alexandria shall form another district:
XXV. The county of Loudoun shall be another district:
XXVI. The counties of Fauquier and Rappahannock shall form another district:
XXVII. The counties of Madison, Culpeper, Orange and Greene shall form another district:
XXVIII. The county of Albemarle shall be another district:
XXIX. The counties of Louisa, Goochland and Fluvanna shall form another district:
XXX. The counties of Nelson, Amherst and Buckingham shall form another district:
XXXI. The counties of Jefferson and Berkeley shall form another district:
XXXII. The counties of Hampshire, Hardy and Morgan shall form another district:
XXXIII. The counties of Frederick, Clarke and Warren shall form another district:
XXXIV. The counties of Shenandoah and Page shall form another district:
XXXV. The counties of Rockingham and Pendleton shall form another district:
XXXVI. The county of Augusta shall be another district:
XXXVII. The counties of Bath, Highland and Rockbridge shall form another district:
XXXVIII. The counties of Botetourt, Alleghany, Roanoke and Craig shall form another district:
XXXIX. The counties of Carroll, Floyd, Grayson, Montgomery and Pulaski shall form another district:
XL. The counties of Mercer, Monroe, Giles and Tazewell shall form another district:*
XLI. The counties of Smyth, Wythe and Washington shall form another district:
XLII. The counties of Scott, Lee and Russell shall form another district:*
XLIII. The counties of Boone, Logan, Kanawha, Putnam and Wyoming shall form another district:*
XLIV. The counties of Nicholas, Fayette, Pocahontas, Raleigh, Braxton and Greenbrier shall form another district:*
XLV. The counties of Mason, Jackson, Cabell, Wayne and Wirt shall form another district:*
XLVI. The counties of Ritchie, Doddridge, Harrison, Pleasants and Wood shall form another district:

* Since the adoption of the constitution, the county of Wise has been attached to the 42d senatorial district. Acts 1855-6, p. 89, § 19. The county of Calhoun, to the 48th district. Id. p. 91, § 10 The county of Roane, to three districts, viz: so much as was taken from Kanawha, belongs to the 43d district; so much as was taken from Jackson, to the 45th district, and so much as was taken from Gilmer, to the 46th district. Id p. 94, § 15. The county of Tucker, to the 48th district. Id. p. 97, § 14. The county of McDowell, to the 40th district. Acts 1857-8, p. 108, ch. 155, § 13. The county of Buchanan, to the 42d district. Id p. 110, § 13. The county of Clay, to the 44th district. Id. p. 113, § 14. The county of Webster is attached to two senatorial districts. The part taken from Nicholas and Braxton votes in the 44th, and the part taken from Randolph, in the 48th districts. Acts 1859-60, p. 156, ch. 17, § 15. So much of Bland county as was taken respectively from Giles, Tazewell and Wythe, shall remain attached to the electoral, congressional and senatorial districts respectively to which the said counties from which it was taken belong, and shall vote with said counties for members of the house of delegates.

XLVII. The counties of Wetzel, Marshall, Marion and Tyler shall form another district:
XLVIII. The counties of Upshur, Barbour, Lewis, Gilmer and Randolph shall form another district:*
XLIX. The counties of Monongalia, Preston and Taylor shall form another district:
L. The counties of Brooke, Hancock and Ohio shall form another district:

Apportionment of Representation.

5. It shall be the duty of the general assembly, in the year one thousand eight hundred and sixty-five, and in every tenth year thereafter, in case it can agree upon a principle of representation, to reapportion representation in the senate and house of delegates in accordance therewith; and in the event the general assembly, at the first or any subsequent period of reapportionment, shall fail to agree upon a principle of representation and to reapportion representation in accordance therewith, each house shall separately propose a scheme of representation, containing a principle or rule for the house of delegates, in connection with a principle or rule for the senate. And it shall be the duty of the general assembly, at the same session, to certify to the governor the principles or rules of representation which the respective houses may separately propose, to be applied in making reapportionments in the senate and in the house of delegates: and the governor shall, as soon thereafter as may be, by proclamation, make known the propositions of the respective houses, and require the voters of the commonwealth to assemble, at such time as he shall appoint, at their lawful places of voting, and decide by their votes between the propositions thus presented. In the event the general assembly shall fail, in the year one thousand eight hundred and sixty-five, or in any tenth year thereafter, to make such reapportionment or certificate, the governor shall, immediately after the adjournment of the general assembly, by proclamation, require the voters of the commonwealth to assemble, at such time as he shall appoint, at their lawful places of voting, and to declare by their votes:

First, whether representation in the senate and house of delegates shall be apportioned on the "Suffrage Basis;" that is, according to the number of voters in the several counties, cities, towns, and senatorial districts of the commonwealth:

Or, second, whether representation in both houses shall be apportioned on the "Mixed Basis;" that is, according to the number of white inhabitants contained, and the amount of all state taxes paid, in the several counties, cities and towns of the commonwealth, deducting therefrom all taxes paid on licenses and law process, and any capitation tax on free negroes, allowing one delegate for every seventy-sixth part of said inhabitants, and one delegate for every seventy-sixth part of said taxes, and distributing the senators in like manner:

Or, third, whether representation shall be apportioned in the senate on taxation; that is, according to the amount of all state taxes paid in the several counties, cities and towns of the commonwealth, deducting therefrom all taxes paid on licenses and law process, and any capitation tax on free negroes, and in the house of delegates on the "Suffrage Basis" as aforesaid:

Or, fourth, whether representation shall be apportioned in the senate on the "Mixed Basis" as aforesaid, and in the house of delegates on the "Suffrage Basis"

* See note on page 12.

as aforesaid: and each voter shall cast his vote in favor of one of said schemes of apportionment, and no more.

6. It shall be the duty of the sheriffs and other officers taking said polls, to keep the same open for the period of three days, and within five days after they are closed, to certify true copies thereof to the governor, who shall, as early as may be, ascertain the result of said vote, and make proclamation thereof; and in case it is ascertained that a majority of all the votes cast is in favor of either of the principles of representation, referred as aforesaid to the choice of the voters, the governor shall communicate the result of such vote to the general assembly, at its first regular session thereafter; but in case it is ascertained that a majority of all the votes cast is not in favor of either of the principles of representation referred as aforesaid to the choice of the voters, it shall be the duty of the governor, as soon as may be after ascertaining that fact, in like manner to cause the voters to decide between the two principles of representation which shall, at such previous voting, have received the greatest number of votes; and he shall ascertain and make proclamation of the result of the said last vote, and communicate the same to the general assembly at its next regular session; and in either case, the general assembly, at the regular session thereof, which shall be held next after the taking of the vote, the result of which shall have been so communicated to it by the governor, shall reapportion representation in the two houses respectively in accordance with the principle of representation in each, for which a majority of the votes cast were given; and it shall be the duty of the general assembly in every tenth year thereafter to reapportion and distribute the number of senators and delegates in accordance with the same principle.

Qualifications of Senators and Delegates.

7. Any person may be elected senator, who, at the time of election, has attained the age of twenty-five years, and is actually a resident within the district, and qualified to vote for members of the general assembly, according to this constitution. And any person may be elected a member of the house of delegates, who, at the time of election, has attained the age of twenty-one years, and is actually a resident within the county, city, town or election district, qualified to vote for members of the general assembly according to this constitution; but no person holding a lucrative office, no minister of the gospel or priest of any religious denomination, no salaried officer of any banking corporation or company, and no attorney for the commonwealth, shall be capable of being elected a member of either house of assembly. The removal of any person elected to either branch of the general assembly from the county, city, town or district for which he was elected, shall vacate his office.

Powers and Duties of the General Assembly.

8. The general assembly shall meet once in every two years, and not oftener, unless convened by the governor in the manner prescribed in this constitution. No session of the general assembly, after the first under this constitution, shall continue longer than ninety days, without the concurrence of three-fifths of the members elected to each house; in which case, the session may be extended for a

further period, not exceeding thirty days. Neither house, during the session of the general assembly, shall, without the consent of the other, adjourn for more than three days, nor to any other place than that in which the two houses shall be sitting. A majority of each house shall constitute a quorum to do business, but a smaller number may adjourn from day to day, and shall be authorized to compel the attendance of absent members in such manner and under such penalties as each house may provide.

9. The house of delegates shall choose its own speaker, and, in the absence of the lieutenant governor, or when he shall exercise the office of governor, the senate shall choose from their own body a president pro tempore; and each house shall appoint its own officers, settle its own rules of proceeding, and direct writs of election for supplying intermediate vacancies: but if vacancies shall occur during the recess of the general assembly, such writs may be issued by the governor, under such regulations as may be prescribed by law. Each house shall judge of the election, qualification and returns of its members, may punish them for disorderly behavior, and, with the concurrence of two-thirds, expel a member, but not a second time for the same offence.

10. The members of the assembly shall receive for their services a compensation, to be ascertained by law, and paid out of the public treasury; but no act increasing such compensation shall take effect until after the end of the term for which the members of the house of delegates voting thereon were elected. And no senator or delegate, during the term for which he shall have been elected, shall be appointed to any civil office of profit under the commonwealth, which has been created, or the emoluments of which have been increased, during such term, except offices filled by elections by the people.

11. Bills and resolutions may originate in either of the two houses of the general assembly, to be approved or rejected by the other, and may be amended by either house, with the consent of the other.

12. Each house of the general assembly shall keep a journal of its proceedings, which shall be published from time to time, and the yeas and nays of the members of either house, on any question, shall, at the desire of one-fifth of those present, be entered on the journal. No bill shall become a law until it has been read on three different days of the session in the house in which it originated, unless two-thirds of the members elected to that house shall otherwise determine.

13. The whole number of members to which the state may at any time be entitled in the house of representatives of the Confederate States, shall be apportioned as nearly as may be amongst the several counties, cities and towns of the state, according to their respective numbers; which shall be determined, by adding to the whole number of free persons, including those bound to service for a term of years, and excluding Indians not taxed, three-fifths of all other persons.

14. In the apportionment, the state shall be divided into districts, corresponding in number with the representatives to which it may be entitled in the house of representatives of the congress of the Confederate States, which shall be formed respectively of contiguous counties, cities and towns, be compact, and include, as nearly as may be, an equal number of the population, upon which is based representation in the house of representatives of the Confederate States.

15. The privilege of the writ of habeas corpus shall not in any case be suspended. The general assembly shall not pass any bill of attainder; or any ex post facto law; or any law impairing the obligation of contracts; or any law whereby private property shall be taken for public uses without just compensation; or any law abridging the freedom of speech or of the press. No man shall be compelled to frequent or support any religious worship, place or ministry whatsoever; nor shall any man be enforced, restrained, molested or burthened in his body or goods, or otherwise suffer, on account of his religious opinions or belief; but all men shall be free to profess, and by argument to maintain their opinions in matters of religion, and the same shall in nowise affect, diminish or enlarge their civil capacities. And the general assembly shall not prescribe any religious test whatever; or confer any peculiar privileges or advantages on any sect or denomination; or pass any law requiring or authorizing any religious society, or the people of any district within this commonwealth, to levy on themselves or others any tax for the erection or repair of any house for public worship, or for the support of any church or ministry; but it shall be left free to every person to select his religious instructor, and to make for his support such private contract as he shall please.

16. No law shall embrace more than one object, which shall be expressed in its title; nor shall any law be revived or amended by reference to its title, but the act revived or section amended shall be re-enacted and published at length.

17. The general assembly may provide that no person shall be capable of holding, or being elected to, any post of profit, trust or emolument, civil or military, legislative, executive or judicial, under the government of this commonwealth, who shall hereafter fight a duel, or send or accept a challenge to fight a duel, the probable issue of which may be the death of the challenger or challenged, or who shall be second to either party, or shall in any manner aid or assist in such duel, or shall be knowingly the bearer of such challenge or acceptance; but no person shall be so disqualified by reason of his having heretofore fought such duel, or sent or accepted such challenge, or been second in such duel, or bearer of such challenge or acceptance.

18. The governor, lieutenant governor, judges, and all others offending against the state, by mal-administration, corruption, neglect of duty, or other high crime or misdemeanor, shall be impeachable by the house of delegates and be prosecuted before the senate, which shall have the sole power to try impeachments. When sitting for that purpose they shall be on oath or affirmation; and no person shall be convicted without the concurrence of two-thirds of the members present. Judgment, in cases of impeachment, shall not extend further than to removal from office, and disqualification to hold and enjoy any office of honor, trust or profit under the commonwealth; but the party convicted shall nevertheless be subject to indictment, trial, judgment and punishment, according to law. The senate may sit, during the recess of the general assembly, for the trial of impeachments.

Slaves and Free Negroes.

19. Slaves hereafter emancipated shall forfeit their freedom by remaining in the commonwealth more than twelve months after they become actually free, and shall be reduced to slavery under such regulation as may be prescribed by law.

20. The general assembly may impose such restrictions and conditions as they shall deem proper on the power of slave owners to emancipate their slaves; and may pass laws for the relief of the commonwealth from the free negro population, by removal or otherwise.

21. The general assembly shall not emancipate any slave, or the descendant of any slave, either before or after the birth of such descendant.

Taxation and Finance.

22, 23, amended by ordinance of state convention, No. 39, which was ratified by vote of the people on the fourth Thursday in May eighteen hundred and sixty-one, to take effect on the first July eighteen hundred and sixty-one, so as to read as follows:

"Taxation shall be equal and uniform throughout the commonwealth; and all property shall be taxed in proportion to its value, which shall be ascertained in such manner as may be prescribed by law; but any property may be exempted from taxation by the vote of a majority of the whole number of members elected to each house of the general assembly."

24. A capitation tax, equal to the tax assessed on land of the value of two hundred dollars, shall be levied on every white male inhabitant who has attained the age of twenty-one years; and one equal moiety of the capitation tax upon white persons shall be applied to the purposes of education in primary and free schools; but nothing herein contained shall prevent exemptions of taxable polls in cases of bodily infirmity.

25. The general assembly may levy a tax on incomes, salaries and licenses; but no tax shall be levied on property from which any income so taxed is derived, or on the capital invested in the trade or business in respect to which the license so taxed is issued.

26. No money shall be drawn from the treasury but in pursuance of appropriations made by law; and a statement of the receipts, disbursements, appropriations and loans shall be published after the adjournment of each session of the general assembly, with the acts and resolutions thereof.

27. On the passage of every act which imposes, continues or revives a tax, or creates a debt or charge, or makes, continues or revives any appropriation of public or trust money or property, or releases, discharges or commutes any claim or demand of the state, the vote shall be determined by yeas and nays, and the names of the persons voting for and against the same shall be entered on the journals of the respective houses, and a majority of all the members elected to each house shall be necessary to give it the force of a law.

28. The liability to the state of any incorporated company or institution to redeem the principal and pay the interest of any loan heretofore made, or which may hereafter be made by the state to such company or institution, shall not be released; and the general assembly shall not pledge the faith of the state, or bind it in any form, for the debts or obligations of any company or corporation.

29. There shall be set apart annually, from the accruing revenues, a sum equal to seven per cent. of the state debt existing on the first day of January in the year one thousand eight hundred and fifty-two. The fund thus set apart shall be called the Sinking fund, and shall be applied to the payment of the interest of the state debt, and the principal of such part as may be redeemable. If no part be redeemable, then the residue of the sinking fund, after the payment of such interest, shall be invested in the bonds or certificates of debt of this commonwealth, or of the Confederate States, or of some of the states of this Confederacy, and applied to the payment of the state debt as it shall become redeemable. Whenever, after the said first day of January, a debt shall be contracted by the commonwealth, there shall be set apart in like manner, annually, for thirty-four years, a sum exceeding by one per cent. the aggregate amount of the annual interest agreed to be paid thereon at the time of its contraction; which sum shall be part of the sinking fund, and shall be applied in the manner before directed. The general assembly shall not otherwise appropriate any part of the sinking fund or its accruing interest, except in time of war, insurrection or invasion.

30. The general assembly may, at any time, direct a sale of the stocks held by the commonwealth in internal improvement and other companies; but the proceeds of such sale, if made before the payment of the public debt, shall constitute a part of the sinking fund, and be applied in like manner.

31. The general assembly shall not contract loans or cause to be issued certificates of debt or bonds of the state, irredeemable for a period greater than thirty-four years.

General Provisions.

32. The general assembly shall not grant a charter of incorporation to any church or religious denomination, but may secure the title to church property to an extent to be limited by law.

33. No lottery shall hereafter be authorized by law; and the buying, selling or transferring of tickets or chances in any lottery not now authorized by a law of this state, shall be prohibited.

34. No new county shall be formed with an area less than six hundred square miles; nor shall the county or counties from which it is formed be reduced below that area; nor shall any county, having a white population less than five thousand, be deprived of more than one fifth of such population; nor shall a county having a larger white population be reduced below four thousand. But any county, the length of which is three times its mean breadth, or which exceeds fifty miles in length, may be divided at the discretion of the general assembly. In all general elections the voters in any county, not entitled to separate representation, shall vote in the same election district.

35. The general assembly shall confer on the courts the power to grant divorces, change the names of persons, and direct the sale of estates belonging to infants and other persons under legal disabilities, but shall not, by special legislation, grant relief in such cases, or in any other case of which the courts or other tribunals may have jurisdiction.

36. The general assembly shall provide for the periodical registration in the several counties, cities and towns, of the voters therein; and for the annual registration of the births, marriages and deaths in the white population, and of the births and deaths in the colored population of the same, distinguishing between the numbers of the free colored persons and slaves.

37. The general assembly, at intervals of five years from the dates of the returns of the census of the Confederate States, shall cause to be taken a census and such statistics of this state as may be prescribed by law; which census and statistics shall be returned to the secretary of the commonwealth, who shall compare and correct the returns and report the same to the general assembly.

38. The manner of conducting and making returns of elections, of determining contested elections, and of filling vacancies in office, in cases not specially provided for by this constitution, shall be prescribed by law; but special elections to fill vacancies in the office of judge of any court shall be for a full term. And the general assembly may declare the cases in which any office shall be deemed vacant, where no provision is made for that purpose in this constitution.

ARTICLE V.

EXECUTIVE DEPARTMENT.

Governor.

1. The chief executive power of this commonwealth shall be vested in a governor. He shall hold the office for the term of four years, to commence on the first day of January next succeeding his election, and be ineligible to the same office for the term next succeeding that for which he was elected, and to any other office during his term of service.

2. The governor shall be elected by the voters, at the times and places of choosing members of the general assembly. Returns of the elections shall be transmitted, under seal, by the proper officers, to the secretary of the commonwealth, who shall deliver them to the speaker of the house of delegates on the first day of the next session of the general assembly. The speaker of the house of delegates shall within one week thereafter, in the presence of a majority of the senate and house of delegates open the said returns, and the votes shall then be counted. The person having the highest number of votes shall be declared elected; but if two or more shall have the highest and an equal number of votes, one of them shall be chosen governor by the joint vote of the two houses of the general assembly. Contested elections for governor shall be decided by a like vote, and the mode of proceeding in such cases shall be prescribed by law.

3. No person shall be eligible to the office of governor unless he has attained the age of thirty years, is a native citizen of the Confederate States, and has been a citizen of Virginia for five years next preceding his election.

4. The governor shall reside at the seat of government; shall receive five thousand dollars for each year of his services, and while in office, shall receive no other emolument from this or any other government.

5. He shall take care that the laws be faithfully executed; communicate to the general assembly at every session the condition of the commonwealth; recommend to their consideration such measures as he may deem expedient; and convene the general assembly on application of a majority of the members of both houses thereof, or when in his opinion the interest of the commonwealth may require it. He shall be commander-in-chief of the land and naval forces of the state; have power to embody the militia to repel invasion, suppress insurrection, and enforce the execution of the laws; conduct, either in person or in such other manner as shall be prescribed by law, all intercourse with other and foreign states; and, during the recess of the general assembly, fill, pro tempore, all vacancies in those offices for which the constitution and laws make no provision: but his appointments to such vacancies shall be by commissions to expire at the end of thirty days after the commencement of the next session of the general assembly. He shall have power to remit fines and penalties in such cases and under such rules and regulations as may be prescribed by law; and, except when the prosecution has been carried on by the house of delegates, or the law shall otherwise particularly direct, to grant reprieves and pardons after conviction, and to commute capital punishment; but he shall communicate to the general assembly, at each session, the particulars of every case of fine or penalty remitted, of reprieve or pardon granted, and of punishment commuted, with his reasons for remitting, granting or commuting the same.

6. He may require information in writing from the officers in the executive department, upon any subject relating to the duties of their respective offices; and may also require the opinion in writing of the attorney general upon any question of law connected with his official duties.

7. Commissions and grants shall run in the name of the commonwealth of Virginia, and be attested by the governor, with the seal of the commonwealth annexed.

Lieutenant Governor.

8. A lieutenant governor shall be elected at the same time, and for the same term as the governor, and his qualification and the manner of his election in all respects shall be the same.

9. In case of the removal of the governor from office, or of his death, failure to qualify, resignation, removal from the state, or inability to discharge the powers and duties of the office, the said office, with its compensation, shall devolve upon the lieutenant governor; and the general assembly shall provide by law for the discharge of the executive functions in other necessary cases.

10. The lieutenant governor shall be president of the senate, but shall have no vote; and while acting as such, shall receive a compensation equal to that allowed to the speaker of the house of delegates.

Secretary of the Commonwealth, Treasurer and Auditor.

11. A secretary of the commonwealth, treasurer and an auditor of public accounts shall be elected by the joint vote of the two houses of the general assembly, and continue in office for the term of two years, unless sooner removed.

12. The secretary shall keep a record of the official acts of the governor, which shall be signed by the governor and attested by the secretary; and when required, he shall lay the same, and any papers, minutes and vouchers pertaining to his office, before either house of the general assembly; and shall perform such other duties as may be prescribed by law.

13. The powers and duties of the treasurer and auditor shall be such as now are, or may be hereafter prescribed by law.

Board of Public Works.

14. There shall be a board of public works, to consist of three commissioners. The state shall be divided into three districts, containing as nearly as may be equal numbers of voters, and the voters of each district shall elect one commissioner, whose term of office shall be six years; but of those first elected, one, to be designated by lot, shall remain in office for two years only, and one other, to be designated in like manner, shall remain in office for four years only.

15. The general assembly, at its first session after the adoption of this constitution, shall provide for the election and compensation of the commissioners, and the organization of the board. The commissioners first elected shall assemble on a day to be appointed by law, and decide by lot the order in which their terms of service shall expire.

16. The board of public works shall appoint all officers employed on the public works, and all persons representing the interest of the commonwealth in works of internal improvement, and shall perform such other duties as may be prescribed by law.

17. The members of the board of public works may be removed by the concurrent vote of a majority of all the members elected to each house of the general assembly; but the cause of removal shall be entered on the journal of each house.

18. The general assembly shall have power, by a vote of three-fifths of the members elected to each house, to abolish said board whenever in their opinion a board of public works shall no longer be necessary.

Militia.

19. The manner of appointing militia officers shall be prescribed by law.

ARTICLE VI.

JUDICIARY DEPARTMENT.

1. There shall be a supreme court of appeals, district courts and circuit courts. The jurisdiction of these tribunals, and of the judges thereof, except so far as the same is conferred by this constitution, shall be regulated by law.

Judicial Divisions.

2. The state shall be divided into twenty-one judicial circuits, ten districts and five sections.

I. The counties of Princess Anne, Norfolk, Nansemond, Isle of Wight, Southampton, Greenesville, Surry and Sussex and the city of Norfolk shall constitute the first circuit

II. The counties of Prince George, Dinwiddie, Brunswick, Mecklenburg, Lunenburg, Nottoway, Amelia, Chesterfield and Powhatan and the city of Petersburg shall constitute the second circuit.

III. The counties of Cumberland, Buckingham, Appomattox, Campbell Prince Edward, Charlotte and Halifax and the town of Lynchburg shall constitute the third circuit.

IV. The counties of Pittsylvania, Bedford, Franklin, Patrick and Henry shall constitute the fourth circuit.

V. The counties of Accomack and Northampton shall constitute the fifth circuit

VI. The counties of Elizabeth City, Warwick, York Gloucester, Matthews, Middlesex, Henrico, New Kent, Charles City and James City and the city of Williamsburg shall constitute the sixth circuit.

VII. The city of Richmond shall be the seventh circuit.

VIII. The counties of Lancaster, Northumberland, Richmond, Westmoreland, King George, Spotsylvania, Caroline, Hanover, King William, King & Queen and Essex shall constitute the eighth circuit.

IX. The counties of Stafford, Prince William, Alexandria Fairfax, Loudoun, Fauquier and Rappahannock shall constitute the ninth circuit.

X. The counties of Culpeper, Madison, Greene, Orange, Albemarle, Louisa, Fluvanna and Goochland shall constitute the tenth circuit.

XI. The counties of Nelson, Amherst, Rockbridge, Augusta and Bath shall constitute the eleventh circuit.

XII The counties of Pendleton, Highland, Rockingham, Page, Shenandoah, Warren and Hardy shall constitute the twelfth circuit.

XIII. The counties of Clarke, Frederick, Hampshire, Morgan, Berkeley and Jefferson shall constitute the thirteenth circuit.

XIV. The counties of Monroe, Greenbrier, Pocahontas, Alleghany, Botetourt, Roanoke and Craig shall constitute the fourteenth circuit.

XV. The counties of Giles, Mercer, Raleigh, Wyoming, Logan, Boone, Fayette and Nicholas shall constitute the fifteenth circuit.*

XVI. The counties of Grayson, Carroll, Wythe, Floyd. Pulaski and Montgomery shall constitute the sixteenth circuit †

XVII The counties of Smyth, Tazewell, Washington, Russell, Scott and Lee shall constitute the seventeenth circuit ‡

XVIII. The counties of Wayne, Cabell, Mason, Jackson, Putnam and Kanawha shall constitute the eighteenth circuit.§

XIX. The counties of Wood, Wirt, Gilmer, Braxton, Lewis, Ritchie, Doddridge and Pleasants shall constitute the nineteenth circuit.‖

XX. The counties of Hancock, Brooke, Ohio, Marshall, Wetzel, Tyler and Monongalia shall constitute the twentieth circuit.

XXI. And the counties of Harrison, Marion, Taylor, Preston, Barbour, Randolph and Upshur shall constitute the twenty-first circuit.¶

3. The first and second circuits shall constitute the first district; the third and fourth circuits the second district; the fifth, sixth and seventh circuits the third district; the eighth and ninth circuits the fourth district; the tenth and eleventh circuits the fifth district; the twelfth and thirteenth circuits the sixth district; the fourteenth and fifteenth circuits the seventh district; the sixteenth and seventeenth circuits the eighth district; the eighteenth and nineteenth circuits the ninth district; and the twentieth and twenty-first circuits the tenth district.

*Clay county is attached to the 15th circuit. Acts 1857-8, ch. 158, § 13, p. 113. Webster county is attached to the same circuit Acts 1859-60, ch. 47, § 14, p. 176
†Bland county is attached to the 16th circuit. Acts 1860-61, ch. 23, § 12, p. 48.
‡Wise county is attached to the 17h circuit. Acts 1855-6 ch 107 § 13, p. 89. McDowell county is attached to the same circuit. Acts 1857-8, ch. 155, § 12, p 107 Buchanan county is attached to the same circuit Acts 1857-8, ch. 156, § 12, p. 110.
§Roane county is attached to the 18th circuit. Acts 1856-7 ch 109, § 14, p. 94
‖Calhoun county is attached to the 19t circuit. Acts 1856-7 ch. 108 § 9, p 91.
¶Tucker county is attached to the 21st circuit. Acts 1856-7, ch. 110, § 13, p. 57.

4. The first and second districts shall constitute the first section; the third and fourth districts the second section; the fifth and sixth districts the third section; the seventh and eighth districts the fourth section; and the ninth and tenth districts the fifth section.

5. The general assembly may, at the end of eight years after the adoption of this constitution, and thereafter at intervals of eight years, rearrange the said circuits, districts and sections, and place any number of circuits in a district, and of districts in a section; but each circuit shall be altogether in one district, and each district in one section; and there shall not be less than two districts and four circuits in a section, and the number of sections shall not be increased or diminished.

Circuit Courts.

6. For each circuit a judge shall be elected by the voters thereof, who shall hold his office for the term of eight years, unless sooner removed in the manner prescribed by this constitution. He shall at the time of his election be at least thirty years of age, and during his continuance in office shall reside in the circuit of which he is judge.

7. A circuit court shall be held at least twice a year by the judge of each circuit, in every county and corporation thereof, wherein a circuit court is now or may hereafter be established. But the judges in the same district may be required or authorized to hold the courts of their respective circuits alternately, and a judge of one circuit to hold a court in any other circuit.

District Courts.

8. A district court shall be held at least once a year in every district, by the judges of the circuits constituting the section and the judge of the supreme court of appeals for the section of which the district forms a part, any three of whom may hold a court; but no judge shall sit or decide upon any appeal taken from his own decision. The judge of the supreme court of appeals of one section may sit in the district courts of another section, when required or authorized by law to do so.

9. The district courts shall not have original jurisdiction, except in cases of habeas corpus, mandamus and prohibition.

Court of Appeals.

10. For each section a judge shall be elected by the voters thereof, who shall hold his office for the term of twelve years, unless sooner removed in the manner prescribed by this constitution. He shall at the time of his election be at least thirty five years of age, and during his continuance in office reside in the section for which he is elected.

11. The supreme court of appeals shall consist of the five judges so elected, any three of whom may hold a court. It shall have appellate jurisdiction only, except in cases of habeas corpus, mandamus and prohibition. It shall not have jurisdiction in civil causes where the matter in controversy, exclusive of costs, is

less in value or amount than five hundred dollars, except in controversies concerning the title or boundaries of land, the probate of a will, the appointment or qualification of a personal representative, guardian, committee or curator; or concerning a mill, road, way, ferry or landing, or the right of a corporation or of a county to levy tolls or taxes; and except in cases of habeas corpus, mandamus and prohibition, and cases involving freedom or the constitutionality of a law.

12. Special courts of appeals, to consist of not less than three nor more than five judges, may be formed of the judges of the supreme court of appeals and of the circuit courts, or any of them, to try any cases remaining on the dockets of the present court of appeals when the judges thereof cease to hold their offices; or to try any cases which may be on the dockets of the supreme court of appeals established by this constitution, in respect to which a majority of the judges of said court may be so situated as to make it improper for them to sit on the hearing thereof.

13. When a judgment or decree is reversed or affirmed by the supreme court of appeals, the reasons therefor shall be stated in writing, and preserved with the record of the case.

General Provisions.

14. Judges shall be commissioned by the governor, and shall receive fixed and adequate salaries, which shall not be diminished during their continuance in office. The salary of a judge of the supreme court of appeals shall not be less than three thousand dollars, and that of a judge of a circuit court not less than two thousand dollars per annum, except that of the judge of the fifth circuit, which shall not be less than fifteen hundred dollars per annum; and each shall receive a reasonable allowance for necessary travel.

15. No judge, during his term of service, shall hold any other office, appointment or public trust, and the acceptance thereof shall vacate his judicial office; nor shall he, during such term, or within one year thereafter, be eligible to any political office.

16. No election of judge shall be held within thirty days of the time of holding any election of electors of president and vice-president of the Confederate States, of members of congress or of the general assembly.

17. Judges may be removed from office by a concurrent vote of both houses of the general assembly, but a majority of all the members elected to each house must concur in such vote; and the cause of removal shall be entered on the journal of each house. The judge against whom the general assembly may be about to proceed, shall receive notice thereof, accompanied by a copy of the causes alleged for his removal, at least twenty days before the day on which either house of the general assembly shall act thereupon.

18. The officers of the supreme court of appeals and of the district courts shall be appointed by the said courts respectively, or by the judges thereof in vacation. Their duties, compensation and tenure of office shall be prescribed by law.

19. The voters of each county or corporation in which a circuit court is held shall elect a clerk of such court, whose term of office shall be six years. The at-

torney for the commonwealth, elected for a county or corporation wherein a circuit court is directed to be held, shall be attorney for the commonwealth for that court; but in case a circuit court is held for a city or for a county and a city, there shall be an attorney for the commonwealth for such, to be elected by the voters of such city or county and city, and to continue in office for the term of four years. The duties and compensation of these officers, and the mode of removing them from office, shall be prescribed by law.

20. When a vacancy shall occur in the office of clerk of any court, such court may appoint a clerk pro tempore, who shall discharge the duties of the office until the vacancy is filled.

21. The general assembly shall provide for the compensation of jurors, but appropriations for that purpose shall not be made from the state treasury, except in prosecutions for felony and misdemeanor.

22. At every election of a governor, an attorney general shall be elected by the voters of the commonwealth for the term of four years. He shall be commissioned by the governor, shall perform such duties and receive such compensation as may be prescribed by law, and be removable in the manner prescribed for the removal of judges.

23. Judges and all other officers, whether elected or appointed, shall continue to discharge the duties of their respective offices after their terms of service have expired, until their successors are qualified.

24. Writs shall run in the name of the commonwealth of Virginia, and be attested by the clerks of the several courts. Indictments shall conclude, against the peace and dignity of the commonwealth.

County Courts.

25. There shall be in each county of the commonwealth a county court, which shall be held monthly, by not less than three nor more than five justices, except when the law shall require the presence of a greater number.

26. The jurisdiction of the said courts shall be the same as that of the existing county courts, except so far as it is modified by this constitution, or may be changed by law.

27. Each county shall be laid off into districts, as nearly equal as may be in territory and population. In each district there shall be elected, by the voters thereof, four justices of the peace, who shall be commissioned by the governor, reside in their respective districts, and hold their offices for the term of four years. The justices so elected shall choose one of their own body, who shall be the presiding justice of the county court, and whose duty it shall be to attend each term of said court. The other justices shall be classified by law for the performance of their duties in court.

28. The justices shall receive for their services in court a per diem compensation, to be ascertained by law, and paid out of the county treasury; and shall not receive any fee or emolument for other judicial services.

29. The power and jurisdiction of justices of the peace within their respective counties shall be prescribed by law.

County Officers.

30. The voters of each county shall elect a clerk of the county court, a surveyor, an attorney for the commonwealth, a sheriff, and so many commissioners of the revenue as may be authorized by law, who shall hold their respective offices as follows: The clerk and the surveyor for the term of six years; the attorney for the term of four years; the sheriff and the commissioners for the term of two years. Constables and overseers of the poor shall be elected by the voters, as may be prescribed by law.

31. The officers mentioned in the preceding section, except the attorneys, shall reside in the counties or districts for which they were respectively elected. No person elected for two successive terms to the office of sheriff, shall be re-eligible to the same office for the next succeeding term; nor shall he, during his term of service, or within one year thereafter, be eligible to any political office.

32. The justices of the peace, sheriffs, attorneys for the commonwealth, clerks of the circuit and county courts, and all other county officers, shall be subject to indictment for malfeasance, misfeasance or neglect of official duty; and upon conviction thereof, their offices shall become vacant.

Corporation Courts and Officers.

33. The general assembly may vest such jurisdiction as shall be deemed necessary in corporation courts, and in the magistrates who may belong to the corporate body.

34. All officers appertaining to the cities and other municipal corporations, shall be elected by the qualified voters, or appointed by the constituted authorities of such cities or corporations, as may be prescribed by law.

Done in convention, in the city of Richmond, on the first day of August, in the year of our Lord one thousand eight hundred and fifty-one, and in the seventy-sixth year of the commonwealth of Virginia.

JOHN Y. MASON,
Pres't of the Convention.

S. D. WHITTLE,
Secretary of the Convention.

SCHEDULE.

Sec.
1. Duty of president of convention.
2. Constitution, how published
3. How submitted to people for ratification or rejection.
4. Regulations for ascertaining sense of voters.
5. Result, how ascertained and proclaimed. General election for legislature and executive officers.
6. Election, how conducted.
7. Return of polls.
8. Officers, when and where to assemble.
9. Legislature, when and where to assemble. Their oaths.

Sec.
10. Legislature under former constitution, abrogated.
11. Term of members of legislature.
12. Term of governor, lieutenant governor and attorney general
13. Terms of judges, when to expire.
14. When former executive office to expire. Other officers, how long to remain in office.
15. How long courts to continue. Laws to remain in force, how long
16. Legislature to carry constitution into effect.

1. It shall be the duty of the president of this convention, immediately on its adjournment, to certify to the governor a copy of the bill of rights and constitution adopted, together with this schedule.

2. Upon the receipt of such certified copy, the governor shall forthwith announce the fact by proclamation, to be published in such newspapers of the state as may be deemed requisite for general information; and shall annex to his proclamation a copy of the bill of rights and constitution, together with this schedule; which proclamation, bill of rights, constitution and schedule shall be published in the manner indicated, for the period of one month; and ten printed copies thereof shall, by the secretary of the commonwealth, be immediately transmitted by mail to the clerk of each county and corporation court in this commonwealth, to be by such clerk submitted to the examination of any person desiring the same.

3. The officers authorized by existing laws to conduct general elections shall, at the places appointed for holding the same, open a poll-book on the fourth Thursday in October next, to be headed "The Constitution as amended and Schedule," and to contain two separate columns; the first column to be headed "For Ratifying;" the other to be headed "For Rejecting." And such officers, keeping said polls open for the space of three days, shall then and there receive and record in said poll-book the votes for and against this constitution and schedule, of all persons qualified, under the existing or amended constitution, to exercise the right of suffrage.

4. The taking of the polls, the duties to be performed by the officers, the privilege of the voters, and the penalties attaching for misconduct on the part of any person, shall be in all things as prescribed by the second, third, fourth, seventh, eighth and ninth sections of the act of the general assembly passed March the fourth, one thousand eight hundred and fifty, entitled "An act to take the sense of the people upon the call of a convention, and providing for organizing the same," so far as the provisions of said sections may be applicable.

SCHEDULE.

5. It shall be the duty of the governor, upon receiving the returns of said officers, to ascertain the result thereof, and forthwith to declare the same by his proclamation, stating the aggregate vote in the state for and against the ratification of the amended constitution and schedule, which shall be published at least once a week until the second Monday in December next, in such newspapers as in his opinion will be best calculated to diffuse general information thereof; and if it appear that a majority of the votes cast is in favor of ratification, the governor, at the same time, and in like manner, shall make proclamation for holding, on the day last mentioned, a general election throughout the state for delegates and senators to the general assembly, according to the apportionment and districts prescribed in this constitution; and also for the election of a governor, lieutenant governor and attorney general.

6. The officers authorized by existing laws to hold and conduct general elections, shall hold and conduct the elections herein required; and such officers and all other persons shall be governed and controlled therein by the provisions of said laws, so far as the same may be applicable to and necessary for the proper conducting of the said elections. Duplicate polls shall be separately kept for governor and lieutenant governor, for attorney general, and for senators and delegates to the general assembly, which shall be verified by the oaths of the officers conducting the elections.

7. The verified duplicate polls for governor, lieutenant governor and attorney general shall be deposited with the clerks of the several counties and cities, who shall retain one in their respective offices, and transmit the other by mail to the secretary of the commonwealth.

8. In the election of senators and delegates for districts formed of more than one county and city, the officers conducting the same at the court-house of the several counties and cities forming each district shall assemble, on the eighth day after the commencement of the said election, at the court-house of the county or city first named as one of the counties of the district; shall compare the polls and ascertain the result, and shall deliver and return certificates of election according to the laws now in force.

9. The members of the general assembly so elected shall meet at the capitol in the city of Richmond on the second Monday in January in the year one thousand eight hundred and fifty-two, and then and there organize as the General Assembly of Virginia; but before such organization, they shall respectively take the oath of fidelity to the commonwealth, and the other oaths of office required by the laws now in force.

10. The election of members of the general assembly under this constitution shall vacate the seats of those elected under the present constitution.

11. The official terms of the delegates first elected to the general assembly under this constitution shall expire on the 30th day of June, in the year one thousand eight hundred and fifty-three.

12. The official terms of the first governor, lieutenant governor and attorney general elected under this constitution shall expire on the thirty-first day of December, in the year one thousand eight hundred and fifty-five.

13. The present judges of the supreme court of appeals and of the circuit courts, and their successors, who may be appointed under the existing constitution, shall remain in office until such time as the law may prescribe for the commencement of the official terms of the judges under the amended constitution, and no longer; which time shall not be more than six months after the termination of the first session of the general assembly under the amended constitution.

14. The executive department of the government shall remain as at present organized; and the governor and councillors of state and their successors appointed under the existing constitution shall continue in office until a governor elected under this constitution shall be qualified; and all other persons in office when this constitution is adopted, except as is herein otherwise expressly directed, shall continue in office until their successors are qualified; and vacancies in office, happening before such qualification, shall be filled in the manner now prescribed by law.

15. All the courts of justice now existing shall continue with their present jurisdiction until and except so far as the judicial system may or shall be otherwise organized; and all laws in force when this constitution is adopted, and not inconsistent therewith, and all rights, prosecutions, actions, claims and contracts shall remain and continue as if this constitution was not adopted.

16. The general assembly shall pass all laws necessary for carrying this constitution into full effect and operation.

Done in convention, in the city of Richmond, on the first day of August, in the year of our Lord one thousand eight hundred and fifty-one, and in the seventy-sixth year of the commonwealth of Virginia.

JOHN Y. MASON,
Pres't of the Convention.

S. D. WHITTLE,
Secretary of the Convention.

www.ingramcontent.com/pod-product-compliance
Lightning Source LLC
Chambersburg PA
CBHW031827230426
43669CB00009B/1255